Lecture Notes in Artificial Intelli

Subseries of Lecture Notes in Computer Scier
Edited by J. G. Carbonell and J. Siekmann

T0238017

Lecture Notes in Computer Science
Edited by G. Goos, J. Hartmanis and J. van Leeuwen

Springer
Berlin
Heidelberg
New York
Barcelona
Hong Kong
London
Milan
Paris
Singapore
Tokyo

Patrick Lambrix

Part-Whole Reasoning in an Object-Centered Framework

 Springer

Series Editors

Jaime G. Carbonell, Carnegie Mellon University, Pittsburgh, PA, USA
Jörg Siekmann, University of Saarland, Saabrücken, Germany

Author

Patrick Lambrix
University of Linköping
Department of Computer and Information Science
581 83 Linköping, Sweden
E-mail: patla@ida.liu.se

Cataloging-in-Publication Data applied for

Die Deutsche Bibliothek - CIP-Einheitsaufnahme

Lambrix, Patrick:
Part-whole reasoning in an object centered framework / Patrick Lambrix. -
Berlin ; Heidelberg ; New York ; Barcelona ; Hong Kong ; London ;
Milan ; Paris ; Singapore ; Tokyo : Springer, 2000
(Lecture notes in computer science ; Vol. 1771 : Lecture notes in
artificial intelligence)
ISBN 3-540-67225-7

CR Subject Classification (1998): I.2, D.1.5, F.4.1, G.2.2

ISBN 3-540-67225-7 Springer-Verlag Berlin Heidelberg New York

Springer-Verlag is a company in the BertelsmannSpringer publishing group
© Springer-Verlag Berlin Heidelberg 2000
Printed in Germany

Typesetting: Camera-ready by author
Printed on acid-free paper   SPIN: 10719774   06/3142   5 4 3 2 1 0

Preface

In many application areas natural models of the domains require the ability to express knowledge about two important relations: is-a and part-of. The is-a relation allows us to organize objects with similar properties in the domain into types. Part-of allows us to organize the objects in terms of composite objects. The is-a relation has received a lot of attention and is well-understood, while part-of has not been studied as extensively. The interaction between these two relations has not been studied in any detail either.

In this book we propose an object-centered framework with specialized support for part-of. The framework is based on description logics. Description logics are a family of object-centered knowledge representation languages tailored for describing knowledge about concepts and is-a hierarchies of these concepts. In addition to the representation and reasoning facilities that description logics provide for is-a, we add representation and reasoning facilities for part-of. We also show the usefulness and feasibility of our approach in a number of application areas.

The work described in this book is based partly on my PhD thesis and partly on recent work within the Laboratory for Intelligent Information Systems at the Department of Computer and Information Science at the University of Linköping. The two persons who have had the largest influence on my work are Lin Padgham and Nahid Shahmehri. A large part of the work reported in this book has been been done in cooperation with them.

Erik Sandewall, Per-Olof Fjällström, Maurizio Lenzerini, Bernhard Nebel, Ralph Rönnquist, Johan Åberg, Cécile Boisson, Silvia Coradeschi, Mats Gustafsson, Anders Haraldsson, Pierpaolo Larocchia, and Ivan Rankin read a previous draft of the book and provided many valuable comments.

As part of our work we extended the CLASSIC description logic system. AT&T Bell Labs provided us with the CLASSIC source code. Deborah McGuinness and Lori Alperin Resnick were very helpful in answering our modeling questions.

The examples in chapters 5 and 6 are based on discussions with Kathleen Lambrix. She clarified for me the workings of a distribution company.

As a basis for the application in chapter 8 we used an existing implementation from the Australian Artificial Intelligence Institute. They provided us with their databases. In particular, we received help from and had interesting discussions with David Kinny, Mike Georgeff, and Ralph Rönnquist.

The application in chapter 9 is based on a manual for project management from Telia Research AB. Peter Lord provided us with this manual.

The work on machine learning described in chapter 10 was carried out in cooperation with Jalal Maleki. Nada Lavrač gave useful comments on an earlier version and encouraged us to pursue this work.

A number of people have contributed to parts of the model and the system described in chapter 11: Jonas Almfeldt, Svend Jacobsen, Johan Lövdahl, Niclas Wahllöf, and Johan Åberg.

The drawings in this book have been made by my friend Hilde Adé.

Part of this work was done during a visit to the Artificial Intelligence Lab of the Computer Science Department at RMIT University, Melbourne, Australia. The Department of Computer and Information Science of the University of Linköping and the Department of Computer Science of RMIT University made this visit possible.

Finally, we acknowledge the financial support of the Swedish Research Council for Engineering Sciences and the Swedish Foundation for Strategic Research.

December 1999   *Patrick Lambrix*

Table of Contents

Part II. Theory

Part III. Application Areas

List of Figures

Are You one of these people who have to talk to a machine quite often? Did you ever have problems explaining to a machine that the tank in a propellant tank assembly is always a propellant tank or that the title in a document has a larger font than the text in the sections or indeed did you need to convey any information about a relation between an entity and its parts to a machine? In the case You answered 'yes' to both questions, this work is written especially for You. In this work we present You with a language for talking to a machine about part-of. The framework we propose supports representing and automated reasoning about part-of. Thereby we support users in modeling domains with part-of, relieve them from implementing some reasoning tasks and relieve them from some of the maintenance of the domain knowledge base.

Part I

Background

1. Introduction

1.1 Motivation

Part-whole hierarchies are a natural way for humans to organize and represent entities in order to manage and reason about the world. Often these hierarchies can be seen in terms of objects composed of other objects. For instance, a document may be seen as a composite object made up of parts. Some of these parts may be sections which themselves are composite objects containing paragraphs. The notion of composite objects is one which is gaining strength in a number of areas. For instance, in the object modeling domain whole-part structures of objects are recognized as one of the important organization techniques and in most object-oriented modeling approaches part-whole relations can be represented in a specialized way (e.g. [CY91, RBPEL91]). In the object-oriented databases area there have been efforts to represent and manage composite objects. Several object-oriented database management systems support some kind of part-whole and some of them allow for variations of the properties of part-whole. Support for composite objects is even regarded as a necessary facility for more complex database systems such as engineering and office databases [St*90, At*89, Cat91]. In document management systems there are international standards such as S-GML and ODA requiring documents to be defined in terms of a structure of parts.

There is also an awareness that part-whole relationships are important for knowledge representation. A knowledge representation system supporting part-whole relations would need to define a flexible representation of different kinds of part-whole relations. We would want to represent such things as the fact that all parts of an object belong to a specific type, or that for objects belonging to a particular type there can be only a certain number of parts for a particular part-whole relation. We might also want to be able to represent constraints between the parts of a composite object. In a way similar to the representation of the is-a relation in object-centered frameworks we may want to be able to determine properties of objects based on inheritance between part and whole. The sort of reasoning we may hope to perform in a knowledge representation system supporting part-whole relations includes such tasks as inferring the existence of composite objects based on the existence of their parts, answering questions such as whether a particular object is a part of

P. Lambrix: Part-Whole Reasoning, LNAI 1771, pp. 5-9, 2000
© Springer-Verlag Berlin Heidelberg 2000

some other object, and determining whether an object could be used in the building of another object belonging to a particular type.

Object-centered models and systems are designed to represent knowledge in the form of objects and types. Knowledge about properties of a particular object is grouped together. By grouping objects into types we can describe the common properties of a group of objects. Further, types are classified in an is-a hierarchy. This allows for an inheritance mechanism to carry over knowledge about the properties of a particular type to a more specific type and thus to the objects of this more specific type. Much work on classification using types has been done in the area of *description logics*. Description logics are a family of object-centered knowledge representation languages with well-defined semantics. Description logics can vary from small-scale languages to very expressive languages. Recently, work has been done on expressing other data models in description logics. For instance, in [BS92] a description logic is proposed that includes the semantics of E/R [BCN92] and DAPLEX [Shi81]. In [CLN94] a framework is given that includes frame systems, E/R and OO-languages. Other work addressing the issue of using description logics as languages for object-centered data modeling can be found in [BJNS94, CDL95, DL95]. An important aspect of description logics is that much attention is given to the services of subsumption checking, i.e. finding out whether a type is more specific than another type, classification of types and recognition of objects, i.e. finding the types of which an object is an instance. Algorithms are provided for these services and for most of them complexity results are known. This has put description logics and classificatory reasoning on a firm theoretical base.

In this work we present an object-centered framework for representation and reasoning about part-of. Given the fact that description logics present a clean object-centered model with a good understanding of the issues regarding types and classification, description logics provide a framework for investigating the issues which appear when we try to integrate classification and other kinds of reasoning. We extend the description logic framework to also deal with part-of. As many object-centered data models can be expressed in description logics we should be able to transfer most of the extensions we propose to these other data models. To study the issues involving is-a and part-of we can extend description logic systems in two ways. The first possibility, which is the approach we follow, is to integrate reasoning about part-of into the actual description logic. This approach makes the issues in the combination of the different kinds of reasoning clearer and therefore leads to a better understanding. Another advantage is that part-of can be handled both on the level of types and on the object level. A more practical advantage is that there are no system integration issues. The second possibility is to combine a description logic system with another system targeted to representing and reasoning about part-of. In this approach the reasoning about is-a and part-of is performed in two different systems and thus we have the advantage of modularity. A major disadvantage is, however, that there is no clear semantics for the combination of the different kinds of reasoning. Indeed, a naive combination of the two kinds of reasoning may give unexpected or unwanted results.[1] Further, it seems that is-a and part-of interact in a number of intricate ways that would require a careful analysis as to whether it is possible at all to represent these interactions using two different systems.

We note that our main interest is in providing part-of first-class citizen status in our framework. It may be possible that some of the extensions in our description logic can be formalized using traditional description logic constructs (such as roles and role constructs), but then part-whole relations are no different from ordinary relations. We want to distinguish part-whole relations from ordinary relations for a number of different reasons including the following. The use of part-whole relations allows for a more natural modeling in many domains. Part-whole relations have particular properties that make it possible to extend a description logic language with constructs that make sense for part-of, but not necessarily for ordinary relations. Finally, giving part-of a first-class status allows for the introduction of special services or inferences regarding part-of.

1.2 Outline

This book consists of five parts. Part I describes the background information. Part II describes an object-centered framework for representing and reasoning with is-a and part-of. A number of application areas and an application, respectively, where the framework has shown to be useful are described in parts III and IV, respectively. The book concludes in part V. Our own contributions can be found mainly in section 3.2 and parts II, III and IV.

In the remainder of part I we present some background to this work. In chapter 2 we describe description logics. In chapter 3 we discuss some approaches to representing part-of in object-centered frameworks. The approaches are in the areas of mereology, cognitive science, knowledge representation and databases. We also define the object-centered model for composite objects that we use in the rest of this book. In chapter 4 we describe the work that has been done to date to integrate part-of in description logics.

Our approach to integrating part-of in description logics[2] is presented in part II. We start in chapter 5 with a simple framework to introduce the most basic notions. In this framework we are able to represent different kinds of part-whole relations. We can define domain restrictions and number restrictions for parts and we can express constraints among the parts of a composite

---

[1] This was shown in [PN93] for the combination of classification and default reasoning.

[2] In the overview article [AFGP96] our approach is discussed as one of the main approaches in the area.

object. The reasoning services are mainly extensions of the standard reasoning services in description logics. This framework is implemented as an extension of the CLASSIC system and is sufficient for some applications. For other applications more specialized representation and reasoning about part-of is needed and we propose an extended framework in chapter 6. In the extended framework we can represent information about the order between parts as well as some inheritance information between parts and wholes. While other approaches up till now have concentrated on the representation of part-of and on extending the standard inferences in description logics to also deal with part-of, we also introduce special services targeted to part-of. In chapter 6 we define new reasoning services which allow building new composite objects given the existence of available parts. In chapter 7 we compare our approach to the approaches described in chapter 4.

In part III and IV we show how the framework introduced in part II can be used in different application areas. We discuss briefly the advantages or added functionality that our description logics for composite objects provide for the applications. However, we do not make a detailed comparison with other approaches in the application area, as this is not the focus of this book. The applications in part III are not fully implemented prototypes. The first and second application are more fully developed than the third. The latter is a sketch of a possible system. The first application, which is described in chapter 8, is an agent-oriented application where we re-model the reaction control system of the space shuttle. We base our model on an existing implementation for which the domain knowledge base contains much hard-coded as well as implicit information about part-of. Then we examine a document management application in chapter 9. We discuss the needs of the application with respect to representation and discuss which reasoning services need to be provided. In chapter 10 we discuss how a description logic for composite objects can be used to learn composite concepts. In part IV we describe a fully implemented system for knowledge-based information retrieval. The system supports a query language that allows for the use of information about content, logical structure and properties about the documents in the queries. The system also takes background knowledge into account during the search.[3]

The book concludes in part V by a chapter stating our main contributions together with pointers to areas for future work.

---

[3] Our framework has also been used in the CODY project at the University of Bielefeld. The knowledge representation system defined within that project allows for the reconstruction of processes of dynamic conceptualization in sequences of mechanical-object assembly. The representation language is roughly a synthesis of the semantic network ERNEST and our own initial work. For more information, see [CJW95, WJ96].

1.3 Conventions

In description logic papers two styles of notation are found. The first style is LISP-like and is more verbose than the other style. The second style uses logical and mathematical notations. For instance, to describe a team that has at least eleven members and for which all members are soccer players we write (**and** *team* (**atleast** *11 member*) (**all** *member soccer-player*)) using the first style. The same description using the second style is written as *team* $\sqcap$ ($\geq$ *11 member*) $\sqcap \forall$ *member.soccer-player*. In this work we use the first style.

In the formal definitions and the structural subsumption rules, normalization rules and combinant inferences rules we use the following conventions.

- a^4 denotes an attribute.
- r denotes a role.
- ap denotes a part-attribute path.
- n denotes a part name.
- p denotes a qualified part name.
- m denotes a number.
- C denotes a concept.

An overview of the symbols that are used in this book, can be found in appendix C.

---

[4] Possibly with subscript. This also holds for the items that follow.

2. Description Logics

Description logics[1] are languages tailored for expressing knowledge about concepts and concept hierarchies. The concept hierarchies represent the is-a relation between concepts. Description logics are usually given a Tarski-style declarative semantics, which allows them to be seen as sub-languages of predicate logic.[2] The main entities in description logics are

- *concepts*, which can be considered as unary predicates which are interpreted as sets of objects over a domain. Examples of concepts are *soccer-team* and *ida-employee*.[3]
- *roles* which can be considered as binary predicates which are interpreted as binary relations between the objects in the domain. An example of a role is *member* which may represent a relation between a team and the persons belonging to the team.
- *individuals* which are interpreted as objects in the domain. For example, a particular member of a team would be represented by an individual.

To build a knowledge base one starts with primitive concepts and roles (see section 2.1.1 for the definition), and can use the language constructs (such as intersection, union or role quantification) to define new concepts and roles. Also information about individuals can be *told* to the knowledge base.

Some of the reasoning tasks that a description logic system supports, are classification, subsumption checking and recognition. Further, the description logic system can be queried using the description logic and some user functions. A large amount of work in description logics has concentrated on investigating the computational complexity of the reasoning tasks (e.g. [Schm89, Neb90a, DLNN91a, DLNN91b, BDS93]) and has put description logics on a firm theoretical basis.

The first description logic system was KL-ONE [BS85]. Nowadays, a whole family of knowledge representation systems has been built using description

---

[1] Description logics have also been referred to as terminological logics, concept languages and KL-ONE-like languages. They have their origin in semantic networks and frame-based systems. The web page of the description logic community is found at address http://dl.kr.org/dl.

[2] See, for instance, [Bor94] for a formal discussion.

[3] IDA is the Swedish name for the department of computer and information science.

P. Lambrix: Part-Whole Reasoning, LNAI 1771, pp. 11-20, 2000
© Springer-Verlag Berlin Heidelberg 2000

logics and for most of them complexity results for the subsumption algorithm are known. The systems differ with respect to expressivity of the description logic and complexity and completeness of the algorithms. Some of the most used systems were BACK (e.g. [Pel91]), CLASSIC (e.g. [Bo*89]), KRIS (e.g. [BH91]) and LOOM (e.g. [MacG91]). Recently, a number of new systems appeared after a system comparison effort in the description logic community (see the systems section in [FDMNW98]).

Description logic systems have been used for building a variety of applications including systems supporting software management (e.g. [DBSB91]), browsing and querying of networked information sources (e.g. [LSK95]), knowledge mining (e.g. [ABN92]), data archeology (e.g. [Br*93]), user interfaces (e.g. [AMSS88]), planning (e.g. [WL92, Koe94]), configuration (e.g. [Ows88, Wr*93]) and natural language understanding (e.g. [BP91, Qua95]). Experience in using description logics in applications has also shown that in many cases we would like to extend the representational and reasoning capabilities of the description logic with other types of reasoning (e.g. [DP91]). Therefore, work has begun on extending description logics with representation and reasoning about, for instance, part-of (see chapter 4), defaults (e.g. [BH92, QR92, BH93, PN93, PZ93, Str93]) and time (e.g. [Schm90, Bet93, LR93, AF94]).

In this chapter we introduce the notions that we need in the remainder of this work. In section 2.1 we discuss how knowledge about concepts and roles can be expressed in a description logic. We use a small description logic as example. For this logic we define syntax and semantics. We introduce the notions of subsumption and classification. How knowledge about individuals can be expressed is discussed in section 2.2. Important inferences are propagation and recognition. Finally, in section 2.3 we briefly discuss the CLASSIC system that we have used as a basis for our implementation.

2.1 Terminological Knowledge

In description logics the distinction between terminological knowledge and assertional knowledge is often made. The terminological knowledge includes knowledge about concepts while the assertional knowledge includes knowledge about individuals. In this section we define a language for the representation of terminological knowledge while in the next section we define a language for the representation of assertional knowledge.

2.1.1 Syntax

In figure 2.1 we define the syntax of the terminological component of a small description logic. We have defined a number of constructs for introducing concepts. The **and** construct allows us to combine information from different

<*concept-descr*> ::=
   ⊤
   | ⊥
   | <*concept-name*>
   | (**and** <*concept-descr*>$^+$)
   | (**all** <*role-name*> <*concept-descr*>)
   | (**atleast** <*positive-integer*> <*role-name*>)
   | (**atmost** <*non-negative-integer*> <*role-name*>)
   | (**fills** <*role-name*> <*individual-name*>$^+$)

<*concept-name*> ::=   <*symbol*>
<*role-name*> ::=   <*symbol*>
<*individual-name*> ::=   <*symbol*>

Fig. 2.1. Syntax of a description logic.

sources. For instance, we may define a concept representing people who are *ida-employee and soccer-player*. Using the **all** construct we can introduce domain restrictions. Representing the fact that in an ida soccer team *all members are ida employees and soccer players* can be done by having (**all** *member* (**and** *ida-employee soccer-player*)) in the definition of the concept *ida-soccer-team*. The **atleast** and **atmost** constructs allow us to introduce number restrictions. For instance, (**atleast** *11 member*) in the definition of a soccer team means that *every soccer team has at least 11 members*. We can also represent the information that a specific individual is a role filler for some specific role. For instance, the fact that *Patrick is a member of an ida soccer team* can be represented by having (**fills** *member Patrick*) in the definition of *ida-soccer-team*.

Terminological axioms are used to introduce names for concepts and definitions of those concepts. Let A be a concept name (<*symbol*>) and C a concept description (<*concept-descr*>). Then terminological axioms can be of the form: $A \dot{\leq} C$ for introducing necessary conditions (primitive concepts), or $A \doteq C$ for introducing necessary and sufficient conditions (defined concepts). A *terminology* or *Tbox T* is a finite set of terminological axioms with the additional restrictions that (i) every concept name used must appear exactly once on the left hand side of a terminological axiom, and (ii) T must not contain cyclic[4] definitions.

In figure 2.2 we show a Tbox. There are three primitive concepts: *team*, *ida-employee* and *soccer-player*. The concepts *soccer-team* and *ida-soccer-team* are defined.

More expressive description logics may introduce other concept-forming constructs as well as role-forming constructs. Examples of role-forming constructs include role conjunction, role disjunction, inverses of roles, composi-

---

[4] Many description logic systems do not allow cyclic definitions. However, see for instance [Neb90b, Baa90, Schi94] for approaches allowing terminological cycles.

$team \stackrel{.}{\leq} \top$

$ida\text{-}employee \stackrel{.}{\leq} \top$

$soccer\text{-}player \stackrel{.}{\leq} \top$

$soccer\text{-}team \stackrel{.}{=}$
      (and   team
             (atleast 11 member)
             (all member soccer-player))

$ida\text{-}soccer\text{-}team \stackrel{.}{=}$
      (and   team
             (atleast 11 member)
             (all member (and ida-employee soccer-player))
             (fills member Patrick))

Fig. 2.2. IDA plays soccer.

tion of roles, transitive closure of roles and creation of roles using a particular concept as domain or range. Examples of concept-forming constructs include exists-restrictions, negation of concepts, disjunction of concepts and role value maps.

2.1.2 Semantics

An *interpretation* of the language consists of a tuple $< \mathcal{D}, \varepsilon >$, where $\mathcal{D}$ is the domain and ε the extension function. The extension function ε maps role names into sub-sets of $\mathcal{D} \times \mathcal{D}$, concept names into sub-sets of $\mathcal{D}$ and individual names into elements of $\mathcal{D}$ such that $\varepsilon[i_1] \neq \varepsilon[i_2]$ whenever $i_1 \neq i_2$.[5] The semantics for the different constructs is shown in figure 2.3.

$\varepsilon[\top] = \mathcal{D}$
$\varepsilon[\bot] = \emptyset$
$\varepsilon[(\textbf{and } A\ B)] = \varepsilon[A] \cap \varepsilon[B]$
$\varepsilon[(\textbf{all } r\ A)] = \{\ x \in \mathcal{D} \mid \forall\ y \in \mathcal{D}: <x,y> \in \varepsilon[r] \rightarrow y \in \varepsilon[A]\}$
$\varepsilon[(\textbf{atleast } m\ r)] = \{\ x \in \mathcal{D} \mid \sharp\ \{\ y \in \mathcal{D} \mid <x,y> \in \varepsilon[r]\} \geq m\ \}$
$\varepsilon[(\textbf{atmost } m\ r)] = \{\ x \in \mathcal{D} \mid \sharp\ \{\ y \in \mathcal{D} \mid <x,y> \in \varepsilon[r]\} \leq m\ \}$
$\varepsilon[(\textbf{fills } r\ i_1\ ...\ i_m)] = \{\ x \in \mathcal{D} \mid <x,\varepsilon[i_1]> \in \varepsilon[r] \wedge\ ...\ \wedge <x,\varepsilon[i_m]> \in \varepsilon[r]\ \}$

Fig. 2.3. Semantics of a description logic.

An interpretation $< \mathcal{D}, \varepsilon >$ is a *model* for a Tbox if for all $A \stackrel{.}{\leq} C$ in the Tbox $\varepsilon[A] \subseteq \varepsilon[C]$ and for all $A \stackrel{.}{=} C$ in the Tbox $\varepsilon[A] = \varepsilon[C]$.

---

[5] The last requirement is the unique name assumption.

2.1.3 Subsumption

For description logics the most important relation between concepts is the is-a relation. This relation is represented by the notion of subsumption. We say that A *subsumes* B, written $B \Rightarrow A$, iff $\varepsilon[B] \subseteq \varepsilon[A]$ for every interpretation $<\mathcal{D},\varepsilon>$. Subsumption between concepts can also be defined with respect to a Tbox, by requiring that the interpretations in the definition of subsumption are models of the Tbox.

Specializing the range of a role leads to a more specialized concept.

$$\frac{\vdash\ C_1 \Rightarrow\ C_2}{\vdash\ (\textbf{all}\ r\ C_1)\ \Rightarrow\ (\textbf{all}\ r\ C_2)}$$

Higher lower bounds are more restrictive.

$$\frac{m_1\ <\ m_2}{\vdash\ (\textbf{atleast}\ m_2\ r)\ \Rightarrow\ (\textbf{atleast}\ m_1\ r)}$$

Higher upper bounds are less restrictive.

$$\frac{m_1\ <\ m_2}{\vdash\ (\textbf{atmost}\ m_1\ r)\ \Rightarrow\ (\textbf{atmost}\ m_2\ r)}$$

Requiring a larger set of role fillers is more restrictive.

$$\frac{\{ii\}\ \subseteq\ \{jj\}}{\vdash\ (\textbf{fills}\ r\ jj)\ \Rightarrow\ (\textbf{fills}\ r\ ii)}$$

Fig. 2.4. Structural subsumption rules for a description logic.

Structural subsumption rules are a convenient way[6] to represent the different reasons why subsumption between two concepts holds. In figures 2.4, 2.5 and 2.6 we show such rules in the style of [Bor92] for our simple language.[7] The rules in figure 2.4 give direct information about subsumption relationships. The rules in figure 2.5 are normalization rules. They define equivalences between concept descriptions and can be used to transform the description of a concept to a normal form. *Combinant inferences* (figure 2.6) use information concerning different kinds of constructs to obtain subsumption relationships.

Using the subsumption relation concepts can be classified into an is-a hierarchy. Most systems classify a concept with respect to is-a when the concept is defined. Definitions of concepts are not allowed to change. For the

---

[6] Another way is to use constraint system propagation rules as, for instance, in [DLNN91a].

[7] $\frac{A}{B}$ can be read as 'if A holds then B also holds'.

and *is distributive over* **all**.

$\vdash$ (**and** (**all** r C_1) (**all** r C_2)) $\equiv$ (**all** r (**and** C_1 C_2))

and *of* **fills** *is like union*.

$\vdash$ (**and** (**fills** r ii) (**fills** r jj)) $\equiv$ (**fills** r $ii \cup jj$)

If you cannot have fillers, then all fillers must belong to the empty set.

$\vdash$ (**all** r $\bot$) $\equiv$ (**atmost** 0 r)

If the fillers can be anything, then this is not really a constraint.

$\vdash$ (**all** r $\top$) $\equiv$ $\top$

Inconsistent upper and lower bounds.

$$\frac{m_1 \; < \; m_2}{\vdash \; (\textbf{and} \; (\textbf{atmost} \; m_1 \; r) \; (\textbf{atleast} \; m_2 \; r)) \; \equiv \; \bot}$$

Fig. 2.5. Normalization rules for a description logic.

Knowing a sub-set of the set of fillers provides a lower bound on the number of fillers.

$$\frac{size(\{ii\}) \; = \; m}{\vdash \; (\textbf{fills} \; r \; ii) \; \Rightarrow \; (\textbf{atleast} \; m \; r)}$$

Fig. 2.6. Combinant inferences for a description logic.

example in figure 2.2 the system classifies *soccer-team* as a specialization of *team* and *ida-soccer-team* as a specialization of *soccer-team*.

2.2 Assertional Knowledge

Assertional statements are used to make statements about individuals. An assertional statement is of the form $i :: C$, where i is an individual name (*<symbol>*) and C a concept description (*<concept-descr>*) as defined before. This means then that $\varepsilon[i] \in \varepsilon[C]$. The information that is explicitly stated in an assertional statement is said to be *told* information. An *Abox* is a finite set of assertional statements. We say that an individual is *defined* in an Abox if it appears in any one of the statements in the Abox. We assume that within one Abox an individual has a unique name. We give an example in figure 2.7.

We say that an interpretation $< \mathcal{D}, \varepsilon >$ is a *model* for an Abox A if $\varepsilon[i] \in \varepsilon[C]$ for every $i :: C$ in the Abox A. A knowledge base is defined as a tuple $< T, A >$ where T is a Tbox and A an Abox. An interpretation is a model for a knowledge base $< T, A >$ if it is a model for T and a model for A. Subsumption can be defined with respect to a knowledge base, by requiring that the interpretations in the definition are models of the knowledge base.

Implemented description logic systems allow a user to assert as well as retract information about individuals from the knowledge base. Thus the Abox can be changed dynamically and is allowed to contain partial information about individuals. Further, in description logics an open world assumption is made.

IDA FC :: *ida-soccer-team*

Patrick :: *ida-employee*

Fig. 2.7. IDA FC.

Two important tasks of a description logic system involving individuals are the propagation of information and the recognition task. *Propagation* computes all the information about an individual that can be deduced from the information in the knowledge base. For instance, given the Tbox in figure 2.2 and the Abox in figure 2.7, we can conclude from the fact that Patrick is a member of IDA FC that he is also a soccer player. *Recognition* is the task of recognizing whether an individual belongs to a particular concept. For instance, in our example the system recognizes that Patrick belongs to (**and** *ida-employee soccer-player*). Rules for reasoning about individuals for the language defined here are given in figure 2.8.[8]

Number of fillers.

$$\frac{kb \;\vdash\; \sharp\{y \;\mid\; r(x,y)\} = m}{kb \;\vdash\; x \;\rightarrow\; (\textbf{atleast } m \; r)}$$

Propagation rule.

$$\frac{kb \;\vdash\; r(x,y), \; kb \;\vdash\; x \;\rightarrow\; (\textbf{all } r \; C)}{kb \;\vdash\; y \;\rightarrow\; C}$$

Fig. 2.8. Reasoning about individuals in a description logic.

2.3 CLASSIC

Our implementation of a description logic system for composite objects is based on the CLASSIC system (e.g. [Bo*89]). The CLASSIC language is quite small and thus provides a basic tool to study the interaction of is-a and part-of. Further, CLASSIC has been used in a number of real applications (e.g. [DBSB91, Br*93, Wr*93, LSK95]) and was until recently[9] the most efficient description logic system ([HKNP92, BHNPF92]). In this section we describe CLASSIC briefly.

As well as the constructs of the simple language above, CLASSIC also defines the **one-of**, **same-as** and **test-c** constructs. The **one-of** construct allows us to collect a number of individuals into a set. For instance, (**all** *member* (**one-of** *John Mary*)) in the definition of a concept would mean that every member is one of the individuals John or Mary. In CLASSIC functional roles are called attributes. The **same-as** construct allows us to compose attributes into paths that are constrained to have the same filler at the end of a path. For instance, assuming that *has-manager, has-coach, belongs-to-team* are attributes, we can say that the manager of a soccer player is also the coach of the team the player is a member of by having (**same-as** *has-manager belongs-to-team.has-coach*) in the definition of *soccer-player*. The **test-c** construct allows us to use programs outside the description logic that return a boolean value as test functions. In the case where we had a function *check-young-team* that computes the average age of all the members of a team

---

[8] *kb* ⊢ in the figure can be read as 'it can be derived from the knowledge base that' while → may be read as 'belongs to'. Observe that when we use → in other situations than these rules, it denotes implication.

[9] See the systems section in [FDMNW98].

and tests whether this is below a certain threshold, we could define a young team using (**test-c** *check-young-team*). Further, it is also possible to assert that a group of concepts are pairwise disjoint. As well as the description logic concepts CLASSIC also defines HOST concepts which are used to represent objects in the host language[10] such as numbers, lists and strings.

In CLASSIC it is possible to introduce *rules*. They can be used to introduce properties for individuals belonging to a specific concept that are not definitional but that happen to hold for all individuals of the concept. For instance, it may be that an *ida-soccer-team* always plays in Linköping, although we do not consider this fact to belong to the definition of *ida-soccer-team*. This can then be handled using a rule **if** *ida-soccer-team* **then** (**fills** *play-in Linköping*).[11] Whenever an individual, e.g. IDA FC, is recognized as an *ida-soccer-team*, the information (**fills** *play-in Linköping*) is added to the individual.

With respect to roles and individuals the notion of closing is defined. It is possible to say that for a particular individual we know all the fillers of a particular role. For instance, we may say that for a particular team all the members are known. Closing of a role for an individual is done using a user function.

CLASSIC's subsumption algorithm is a structural subsumption algorithm. It contains two steps: a normalization step and a comparison step. During normalization a concept description is transformed into an equivalent concept description using rules as in figure 2.5. In the comparison phase subsumption is tested using rules as in figures 2.4 and 2.6. The algorithm is, however, incomplete with respect to the semantics as defined above. The incompleteness originates from the fact that individuals are allowed in the concept definitions and can thus influence subsumption. This means that the concept hierarchy could change when individuals change. Therefore, subsumption is usually defined as being independent of these assertions. Introducing individuals in concept descriptions also leads to intractability of the subsumption algorithm. In [BP94] a modified semantics for individuals is given for which the polynomial subsumption algorithm implemented in CLASSIC is complete.

The interaction with CLASSIC is handled via user functions. These user functions are used to define concepts, roles, individuals and rules. For individuals they are also used to assert and retract information. To define the primitive concept *team*, for example, we can write *(cl-define-primitive-concept 'team 'classic-thing)*. To introduce *soccer-team*[12] we can write *(cl-define-concept 'soccer-team '(and team (atleast 11 member) (all member soccer-player)))*. Further, at each point in time it is possible to retrieve all information about concepts, roles and individuals. For concepts this information includes a description of the concept, the more general concepts in the knowl-

---

[10] In the version of CLASSIC we use, the host language is LISP.
[11] This is not the CLASSIC syntax.
[12] We assume that *team*, *soccer-player* and *member* are already introduced before.

edge base, the more specific concepts and the individuals that belong to the concept. For individuals this information includes a description of the individual, the concepts the individual belongs to and the fillers for roles. Different kinds of questions can also be asked. For instance, we can ask whether a concept subsumes another concept, whether two concepts are disjoint, whether an individual belongs to a concept or whether a role is closed for a particular individual.

In chapter 5 we use the language defined in this chapter as a basis for defining a description logic for composite objects. For this description logic for composite objects we have based our implementation on the COMMON LISP implementation version 2.2 of CLASSIC. We extend the CLASSIC algorithms and define some new functionality.

3. Composite Objects

In this chapter we describe some of the approaches that deal with composite objects. We start out with mereology where a formal theory of parts and wholes is given. In mereological theories it is assumed that there is one basic part-of relation for which a number of axioms can be stated. This point of view has been challenged in the cognitive science and linguistics areas, where it is claimed that there exist different part-of relations each having their own properties. Nowadays, several authors subscribe to the view that there is one basic part-of relation which is then specialized into different part-whole relations.[1] These part-whole relations can have properties different from the part-of relation. In the next section we discuss both areas. We describe the most common mereological theory (section 3.1.1) and the most common taxonomies of part-whole as they appear in the literature (section 3.1.2).

In the database community there is also an awareness that information about parts and wholes is needed for complex applications. Several systems allow for some kind of specialized representation and handling of part-of. We discuss some of these systems in section 3.1.3.

In this book we propose a framework and knowledge representation system to deal with part-of. In section 3.1.4 we review some of the earlier approaches in the knowledge representation area where support for part-of is provided. Recently, most of the work in this area has been done using description logics. These approaches are discussed in the next chapter.

In section 3.2 we describe the basis for our framework. Based on the requirements of different applications (see parts III and IV) we found that there was a need for representing different named part-whole relations as well as a more basic relation with part-of intuition. We describe the different properties that we assume for those relations and discuss which classes of part-whole relations are supported.

---

[1] This view is also proposed in the overview article [AFGP96].

P. Lambrix: Part-Whole Reasoning, LNAI 1771, pp. 21-30, 2000
© Springer-Verlag Berlin Heidelberg 2000

3.1 Composite Objects in Different Areas

3.1.1 Mereology

The earliest formal theories about parts and wholes are the Mereology of Leśniewski and the Calculus of Individuals by Leonard and Goodman. Since then a number of other theories have been proposed, many of which are variants of the earlier works. A unified minimal mereology is given by the Classical Extensional Mereology. In [Var96] we find a taxonomy of mereologies. Ground Mereology is the theory that defines parthood to be a partial order (reflexive, antisymmetric and transitive). A proper part can be defined as a part which is not itself. This is the basis for every mereological theory. Each theory can then add further principles. However, even this very basic theory is not unchallenged. The issue is whether part-of is transitive. For example, assume a house has a door and the door has a handle [Lyo77]. The question is then whether the handle is also a part of the house. Many authors argue that part-of is not transitive (e.g. [Res55, Lyo77, Cru79, WCH87, ILE88]). For instance, in [WCH87] different kinds of part-whole relations are proposed (see next section) and it is argued that part-whole is transitive when one combines part-whole relations in the same class. However, when we mix part-whole relations from different classes we no longer have transitivity. Other authors (e.g. [Sim87, AFGP96, Var96, Sat98]) argue that transitivity does not hold for the case where one does not only consider the part-of relation between whole and parts, but also attributes some functionality to the parts. Mereologists then claim that there exists a basic part-of relation for which transitivity holds and of which part-whole relations are a kind of specialization.[2]

Extensional Mereology is obtained from Ground Mereology by adding the *strong supplementation principle*. This principle states that if all parts of an object x overlap with another object y, then object x is a part of object y. This principle implies the *extensionality principle* that states that two objects are identical if they have the same parts. In practice, this principle turns out to be too strong. For instance, in the case where objects are not only described by their parts but also by their properties, it may well be that two different objects share all their parts. An example is where two different committees share the same members. It can be the case that the secretary of the first committee is the chairperson of the second committee and vice versa and thus it is obvious that the two committees are different. A weaker constraint is the *weak supplementation principle*. This principle states that if an object has a proper part then it has more than one.

---

[2] In the following we use 'part-of' as a general term. When we use 'part-of relation' we assume that we talk about a basic relation as in mereology. In section 3.2 we define our own 'part-of relation'. The term 'part-whole relation' is used for a relation with part-of intuition. Different part-whole relations may have different behaviors.

Classical Extensional Mereology is an extension of Extensional Mereology. An important addition in this framework is the *principle of sum*, stating the fact that there always exists a mereological sum, i.e. there always exists an object that is composed of any two objects in the theory. This principle is too strong in practice as well. One example is in the case of scattered entities. For instance, it may not make any sense to denote the object composed of this book and Sweden. For an overview of classical as well as non-classical[3] extensional mereologies we refer to [Sim87].

3.1.2 Cognitive Science and Linguistics

In cognitive science and linguistics there seems to be a consensus that there is a need for a classification of different part-whole relations, each class having its own properties. An elaborate taxonomy is given in [WCH87]. The authors differentiate the part-whole relations from other semantic relations such as attribution, possession, the class-subclass relation and spatial inclusion. Attributes are properties of objects which do not have the part-whole intuition. For instance, the height of a tower is an attribute but not a part. An example of possession is 'John has a bicycle'. The class-subclass relation is actually the is-a relation. An (out of date) example of spatial inclusion is the following: West Berlin is in East Germany. Compare this with: East Berlin is in (and part of) East Germany.

The classification of part-whole relations in [WCH87] is based on three different properties. A part can be *functional* or not. Functional parts are restricted by their function or in their spatial or temporal location. Parts can be *separable* in which case they can be separated from the whole. *Homeomerous* parts are the same kind of thing as their wholes. With respect to these properties six[4] different classes of part-whole are defined.

– component/integral object (example: pedal/bike)
  Integral objects exhibit some kind of patterned organization or structure. The nature of the integral object is defined by this organization. The components are also patterned and bear specific functional and structural relationships to one another and to the whole. The parts are functional and separable but are not homeomerous.
– member/collection (example: ship/fleet)
  Members in a collection do not need to have any functional relationship to the collection. We note that collections are different from classes. The members in a class share some properties and membership in the class is thus based on a similarity principle. Membership in a collection is based

---

[3] In the non-classical extensional mereologies the principle of sum is rejected.
[4] The taxonomy in [WCH87] does not define classes with the properties *functional* and *homeomerous*. The authors in [GP95] suggest that it may be that functional implies not homeomerous and homeomerous implies not functional.

on spatial proximity or by social connection. The parts in a collection are not functional and not homeomerous, but are separable.
- portion/mass (example: slice/pie)
  Portions of a mass are homogeneous and are comprised in the whole. They are not functional, but are homeomerous and separable.
- stuff/object (example: steel/car)
  The object partly is or is made of the stuff. The parts are not functional, not homeomerous, and not separable.
- feature/activity (example: paying/shopping)
  The features are the different phases of the activity or process. The parts are functional, but are not homeomerous and not separable.
- place/area (example: Linköping/Sweden)
  This is the relation between areas and the places and locations within them. The parts are not functional and not separable but are homeomerous.

With respect to transitivity it is suggested that combining different kinds of part-whole results in non-transitivity, while combining part-whole relations in the same class results in transitivity.

Another classification of part-whole relations is given in [ILE88] where four different different types of part-whole relations are identified. In the functional component type the part contributes to the composition, not only as a structural unit, but the part is also essential to the purposeful activity of the composition. An example is the bike/wheel relation. The segmented whole type is exemplified by a pie and its pieces. This relation implies a kind of removability or separability of the parts from the whole. It also seems that the whole must exist before the part. The other types of part-whole relation are the member/group relation and the set/sub-set relation. The first three types of part-whole relations are similar to types in [WCH87]. The authors of [ILE88] argue that the stuff/object type in [WCH87] is better modeled not using part-of and that the feature/activity type in [WCH87] may be handled by some combination of functional part and sequencing.[5] With respect to transitivity they observe that, in general, transitivity does not hold for functional parts. Nor does it hold for the member-group relation. On the other hand, transitivity holds for the set/sub-set relation and for the segmented whole relation.

In [GP95] the authors propose classifying part-whole relations into relations that are induced by the compositional structure of the whole and relations that are independent of this structure. With respect to compositional structure, the following types are introduced. Complexes have a heterogeneous structure and their parts are called components. There are functional, temporal and spatial relations between the components and the whole. Collections consist of elements which are all related to the whole in the same way. Masses are homogeneous and can be divided into quantities. The fact that different views on an entity are allowed is interesting. For instance, the

---

[5] Sequencing is another type of relation, not having the part-of intuition.

relation between a fleet and its ships can be seen as a collection/element relation in the case where the members play no specific roles. The fleet may also be considered a complex in the case where each ship has a specific location or function. With respect to relations independent of the compositional structure we have segments and portions. Segments are parts that result from the application of an external scheme. An example is 'the beginning of a story'. In the case of portions, parts are selected from the whole using a property dimension. An example is 'the red parts of a particular painting'.

3.1.3 Databases

Support for composite objects is needed for complex applications in object-centered[6] database management systems [St*90, At*89, Cat91]. One reason for this is that the system can then provide for specialized support based on part-of. For instance, one could define the semantics of a copy function for composite objects as copying the object together with its parts. Also, some kinds of objects can exist only when they belong to a whole. In this case when the whole is deleted, the part should be deleted automatically. Another reason for support for composite objects is that the composite objects hierarchy can be used for a number of tasks. For instance, considering the fact that whenever a composite object is accessed, there is a good chance that the parts are also accessed, clustering with respect to composite objects may give the database an increase in access performance. The composite objects hierarchy may also be used as a basis for defining authorization or access control. Most systems that support composite objects nowadays allow users to define and name the different kinds of part-whole [Cat91].

In [Da*90] a list of requirements for databases supporting composite objects is provided. The system must support object identity to which parts and attributes can be assigned. Further, the system should allow modeling of part-whole relationships. Derived values in wholes and parts must also be supported. For instance, the weight of an assembly could be derived as the sum of the weights of the parts. The dependency can also go from whole to part. For instance, the location of a part may be derived from the location of the whole. The most fundamental requirement is the fact that wholes can be manipulated as a whole. For instance, when displaying a composite object one may want to display all its parts too. A further requirement is the ability to express constraints on the part-whole relationships. For instance, in the design of a product, connection requirements may be specified between the different parts of the product. It should also be possible to view composite objects at different levels of abstraction. In a document database, for instance, it should be possible to view the complete text of a document or just a table of contents. To be able to define composite objects with arbitrary

---

[6] Including object-oriented and extended-relational.

levels, recursion must be allowed in the definition of composite objects. Finally, there should also be support for flexible transaction management where transactions can be performed on a composite object together with its parts. Although the authors have listed these requirements for composite objects, they argue that many of them are also useful in other situations. Therefore, their approach is to incorporate support for these requirements into the data model and they do not restrict their use to part-of. A similar approach is followed by POSTGRESS [SK91].

An object-oriented system that provides much support for part-of is O-RION. Parts of a composite object in ORION are classified with respect to two properties. First, the parts of a composite object can be dependent or independent. A dependent part is an object whose existence is based on the existence of a whole to which it belongs. For instance, the roof of a car may not exist if the car does not exist. This gives a special semantics to the delete operation. Further, a part can be exclusive or shared. In the first case the part can belong to only one whole at a time. In the case of shared parts, different wholes may contain the same part. Support for these different properties of parts is implemented in the ORION system [KBG89]. Further, query facilities for traversing the composite objects hierarchy have been implemented. The hierarchy is also used for authorization [RBKW91], clustering [Ba*87] and locking [KBG89].

In [KC90] composite objects are connected to their parts by is-component-of and is-composed-of relationships. Special attention is given to propagation of change from parts to wholes. The latter problem has also been studied by other authors. For instance, in [Zdo86] the authors argue that a change in a part should not always be propagated to the whole. IRIS is a system that allows the freezing of a composite object so that when a part is changed, new versions of the whole are also created [BM88]. In [Lam92] we studied the temporal aspects of composite objects. We identified two classes of composite objects. On one hand there are composite objects such as folders, where the composite object is considered to have changed only if things are added or removed from the whole. On the other hand we have composite objects such as documents where the whole (the document) is considered to have changed whenever one of its parts (e.g. a paragraph) changes internally. We formalized the relations connecting such compositions and developed synchronization rules which are capable of maintaining the desired relations as parts of the database change over time.

3.1.4 Early Approaches in Knowledge Representation

In the area of knowledge representation the part-of relation has received attention in a number of systems. In this section we describe some of the early approaches. In these approaches it is recognized that part-of plays an important role in modeling, but there is not always specialized support for part-of. More recently, most of the work on part-of in knowledge representation has been done in the area of description logics. These approaches are described in the next chapter.

In the NETL system [Fah79] it is possible to represent the part-of relation. This relation is considered to be transitive. Part-of is represented by creating a PART role. By using roles NETL can use its inheritance machinery. The PART roles are, however, treated in a special way. It is only for these roles that a transitive closure is defined. A part-of hierarchy is integrated in the semantic network.

The CSAW knowledge representation system, which is based on semantic nets, is presented in [Hay77]. There, the part-whole relations are considered next to the is-a relation to be the most important structural relations in a CSAW knowledge base. They are represented by the PART-OF role. These PART-OF relations can be defined at the type level as well as at the object level. Special attention is also given to the dependence relation where the existence of some object implies the existence of a composite of which the object is a part.

In [Schu79] it is assumed that the part-of relation is at least a partial ordering, that the extensionality property holds, that there exists a unique empty part and that overlap, merging and difference operators exist. It is argued that people tend to conceptualize objects in terms of pairwise disjoint, jointly exhaustive parts and thus in terms of partitionings. The representation of the part-of relation is then also based on the notion of partitioning. Sets of partitionings can be represented by a *parts graph*. It is shown that the problem of confirming that an object is part of another object is co-NP-complete in the framework. Therefore *closed* parts graphs are suggested. A parts graph is closed if all parts can be decomposed into a sub-set of a fixed set of ultimate parts. These graphs allow for a linear space-time algorithm for the problem of confirming that an object is part of another object. It is also shown that for every parts graph there is a logically equivalent closed parts graph the size of which may be exponential with respect to the size of the original graph. In [PS81] the class of part graphs with efficient retrieval is extended from closed parts graphs to *semi-closed parts graphs*. A serious limitation that the authors of [PS81] observe, is that parts are not considered on the level of concepts, but only on the object level.

3.1.5 Summary

In this section we have seen different views on part-of. Some authors consider that there is one basic part-of relation. In practice, however, it seems necessary to be able to distinguish between different kinds of part-whole relations. We have seen different taxonomies of part-whole relations. The behaviors of these part-whole relations are not the same for every class. For instance, some part-whole relations are transitive, while others are not. In some cases a composite object can be looked upon in different ways. We argue that in a knowledge representation system supporting part-of, a user should have the ability to define different kinds of part-whole relations. However, at the same time it can be useful to support a basic transitive part-of relation.

The basic part-of model can be described as a partial order. Further, one can add supplementation principles and the sum principle. The resulting model may incorporate the extensionality property or not.

Parts can have different properties. They can be exclusively owned or shared. Their existence may be dependent on the existence of a whole to which they belong. Values of attributes of parts and wholes can be inherited via part-of. Constraints may be defined both between parts and also between parts and wholes. Parts can also differ with respect to temporal properties.

Composite objects should be first-class citizens in a knowledge representation system. This means that they have their own identity and that they can be operated on and reasoned about as one entity. It is, then, also important to allow for a query facility that takes into account information about part-of.

In this work we have chosen to start with a language with limited representational capability in order to develop a clear understanding of the issues involved. We introduce a framework based on the needs of a number of applications (see parts III and IV). One advantage of this approach is that we are able to define specialized reasoning techniques for part-of. In the next section we discuss the basis of our part-of representation. In chapters 5 and 6 we then introduce a description logic for composite objects.

3.2 A Basis for Part-of Representation

3.2.1 Mereological Assumptions

We decided to allow for a representation of different kinds of part-whole relations. In our framework we can say such things as the string t is a *title* part of the document d. This we write as $t \triangleleft_{title} d$ and we say that t is a *direct (title) part* of d. Thus the part-whole relations are *named*, i.e. whenever we introduce a part-whole relation between different objects this relation receives a part name. By naming the relations we are able to distinguish between different kinds of part-whole relations. Different parts can be connected to the same part name. For instance, different pieces of text may be section parts of one document. An object that has direct parts is a *composite object*. We also define a transitive relation with part-of intuition that in the rest of this work is called *part-of*. We define the part-of relation[7] to be the transitive closure over all the direct parts.

Definition 3.2.1. $x \triangleleft^* y$ *iff*

$\exists\ n_1,...,n_m,x_1,...,x_{m-1}\colon x \triangleleft_{n_1} x_1 \triangleleft_{n_2} \ldots \triangleleft_{n_{m-1}} x_{m-1} \triangleleft_{n_m} y$

---

[7] This relation can be seen as a sub-relation of the basic part-of relation as proposed in [Sim87, Var96, AFGP96]. In chapter 6 we describe another relation with part-of intuition that includes our part-of relation.

Thus, we also have that a direct part is a part. Further, it is easy to see that $\lhd^*$ is transitive.

We assume that an object cannot be a part of itself.[8] Clearly, with this assumption an object cannot be a direct part of itself. The assumption also implies that there are no cycles in the part-of relation. Further, together with the transitivity of part-of, the assumption implies the antisymmetry of part-of.

Assumption 1. $\forall\ x: \neg(x\ \lhd^*\ x)$

The weak supplementation principle states that an object cannot have just one direct part.[9] Every composite object has at least two direct parts. This assumption is formulated as follows:

Assumption 2. $\forall\ x,y,n_1: x \lhd_{n_1} y \rightarrow (\exists\ z,n_2: z \neq x \wedge z \lhd_{n_2} y)$

The following assumption intends to capture the intuition behind the meaning of *direct* part. If a part y is a direct part of an object x, then there can be no other object z such that y is a part of z and z is a part of x.

Assumption 3. $\forall\ x,y: (\exists\ n: y \lhd_n x) \rightarrow \neg(\exists\ z: y \lhd^* z \wedge z \lhd^* x)$

This assumption also leads us to the following. If an object x has a part y, then the direct parts of y are not direct parts of x.[10]

We do not assume the extensionality property. In our model, objects are not only described by their structure, but also by their properties. Thus, we allow two different composite objects to share all their parts. We do not assume the principle of sum either. Thus, it is not the case that there is always an object composed of two other given objects. In some applications, however, a variant of the principle of sum may be useful. For instance, in the bottom-up instantiation of documents, it may be useful to be able to infer the existence of the whole on the basis of the existence of the parts. In chapter 6 a specialized inference is defined that allows for this instantiation in certain cases.

3.2.2 Scope of the Framework

In our framework we allow the definition of different kinds of part-whole relations. However, in the description logic for composite objects that we introduce later, no properties can be attributed to the different kinds. For instance, it is not possible to say that a particular kind of part-whole is transitive. Neither is there an is-a hierarchy of part-whole relations. So it

---

[8] Thus, our part-of relation has the same properties as the proper part relation in mereology.

[9] Although this assumption looks reasonable, we see later that it actually cannot be checked for individuals.

[10] The direct parts of y are, of course, parts of x.

is not possible to say that a particular kind of part-whole relation is more specific than another. In section 12.2 we discuss these issues briefly. It is possible, however, to define domain constraints and number restrictions for parts. Further, we also allow representation of constraints between parts, order information and some inheritance via part-whole relations.

Parts can be shared between different composite objects. We have no way of defining them to be exclusive. However, in some specialized inferences (chapter 6) we assume exclusivity of the parts except where sharing is stated explicitly.

In the applications described in parts III and IV we have mainly concentrated on modeling the composition/(functional) component type of part-whole relations. In the application in chapter 8 we model a physical system. In chapters 9 and 11 the composite objects are folders, documents and their parts.

The knowledge representation system that we propose is a description logic system. Therefore, the standard inference procedures are available. These include subsumption, classification and recognition. We also have the possibility of querying the knowledge base using information about the structure of the objects. We have added capabilities to traverse a part-of hierarchy for objects. Further, in chapter 6 we define some specialized inferences based on part-of.

4. Part-of in Description Logics

In this chapter we describe the existing approaches for integrating features for representing and reasoning about part-of in description logics. In all these approaches the description logic system has been extended with special constructs or mechanisms. We describe first the approaches which propose a general framework and then the approaches which concentrate on specific issues in the interaction between is-a and part-of. None of the approaches defines specialized inferences with respect to part-of.

4.1 General Frameworks

4.1.1 A Framework for Physical Whole-Part Relations

The approach in [SP94a, SP94b] is inspired by three applications: a stereo system application [MRI95], a telephone switching application [Wr*93], and the Plinius project [SVSM93]. The approach is targeted at 'physical whole-part relations' having the following properties: a physically composed object has a number of components, it cannot be part of itself, each part is connected to at least one other part and the properties of the whole are constrained by properties of the parts. The underlying part-of model introduces a *directly contains* relation and a *contains* relation. The contains relation is asymmetric and transitive. Part-of is, then, the inverse of contains. A contains and part-of relation is also defined between concepts with the intuition that C_1 contains or is part of C_2 if every individual in C_1 contains or is part of an individual in C_2 respectively. These relations between concepts are transitive, but not asymmetric. Similar relations are defined with intuitive meanings 'may be part of' and 'may contain'.

The proposed language is an extension of CLASSIC. To represent part-of, whole-part roles and part-whole roles which are different from ordinary roles are introduced. The language allows for domain restrictions and number restrictions on the whole-part roles. Fillers for the whole-part roles can be asserted as well. The whole-part roles form a whole-part role hierarchy. The whole-part roles not only represent structural information, but also include a functional aspect. Therefore, the whole-part roles are not transitive. It is also assumed that individuals cannot participate in a cycle via part-whole roles.

P. Lambrix: Part-Whole Reasoning, LNAI 1771, pp. 31-37, 2000
© Springer-Verlag Berlin Heidelberg 2000

The system needs, then, to be able to answer various queries including containment queries. Further, three different kinds of inferences are recognized. The completion inferences include inheritance via part-of and calculations of the transitive closure of part-of. The contradiction detection mechanisms include detection of cycles in the part-whole relations. Finally, there are the classification and subsumption inferences in which information about part-of needs to be taken into account. It is observed that since whole-part roles are not transitive, they do not influence subsumption with respect to transitive closure calculations. A prototype has been implemented.

4.1.2 A Framework with Specialized Role Constructors and Quantifiers

In [Fra93] an extension of $\mathcal{ALC}$ is presented to represent and reason about collective entities. The application in mind is the representation of plurals and plural quantifiers in natural language. First a *Collection Theory* is introduced which allows for complete reasoning and extends $\mathcal{ALC}$ to embed this collection theory. A sound and complete subsumption algorithm for a slightly weaker variant of this new language exists. Then it is argued that a theory of part-whole is more expressive and more adequate than an element-based collection theory. We briefly describe this mereology.

The basic relation is $\geq$ and should be read as *has-part*. The has-part relation is reflexive, anti-symmetric and transitive.

A complete new set of role constructors is defined. Using the notation of [Fra93] a role is defined as a primitive role, $\geq$, $\lhd$ C.R, $\unlhd$ C.R, $\lhd\!\!\!| $ C.R, $\rhd$ C.R, $\unrhd$ C.R, $|\!\!\!\rhd$ C.R.

The $\lhd$ and $\rhd$ are quantifiers that specify that a relation necessarily holds for all the parts of a certain type. For instance, $\lhd$ C.R(a,b) holds iff $\forall$ x: $(\geq(a,x) \wedge C(x)) \rightarrow R(x,b)$. This allows us to express items such as "The Beatles were born in Liverpool" as ($\lhd$ Person.Born-in)(beatles,liverpool).

The $\unlhd$ and $\unrhd$ quantifiers specify that a relation necessarily holds for some parts including all the parts of a certain type. For instance, $\unlhd$ C.R(a,b) holds iff $\forall$ x: $(\geq(a,x) \wedge C(x)) \rightarrow (\exists s: \geq(s,x) \wedge R(s,b))$. The fact that the Beatles sing "Yesterday" can be represented by ($\unlhd$ Person.Sing) (beatles,yesterday).

The $\lhd\!\!\!|$ and $|\!\!\!\rhd$ quantifiers represent the group reading of a relation. They specify that a relation possibly holds for some part of a certain type. For instance, $\lhd\!\!\!|$ C.R(a,b) holds iff $\exists$ x: $(\geq(a,x) \wedge C(x) \wedge R(x,b))$. ($\lhd\!\!\!|$ People.Play-in)(beatles,london) represents the fact that the Beatles played in London, but it is actually unknown whether the group that played in London was actually composed of all the members of the Beatles.

A plural operator $\star$ is defined as $\star P(a)$ iff $\forall$ x: $\geq(a,x) \rightarrow (\exists$ y: $P(y) \wedge (\geq(x,y) \vee \geq(y,x)))$ This operator allows for the construction of plural collective entities having singular objects of a certain type as their parts. For instance, we can define People as $\star$Person.

The resulting mereology does not satisfy the extensionality property. The author also mentions that several issues still need to be addressed: the existence of atoms (entities that have no parts), the possible inclusion of different part-whole relations, and the calculus.

4.1.3 A Framework for Part-of in Engineering Applications

In [Sat95, Sat98] support for part-of is needed to model an engineering application. The author argues that a description logic system supporting composite objects should allow for

1. handling of different kinds of part-of relations,
2. representation of inverses of part-of relations,
3. modeling of transitivity-like interactions between part-of relations and
4. representation of special characteristics of part-of relations.

In the early version of the framework [Sat95] the taxonomy defined in [WCH87] is used as a basis. The different kinds of part-of relation that are considered consist of component/composition, member/collection, segment/entity, quantity/mass, stuff/object and ingredient/object. Then the results[1] of combining different kinds of part-of relations are investigated. For instance, if a is a component of b and b is of stuff c, then a is of stuff c. For each of these six kinds of part-of relations a predefined primitive role (*is-d-composite*, *is-d-member* etc.) is introduced, each representing a direct part-of relationship. Then six roles are defined (one for each kind of part-of relation) as the transitive closure of the respective direct roles and the results of the combinations. The characteristics that are to be represented are exclusive parts, multi-possessed parts, owner-restricted parts, essential parts and dependent parts. Finally, the part-of relations are also considered to be acyclic. To be able to satisfy these requirements a highly expressive language is proposed with the role-forming operators for a top role, inverse, conjunction, disjunction, composition and transitive closure and the concept-forming operators for conjunction, primitive negation, exists restriction, value restriction and primitive single restriction. This language allows us to express all the properties and characteristics of the six relations and their interactions. A consequence of this expressivity is, however, that subsumption becomes undecidable.

In a later version of the framework [Sat98] a new taxonomy of part-whole relations is proposed. The general part-whole relation is a partial order (i.e. transitive and reflexive). A first specialization of this general relation is the integral part-whole relation which involves integrity conditions on the parts. The integrity conditions are only imposed on the parts and not on the wholes. On the other hand, the composed part-whole relation is a specialization of the general part-whole relation which requires an additional relation to hold

---

[1] These are the transitivity-like interactions.

between a part and its whole. The thesis [Sat98] investigates some of the influences of the requirements of the different classes of part-whole relations on the required expressive power of representation languages. The focus is on extending description logics with transitive relations and to relate transitive relations to other, possibly non-transitive relations. A number of complexity results are provided.

4.2 Specific Issues

4.2.1 Composition Constructor

In [ACGPS94] the authors propose a new constructor for description logics to deal with the component-object relation. The new construct has the form

$$(\textbf{compos } (n_1, C_1) + ... + (n_m, C_m))$$

and defines a concept that is made up of at least n_1 parts belonging to C_1 *plus* ... *plus* at least n_m parts belonging to C_m. The meaning of the plus operator needs more attention. For instance, let manager and secretary be concepts subsumed by the concept employee and assume a working-group is defined as follows.

$manager \stackrel{.}{\leq} employee$
$secretary \stackrel{.}{\leq} employee$
$working\text{-}group \stackrel{.}{=} (\textbf{compos } (1, manager) + (1, secretary) + (2, employee))$

Let Mary be a manager, Jane a secretary and John and Marc be employees. Then there are two ways to interpret the definition of a working-group. The first interpretation would allow a working-group to be composed of only Jane and Mary as there are then a manager, a secretary and two employees. However, the intended meaning of the operator is the case where every individual is counted only once among the parts. So, a working-group has to have at least four people. A group containing Mary, Jane, John and Marc would be a valid instantiation of a working-group.

Observe that there are no maximum restrictions for the number of components of a concept. So, for instance, a valid instantiation of working-group can have more than one manager or secretary and more than two employees. There may also be extra components that do not belong to the specified domains.

The **compos** constructor is defined on the whole set of components of a concept and therefore inheritance of this restriction is not allowed.

The resulting subsumption algorithm requires in the general case exponential time with respect to the number of components of the more general concept.

4.2.2 Transitivity Aspects

In [HPS88] the authors report on an attempt to represent the ABEL knowledge base in the knowledge representation system NIKL. ABEL is a knowledge-based system for diagnosis of acid-base and electrolyte disorders. One of the main problems with respect to representation they found was the lack of support for part-of. For instance, the following particular interaction between subsumption and the part-of relation was needed. In this domain in some cases one wants to deduce the presence of diseases of organs from the presence of diseases of parts of these organs. For instance, let the concepts urinary-system, kidney, nephron, kidney-disease and nephron-disease be as follows.

$urinary\text{-}system \doteq anatomical\text{-}entity$
$kidney \doteq (\textbf{and } anatomical\text{-}entity \text{ } (\textbf{all } is\text{-}part\text{-}of \text{ } urinary\text{-}system))$
$nephron \doteq (\textbf{and } anatomical\text{-}entity \text{ } (\textbf{all } is\text{-}part\text{-}of \text{ } kidney))$
$kidney\text{-}disease \doteq (\textbf{and } disease \text{ } (\textbf{all } anat\text{-}involvement \text{ } kidney))$
$nephron\text{-}disease \doteq (\textbf{and } disease \text{ } (\textbf{all } anat\text{-}involvement \text{ } nephron))$

In this case we would like to be able to deduce the fact that a nephron-disease is also a kidney-disease.

In [SM91] a possible way of introducing part-of in NIKL is introduced. The authors propose introducing for each concept for which the individuals have parts also another concept representing these parts. For instance, for the concept *kidney* the concept *kidney-part* is introduced too. The transitivity of part-of can then be obtained via subsumption. For instance, assume that we also have the concepts *nephron*, *body* and *body-part*. We assert that a kidney is a body part and that a nephron is a kidney part. Assume also that an individual is connected to its parts via the role *Has-Part*. Then to answer the question whether a nephron is a part of body, we need to ask NIKL whether the domain for the *Has-Part* role in *body* subsumes *nephron*. The authors agree that this is not an ideal method for representing part-of and much of the reasoning and representation has to be done by the user.

The work in [Jan88, JP89] aims at extending the expressive capabilities of NIKL to deal with the limitations described in [HPS88]. The new system is called KOLA. The part-of relations are treated as ordinary roles. Part-of is assumed to be transitive and it is possible to state this in the language using the **Transitive** constructor. For instance, (**Transitive** anatomical-part-of) asserts that the anatomical part-of relation is transitive.

Further, the authors note that special attention has to be paid to the interaction between subsumption and the part-of relation as in the example above, where in some cases one wants to deduce diseases of organs from diseases of parts of these organs. To be able to perform this kind of inferencing the notion of *indirect transitivity* is introduced:

A relation r_1 is indirectly transitive via relation r_2 if in the course of inferential operations on a concept involving r_1 a search of the role restriction of r_1 via the transitive relation r_2 is necessary.

In the example above we could define *anat-involvement* to be indirectly transitive via *is-part-of*. To answer the question whether a nephron disease is a kidney disease involves searching for a chain of *is-part-of* relations between the role restrictions of the *anat-involvement* role of *nephron-disease* (i.e. *nephron*) and *kidney-disease* (i.e. *kidney*). The constructor **Indir-Trans** allows a user to state the indirect transitivity.

Also in [Ber94] the part-of relation is used in a medical domain application. The authors note that all different types of part-whole relations as defined in [WCH87] also occur in their domain. However, they argue that the component/integral object and place/area relations are predominant and the transitive connection of these relations is often acceptable. Thus they decide to use one part-of relation which is a partial order. The part-of relation between concepts is represented by a partonomy.

The language has limited expressivity. A concept description consists of a base concept and a set of role restrictions. One of the role restrictions may involve the part-of role. The domain of the part-of restriction refers to the whole of the concept. The subsumption algorithm does not compute all subsumption relations as the transitivity of the part-of relation is not taken into consideration.

In some cases the disease of an organ component must be considered as a disease of an organ. However, this should not always be done. Therefore, the notion of part-sensitive subsumption is introduced in which the part-of relation is taken into consideration during subsumption.

As an extension of the part-of relation, the subsumptive part-of relation is introduced. Essentially, a concept C_1 is a subsumptive part of a concept C_2 if there is another concept C such that C_1 is subsumed by C and C is a part of C_2 or C_1 is a part of C and C is subsumed by C_2.

4.2.3 Part-of in an Object-Based Framework

The work in [Nap92, NLD94] aims at integrating general object-based methods and description logics into one framework. An example of this is the introduction of the notion of *o-subsumption* that defines the notion of subsumption for objects in the context of object-based representation systems.

In [NLD94] the aim is to model a domain for organic synthesis planning where the objects are molecular structures. The molecular structures are represented by graphs. In this context the part-of relation in the form of sub-structure relation becomes important. This relation is defined using a specialized kind of o-subsumption called *co-subsumption*. A structured object o_1 co-subsumes a structured object o_2 if o_1 describes a part of the structure of o_2. Essentially, co-subsumption captures the sub-graph relation. The co-subsumption relation is used as a basis for the *functional partonomy*. This hierarchy is then used in the planning cycle to find which structures can be used to build a given target structure.

4.3 Summary

We have seen that different authors represent part-of in different ways. Some authors represent only one part-of relation, others allow the representation of different part-whole relations. In the latter case some authors have predefined kinds of part-whole relations while others allow full flexibility with part-whole hierarchies. Most authors concentrate on the relation between a whole and its parts (i.e. a whole has parts) while only few concentrate on the relation between the parts and their wholes (i.e. parts are included in wholes).

Few authors provide an underlying framework for their part-of representation. This means that for several authors unintended models can arise.

The support for representing part-of is usually motivated in terms of applications. They include telephone switching applications, medical applications, applications in natural language processing and applications in chemistry.

Some authors restrict themselves to some specialized inferences or properties with respect to part-of, while other authors try to model part-of as generally as possible. The properties include transitivity, exclusive parts, essential parts and dependent parts. The languages that support composite objects range from relatively small and efficient languages to very expressive but undecidable languages. For some description logics prototypes have been implemented.

In chapters 5 and 6 we propose our own framework. We allow the representation of information about different kinds of part-whole relations. The underlying framework for part-of is as defined in section 3.2. We concentrate on the relation between wholes and their parts. The language we propose is also motivated by various applications (see chapters 8, 9 and 11). In chapter 5 we present a rather simple description logic for which an implementation exists. In chapter 6 we present a more expressive language that deals with a number of other properties. There we also propose new reasoning services targeted at part-of.

Part II

Theory

5. A Framework for Part-of Reasoning in Description Logics

5.1 Introduction

For many domains natural models require the ability to represent information about is-a as well as about part-of. A knowledge representation system supporting these relations needs a flexible representation as well as specialized services. For instance, with respect to representation we would like to be able to represent such items as the fact that all parts of an object or all objects in a certain relation to an object belong to a specific type, or that there are only a certain number of parts for a particular part-whole relation. The desired services may include checking whether one type is a sub-type of another, recognizing whether an object belongs to a particular type and support for instantiation of composite objects.

In this chapter and the next chapter we present a framework that integrates part-of in description logics. This framework provides support for many of the features that are desired in a knowledge representation system for composite objects. In this chapter we discuss a simple framework in which we define the basic notions of our description logic for composite objects. In the next chapter we extend the representational and reasoning capabilities of the framework.

As we have seen in section 3.2, our part-of model is based on the notion of direct parts which have names. This allows us to conceptualize different part-whole relations in our models. We can distinguish between part-whole relations and other relations as well as between different kinds of parts.

In sections 5.2 and 5.3 we extend a standard description logic in two ways. First, we use the notion of *part name* that allows us to distinguish among different kinds of parts in a similar way as the notion of roles allows us to distinguish among different binary relations.

For these part names we define analogues for the constructs that are available for roles. Thus we are able to express domain restrictions and number restrictions for part names. We can also express that certain part names have certain fillers. Further, we define a new construct which allows us to define constraints between the different parts of a composite. It is a step towards allowing for specialized reasoning and inferencing involving the part-of relation.

P. Lambrix: Part-Whole Reasoning, LNAI 1771, pp. 41-53, 2000
© Springer-Verlag Berlin Heidelberg 2000

In section 5.4 we define a part-of hierarchy for individuals based on the direct parts. It allows us to represent and query the structure of composite individuals. By traversing the part-of hierarchy we can obtain information about composite individuals and parts at different levels.

We have implemented the notions defined in this chapter as an extension to CLASSIC. In section 5.5 we discuss the implemented functionality of the new system, CLASSIC($\triangleleft$).

The examples that we use in this chapter and the next chapter are based on the activities in a distribution company. A distribution company receives goods which are to be redistributed to clients. Whenever a new load of goods arrives, the goods are stored. This can be done in parcels (a pallet with goods of the same kind) or as loose items. When an order is received from a client, the necessary goods are taken from the store and shipped. The examples that we use only describe a part of the activities of a distribution company and in a much simplified manner. However, they are sufficient for our purposes here.

5.2 Terminological Knowledge

Part-whole relations capture structural information about objects. In a system supporting part-whole relations it is therefore important to be able to distinguish between part-whole relations, such as the relation between a truck and its doors, and other relations, such as the relation between a truck and its driver. Further, different kinds of parts can have different properties. Thus it is important to be able to distinguish between different kinds of parts. We do this by defining the notion of *part name* in the description logic. Part names are similar to roles in standard description logics in the sense that they can be seen as binary relations over a domain of individuals.

Obviously, in a way similar to roles, it is important to be able to define domains to which the different parts in a composition must belong. We do this using the **allp** construct which is similar to the **all** construct for roles. For instance, (**allp** *pallet-p Australian-pallet*) in the definition of an *Australian-parcel* would mean that all pallet parts are Australian pallets.[1] Also in a way similar to roles, we introduce constructs for giving number restrictions for parts. These are the **atleastp** and **atmostp** constructs. This enables us to make statements such as (**atmostp** *60 parcel-p*), indicating that there are at most sixty parcel parts. If no explicit range is given for a part name, it is assumed that an individual belonging to that concept can have any number of parts for that part name.

In cases where we want a particular individual to be a filler for a part name, we can use the **part-fills** construct. For instance, (**part-fills** *parcel-p p*) would mean that the individual *p* is a parcel part. For concepts this

---

[1] To ship goods to Australia different pallets must be used than for the goods shipped to European destinations.

construct makes sense in the case where all individuals belonging to that concept share a particular individual as a direct part with the same part name.[2] As we describe later, this language is also used to describe information about individuals. This construct is a natural way to state that a particular individual is a direct part with a particular part name of another individual.

Further, we found the ability to express constraints between the different parts of a composite to be useful in several domains. We define the **pp-constraint** construct[3] to allow for this expressivity. For instance, specifying that the leader part of a standard work group must be the boss of the members of the group can be done by having (**pp-constraint** *is-boss-of leader-p member-p*) in the definition of standard work group.

5.2.1 Syntax

$<$*concept-descr*$>$ ::=
    $\top$
    | $\bot$
    | $<$*concept-name*$>$
    | (**and** $<$*concept-descr*$>^{+}$)
    | (**all** $<$*role-name*$>$ $<$*concept-descr*$>$)
    | (**atleast** $<$*positive-integer*$>$ $<$*role-name*$>$)
    | (**atmost** $<$*non-negative-integer*$>$ $<$*role-name*$>$)
    | (**fills** $<$*role-name*$>$ $<$*individual-name*$>^{+}$)
    | (**allp** $<$*part-name-name*$>$ $<$*concept-descr*$>$)
    | (**atleastp** $<$*positive-integer*$>$ $<$*part-name-name*$>$)
    | (**atmostp** $<$*non-negative-integer*$>$ $<$*part-name-name*$>$)
    | (**part-fills** $<$*part-name-name*$>$ $<$*individual-name*$>^{+}$)
    | (**pp-constraint** $<$*role-name*$>$ $<$*part-name-name*$>$ $<$*part-name-name*$>$)

$<$*concept-name*$>$ ::=	$<$*symbol*$>$	
$<$*role-name*$>$ ::=	$<$*symbol*$>$	
$<$*part-name-name*$>$ ::=	$<$*symbol*$>$	
$<$*individual-name*$>$ ::=	$<$*symbol*$>$	

Fig. 5.1. Syntax of a description logic for composite objects.

The syntax of the language is defined in figure 5.1. *Terminological axioms*[4] are used to introduce names for concepts and definitions of those concepts.

---

[2] In an electronic document domain, the departmental logo might be shared by all departmental reports as a logo part.

[3] This construct may be seen as a variant of the generalized value restriction in [Han92].

[4] These definitions are standard for the standard part of our language (see section 2.1.1). For a *terminology* we add to the requirement that there are no cycles via is-a the requirement that there are no cycles via part-of and via the combination of is-a and part-of.

$employee \mathbin{\dot{\leq}} \top$

$item \mathbin{\dot{\leq}}$
> (**and** (**atleast** *1 item-number*)
>   (**atmost** *1 item-number*))

$pallet \mathbin{\dot{\leq}}$
> (**and** (**atleast** *1 pallet-number*)
>   (**atmost** *1 pallet-number*))

$parcel\text{-}card \doteq$
> (**and** (**atleast** *1 card-number*)
>   (**atmost** *1 card-number*)
>   (**atleast** *1 item-number*)
>   (**atmost** *1 item-number*)
>   (**atleast** *1 pick-location-number*)
>   (**atmost** *1 pick-location-number*)
>   (**atleast** *1 quantity*)
>   (**atmost** *1 quantity*))

$parcel \doteq$
> (**and** (**atleast** *1 item-number*)
>   (**atmost** *1 item-number*)
>   (**atleastp** *1 card-p*)
>   (**atmostp** *1 card-p*)
>   (**allp** *card-p parcel-card*)
>   (**atleastp** *1 pallet-p*)
>   (**atmostp** *1 pallet-p*)
>   (**allp** *pallet-p pallet*)
>   (**allp** *item-p item*))

$pick\text{-}location \doteq$
> (**and** (**atleast** *1 capacity*)
>   (**atmost** *1 capacity*)
>   (**atleast** *1 location-number*)
>   (**atmost** *1 location-number*)
>   (**atleast** *1 location-supervisor*)
>   (**atmost** *1 location-supervisor*))

$standard\text{-}work\text{-}group \doteq$
> (**and** (**atleastp** *1 leader-p*)
>   (**atmostp** *1 leader-p*)
>   (**allp** *leader-p employee*)
>   (**allp** *member-p employee*)
>   (**pp-constraint** *is-boss-of leader-p member-p*))

Fig. 5.2. Concept definitions in a distribution company domain.

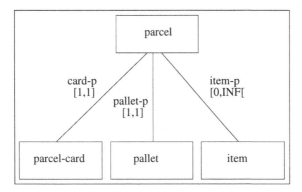

Fig. 5.3. Parcel.

Let A be a concept name (<*symbol*>) and C a concept description (<*concept-descr*>). Then terminological axioms can be of the form: A $\dot{\leq}$ C for introducing necessary conditions (primitive concepts), or A $\dot{=}$ C for introducing necessary and sufficient conditions (defined concepts). A *terminology* (*Tbox*) T is a finite set of terminological axioms with the additional restrictions that (i) every concept name used must appear exactly once on the left-hand side of a terminological axiom, and (ii) T must not contain cyclic definitions directly or indirectly, via either $\dot{=}$, $\dot{\leq}$, an **allp** construct or any combination of these.

This language allows us then to define concepts[5] as in figure 5.2. The concepts *item* and *pallet* are defined as primitive concepts. Items have exactly one filler for the *item-number* role and pallets have exactly one filler for the *pallet-number* role. The other concepts are defined concepts. A *parcel-card* has a number of different roles with exactly one filler per role (*card-number*, *item-number*, *pick-location-number* and *quantity*). *Parcels* contain one parcel card, one pallet part and item parts. The domain constraints are given. Parcels also have an item number representing the kind of goods that the parcel consists of. Figure 5.3 shows the properties of a parcel that are related to part names. A *pick-location* is a place in the store where goods can be retrieved. A pick location has a capacity, a location number and a location supervisor. A *standard-work-group* has exactly one leader part. All member parts and the leader part must be employees. Further, the leader part must be the boss of the member parts.

5.2.2 Semantics

An interpretation of the language consists of a tuple $< \mathcal{D}, \varepsilon >$, where $\mathcal{D}$ is the domain and ε the extension function. The extension function is defined in

---

[5] Some of the concepts are redefined in the next chapter where we have a more expressive language at our disposal.

the standard way for description logics (as in section 2.1.2), but extended to also deal with part names. The extension function ε maps part name names and role names into sub-sets of $\mathcal{D} \times \mathcal{D}$, concept names into sub-sets of $\mathcal{D}$ and individual names into elements of $\mathcal{D}$ such that $\varepsilon[i_1] \neq \varepsilon[i_2]$ whenever $i_1 \neq i_2$. The semantics for the different constructs are shown in figure 5.4. We assume that in a domain for an interpretation the assumptions in section 3.2 about parts hold. Thus in a domain (i) part-of is a strict partial order, (ii) every composite has at least two parts and (iii) there are no parts between a composite and its direct parts. We have a standard semantics for the standard part of our language. For convenience we write $y \lhd_n x$ to denote $<y,x> \in \varepsilon[n]$ where n is a part name name. If $y \lhd_n x$, we say that y is a direct part of x with name n or y is an n-part of x.

$$\varepsilon[\top] = \mathcal{D}$$
$$\varepsilon[\bot] = \emptyset$$
$$\varepsilon[(\textbf{and } A\ B)] = \varepsilon[A] \cap \varepsilon[B]$$
$$\varepsilon[(\textbf{all } r\ A)] = \{\ x \in \mathcal{D} \mid \forall\ y \in \mathcal{D}\colon <x,y> \in \varepsilon[r] \rightarrow y \in \varepsilon[A]\}$$
$$\varepsilon[(\textbf{atleast } m\ r)] = \{\ x \in \mathcal{D} \mid \sharp\ \{\ y \in \mathcal{D} \mid <x,y> \in \varepsilon[r]\} \geq m\ \}$$
$$\varepsilon[(\textbf{atmost } m\ r)] = \{\ x \in \mathcal{D} \mid \sharp\ \{\ y \in \mathcal{D} \mid <x,y> \in \varepsilon[r]\} \leq m\ \}$$
$$\varepsilon[(\textbf{fills } r\ i_1\ ...\ i_m)] = \{\ x \in \mathcal{D} \mid <x,\varepsilon[i_1]> \in \varepsilon[r] \wedge\ ...\ \wedge <x,\varepsilon[i_m]> \in \varepsilon[r]\ \}$$
$$\varepsilon[(\textbf{allp } n\ A)] = \{\ x \in \mathcal{D} \mid \forall\ y \in \mathcal{D}\colon y \lhd_n x \rightarrow y \in \varepsilon[A]\}$$
$$\varepsilon[(\textbf{atleastp } m\ n)] = \{\ x \in \mathcal{D} \mid \sharp\ \{\ y \in \mathcal{D} \mid y \lhd_n x\ \} \geq m\ \}$$
$$\varepsilon[(\textbf{atmostp } m\ n)] = \{\ x \in \mathcal{D} \mid \sharp\ \{\ y \in \mathcal{D} \mid y \lhd_n x\ \} \leq m\ \}$$
$$\varepsilon[(\textbf{part-fills } n\ i_1\ ...\ i_m)] = \{\ x \in \mathcal{D} \mid \varepsilon[i_1] \lhd_n x \wedge\ ...\ \wedge \varepsilon[i_m] \lhd_n x\ \}$$
$$\varepsilon[(\textbf{pp-constraint } r\ n_1\ n_2)] = \{\ x \in \mathcal{D} \mid \forall\ y_1,y_2 \in \mathcal{D}\colon$$
$$(y_1 \lhd_{n_1} x \wedge y_2 \lhd_{n_2} x) \rightarrow <y_1,y_2> \in \varepsilon[r]\}$$

Fig. 5.4. Semantics of a description logic for composite objects.

As noted before, part names are similar to roles in standard description logics. Therefore the semantics of the **allp**, **atleastp**, **atmostp** and **part-fills** constructs are part name analogues of the **all**, **atleast**, **atmost** and **fills** constructs which involve roles. However, by distinguishing between part names and roles we can treat the part names and thus the part-of relation in a special way. For instance, this allows us to define constraints between the parts of a composition (**pp-constraint**s), whereas we cannot define constraints between the fillers of ordinary roles. Essentially, part-of can be seen as a labeling on certain roles, giving them a more specific semantics than other roles.

An interpretation $<\mathcal{D}, \varepsilon>$ is a *model* for a Tbox if for all $A \dot{\leq} C$ in the Tbox $\varepsilon[A] \subseteq \varepsilon[C]$ and for all $A \doteq C$ in the Tbox $\varepsilon[A] = \varepsilon[C]$.

5.2.3 Subsumption

Subsumption is defined as usual for description logics. A subsumes B, written $B \Rightarrow A$, iff $\varepsilon[B] \subseteq \varepsilon[A]$ for every interpretation $<\mathcal{D},\varepsilon>$. Subsumption between concepts can also be defined with respect to a Tbox, by requiring that the interpretations in the definition are models of the Tbox.

Structural subsumption rules for the aspects of the language involving part-of are given in figure 5.5 in the style of [Bor92]. Normalization rules can be found in figure 5.6 and combinant inference rules in figure 5.7. For the rules of the standard part of the language, we refer to [Bor92].

Specializing the range of a part name leads to a more specialized concept.

$$\frac{\vdash\ C_1\ \Rightarrow\ C_2}{\vdash\ (\textbf{allp}\ n\ C_1)\ \Rightarrow\ (\textbf{allp}\ n\ C_2)}$$

Higher lower bounds are more restrictive.

$$\frac{m_1\ <\ m_2}{\vdash\ (\textbf{atleastp}\ m_2\ n)\ \Rightarrow\ (\textbf{atleastp}\ m_1\ n)}$$

Higher upper bounds are less restrictive.

$$\frac{m_1\ <\ m_2}{\vdash\ (\textbf{atmostp}\ m_1\ n)\ \Rightarrow\ (\textbf{atmostp}\ m_2\ n)}$$

Requiring a larger set of part fillers is more restrictive.

$$\frac{\{ii\}\ \subseteq\ \{jj\}}{\vdash\ (\textbf{part}-\textbf{fills}\ n\ jj)\ \Rightarrow\ (\textbf{part}-\textbf{fills}\ n\ ii)}$$

Fig. 5.5. Structural subsumption rules for a description logic for composite objects.

With respect to parts we obtain the semantics that if A subsumes B, then B may have additional kinds of parts, more known part fillers, or more specialized parts than A, and the constraints (**pp-constraints**) between the parts of B may be stronger than those between the parts of A. Further, the possible numbers of direct parts with a particular part name defined in B are all in the interval of possible numbers of direct parts with the same part name defined in A.

5.3 Assertional Knowledge

Assertional statements are similar to terminological axioms but are used to make statements about individuals rather than about concept definitions. An assertional statement is of the form $i :: C$, where i is an individual name (<*symbol*>) and C a concept description (<*concept-descr*>) as defined before. This means then that $\varepsilon[i] \in \varepsilon[C]$. An *Abox* is a finite set of assertional statements.

and *is distributive over* **allp**.

$\vdash$ (**and** (**allp** n C_1) (**allp** n C_2)) $\equiv$ (**allp** n (**and** C_1 C_2))

and *of* **part-fills** *is like union*.

$\vdash$ (**and** (**part-fills** n ii) (**part-fills** n jj)) $\equiv$ (**part-fills** n $ii \cup jj$)

If you cannot have parts, then all parts must belong to the empty set.

$\vdash$ (**allp** n $\bot$) $\equiv$ (**atmostp** 0 n)

If the parts can be anything, then this is not really a constraint.

$\vdash$ (**allp** n $\top$) $\equiv$ $\top$

Inconsistent upper and lower bounds.

$$\frac{m_1 < m_2}{\vdash (\text{\textbf{and} } (\textbf{atmostp } m_1 \ n) \ (\textbf{atleastp } m_2 \ n)) \ \equiv \ \bot}$$

Fig. 5.6. Normalization rules for a description logic for composite objects.

Knowing a sub-set of the set of part fillers provides a lower bound on the number of part fillers.

$$\frac{size(\{ii\}) \ = \ m}{\vdash (\textbf{part} - \textbf{fills } n \ ii) \ \Rightarrow \ (\textbf{atleastp } m \ n)}$$

Constraints and roles - 1.

$\vdash$ (**and** (**pp-constraint** r n_1 n_2) (**atleastp** 1 n_1) (**allp** n_1 (**atmost** m r)))
$\Rightarrow$ (**atmostp** m n_2)

$\vdash$ (**and** (**pp-constraint** r n_1 n_2) (**atleastp** 1 n_1) (**allp** n_1 (**all** r C)))
$\Rightarrow$ (**allp** n_2 C)

Constraints and roles - 2.

$\vdash$ (**and** (**pp-constraint** r n_1 n_2) (**atleastp** m n_2))
$\Rightarrow$ (**allp** n_1 (**atleast** m r))

$\vdash$ (**and** (**pp-constraint** r n_1 n_2) (**part-fills** n_2 $i_1...i_k$))
$\Rightarrow$ (**allp** n_1 (**fills** r $i_1...i_k$))

Fig. 5.7. Combinant inferences for a description logic for composite objects.

We say that an individual is *defined* in an Abox if it appears in any one of the statements in the Abox. We assume that within one Abox an individual has a unique name.

In figure 5.8 we give an example of an Abox. The Abox defines a parcel p (as defined in figure 5.2) and its different known parts: a parcel card pc and a pallet *pal*. Figure 5.9 shows the parcel individual with its parts.

p ::

    (**and** *parcel*
        (**fills** *item-number in*)
        (**part-fills** *card-p pc*)
        (**part-fills** *pallet-p pal*))

pc ::

    (**and** *parcel-card*
        (**fills** *card-number cn*)
        (**fills** *item-number-p in*)
        (**fills** *pick-location-number-p pln*)
        (**fills** *quantity-p q*))

Fig. 5.8. A parcel individual - 1.

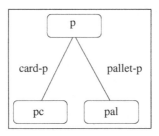

Fig. 5.9. A parcel individual - 2.

We say that an interpretation $< \mathcal{D}, \varepsilon >$ is a *model* for an Abox A if $\varepsilon[i] \in \varepsilon[C]$ for every $i :: C$ in the Abox A. A knowledge base is defined as a tuple $< T, A >$ where T is a Tbox and A an Abox. An interpretation is a model for a knowledge base $< T, A >$ if it is a model for T and a model for A. Subsumption can be defined with respect to a knowledge base, by requiring that the interpretations in the definition of subsumption are models of the knowledge base.

Rules for reasoning about individuals in the standard part of the language can be found in [Bor92]. In figure 5.10 we show the rules that are specific for our language and that involve the part-of relation.

Number of parts.

$$\frac{kb \;\vdash\; \sharp\{x \mid x \vartriangleleft_n y\} = m}{kb \;\vdash\; y \;\rightarrow\; (\textbf{atleastp}\; m\; n)}$$

Propagation rules.

$$\frac{kb \;\vdash\; x \vartriangleleft_n y,\; kb \;\vdash\; y \;\rightarrow\; (\textbf{allp}\; n\; C)}{kb \;\vdash\; x \;\rightarrow\; C}$$

$$\frac{kb \;\vdash\; x_1 \vartriangleleft_{n_1} y,\; kb \;\vdash\; x_2 \vartriangleleft_{n_2} y\,,\; kb \;\vdash\; y \;\rightarrow\; (\textbf{pp}-\textbf{constraint}\; r\; n_1\; n_2)}{kb \;\vdash\; r(x_1, x_2)}$$

Fig. 5.10. Reasoning about individuals in a description logic for composite objects.

5.4 Part-of Hierarchy for Individuals

In applications it is sometimes necessary to know which individuals contain a particular individual and which individuals are contained in a particular individual. For instance, if a particular part of a car is broken, then assuming that there is no malfunction procedure involving alternative parts, all the composites containing that part also have to be considered as broken. However, while diagnosing the fault, we may start with the most composite individual and test its parts and then the parts of the parts and so on until the fault is found. In these cases we need to find the parts at different levels while the part name is not so important. To be able to support these queries we introduce the notion of *part-of* which is based on the notion of direct part.

Definition 5.4.1. *An individual i_1 is a* **direct part with part name** n *of individual i_2 with respect to knowledge base $< T, A >$ (notation $i_1 \vartriangleleft_n {}_{<T,A>} i_2$)[6] iff $\varepsilon[i_1] \vartriangleleft_n \varepsilon[i_2]$ for every model $<\mathcal{D},\varepsilon>$ of $< T, A >$.*

An individual i_1 is a **part** *of individual i_2 with respect to knowledge base $< T, A >$ (notation $i_1 \vartriangleleft^* {}_{<T,A>} i_2$) iff $\varepsilon[i_1] \vartriangleleft^* \varepsilon[i_2]$ for every model $<\mathcal{D},\varepsilon>$ of $< T, A >$.*

An individual having parts is called a **composite individual**.

Thus the part-of relation is defined as the transitive closure over all the direct part relations. It follows from the definition that the part-of relation for individuals with respect to a knowledge base is a strict partial order, i.e. irreflexive and transitive.

The part-of hierarchy that is based on the part-of relation supports reasoning about the part-of relation for individuals in a similar way as the subsumption hierarchy supports reasoning about the is-a relation for concepts. The question as to which composite individuals the individual i is a part

---

[6] We sometimes also write $i_1 \vartriangleleft_n i_2$ in $< T, A >$. When it is clear which knowledge base we are using, we often do not mention the knowledge base in the symbols for direct part and part.

of is answered by identifying all individuals i' such that $i \lhd^* i'$. Similarly, the question as to which individuals are part of individual i is answered by identifying all individuals i' such that $i' \lhd^* i$. Both queries simply involve following paths up and down respectively, in the part-of hierarchy starting at the individual i. The information is directly available using Abox statements and the semantics of the language.

5.5 Implemented Functionality

As a basis for our implementation we use the COMMON LISP implementation, version 2.2 of the CLASSIC system [Re*93]. This version of the system is made available to academic researchers by AT&T Bell Laboratories. A description of the subsumption algorithm can be found in, for example, [BP94].

The subsumption algorithm for the extended system, CLASSIC($\lhd$), is very similar to CLASSIC's subsumption algorithm. We have extended the original algorithm in the following way. In the normalization step we have added an implementation of the rules in 5.6 which are part name analogues of existing rules for roles. In the inferences step we have added the rules in figure 5.7. The first rule is again a part name analogue of an existing rule for roles. The other rules require going through a list of pp-constraints and for each of them looking for a restriction for the domain of a part name. The subsumption step is extended with an implementation of the rules in figure 5.5. Again, they are part name analogues of existing rules for roles. All the additional computations can be done in polynomial time so that the complexity of the algorithm for CLASSIC($\lhd$) is still polynomial.

With respect to individuals we have added an implementation of the rules in figure 5.10. While we have again part name analogues of rules for roles, we also have a new propagation rule for the constraints between parts. For each (**pp-constraint** $r\ n_1\ n_2$) in the description of an individual, we have to find all its part-fillers for part names n_1 and n_2 and add the n_2-parts as r-fillers to the n_1-parts. Recognizing individuals is very similar to recognizing the corresponding constructs for roles for the **allp, atleastp, atmostp** and **part-fills** constructs. An individual i belongs to (**pp-constraint** $r\ n_1\ n_2$) if it is told to be so, can be inferred from the told information, or when all its n_1-parts have all its n_2-parts as r-fillers. The latter can only be checked in the case where we know all the n_1-parts and n_2-parts of i.

The system also checks that the part-whole relations satisfy the model as described in chapter 3. In particular, a check is made to ensure that no cycles occur in the part-of hierarchy. We also check to ensure that two direct parts of an individual are not in a part-of relation with each other. Because of the open-world assumption in description logics, we do not check the assumption that an individual cannot have only one part.

To maintain the part-of hierarchy we need to do the following (see figure 5.11). Whenever we know that an individual is a part filler for another individual (by being told or by propagation) then it is also a part. Further, parts of parts are also parts, i.e. part-of is transitive. Another way that an individual can be part of another individual is when the first individual belongs to a concept of which the other individual is a part. This happens, for instance, when we have i_1 :: (**and** (**atleastp** 1 n_1) (**allp** n_1 (**part-fills** n_2 i_2))). In this case we know that in every interpretation $\varepsilon[i_2] \lhd^* \varepsilon[i_1]$.[7] More generally, if the first individual belongs to a concept that defines a chain of part names for which there is at least one part and the chains ends with a **part-fills** construct involving another individual, then the other individual is a part of the first individual. When creating a new individual or adding information to an individual, the part-of hierarchy is updated.

A direct part is a part.

$$\frac{kb \;\vdash\; x \lhd_n y}{kb \;\vdash\; x \lhd^* y}$$

Transitivity of part.

$$\frac{kb \;\vdash\; x \lhd^* y, kb \;\vdash\; y \lhd^* z}{kb \;\vdash\; x \lhd^* z}$$

Parts through concepts.

$$\frac{kb \;\vdash\; x \;\rightarrow\; (\textbf{and} \; (\textbf{atleastp} \; 1 \; n_1) \; (\textbf{allp} \; n_1 \; (\textbf{part} - \textbf{fills} \; n_2 \; y)))}{kb \;\vdash\; y \lhd^* x}$$

$$\frac{\begin{array}{l} kb \;\vdash\; x \;\rightarrow\; (\textbf{and} \; (\textbf{atleastp} \; 1 \; n_1) \\ (\textbf{allp} \; n_1 \; (\; ... \; (\textbf{and} \; (\textbf{atleastp} \; 1 \; n_m) \; (\textbf{allp} \; n_m \; (\textbf{part} - \textbf{fills} \; n_2 \; y))))...))) \end{array}}{kb \;\vdash\; y \lhd^* x}$$

Fig. 5.11. Maintaining the part-of hierarchy for individuals.

To be able to use and traverse the part-of hierarchy we implemented user functions for CLASSIC($\lhd$). They include questions such as finding out whether one individual is a part or a direct part of another individual. We can also obtain a list of individuals that are part of another individual or a list of individuals of which a particular individual is a part. More complex functions return a list of individuals that are higher up or lower down in the part-of hierarchy than a particular individual and belong to a particular concept. In appendix A we list the functionality that we have added to CLASSIC.

---

[7] Consider as example a non-empty folder with departmental reports. Each of the departmental reports contains the departmental logo as a part. Then we also know that the departmental logo is included in every non-empty folder of departmental reports.

5.6 Summary

We have extended a standard description logic with part names and constructs involving part names, thus allowing for the representation of part-whole relations in description logics. For the language, the constructs for roles received analogues for part names and we added the notion of constraints between parts. We defined a part-of hierarchy that allows for reasoning about the part-of relation for individuals. We implemented these notions as an addition to CLASSIC which we call CLASSIC($\lhd$).

The framework defined here can be used as a basis for different applications. In chapter 8 we describe an agent-oriented application which has benefited from modeling the application in a small extension of this description logic. In chapter 10 we use the framework defined here in a machine learning application. For other applications (see chapters 9 and 11) more specialized constructs in the language and specialized inferencing involving part-of are needed. In the next chapter we extend our framework in various ways.

6. Extending the Framework

6.1 Introduction

In the previous chapter we extended a description logic system to provide support for representation of and inferencing with composite objects. In a similar way as standard description logic systems provide services for the is-a relation, a description logic for composite objects needs to provide specialized services for part-of. However, up till now, no other approach that combines description logics with part-of has provided any such services. A natural class of services concerning part-of are services that provide support for the instantiation or building of composite objects. In this chapter we propose a number of services in this class: *composes, assembly* and *completion*. The *composes* relation allows checking whether a set of individuals can be used as parts and modules for an individual belonging to a particular concept. The *assembly* inference extends a given knowledge base by inferring new individuals given the existence of individuals that can be used as parts and modules. Finally, *completions* allow for finding out given some parts what parts are still missing to be able to build an individual of a certain type.

In this chapter we also extend the description logic in different ways with respect to representational capabilities. A first extension allows representation of ordering information. In some application domains such as a document domain, there is a need for this kind of information. For instance, in a document domain the order in which sections or paragraphs occur in a document is important. In a way similar to propagation of information via is-a, propagation of information via part-of can also be useful. For instance, we may want to express a constraint between parts and whole such as the fact that people writing some sections in a document are also authors of the document. In this chapter we introduce some limited support for this kind of propagation of information via part-of.

Further, we introduce a new relation with part-of intuition. We found that in some cases we have a containment relation between objects which should not be expressed using a direct part or part-of relation as defined in the previous chapter. For instance, assume that a delivery is defined as containing a number of parcels and assume we have a particular delivery d that contains twenty parcels. Then the aggregation of ten of these parcels is also contained in the delivery, but we would not call the aggregation a part

P. Lambrix: Part-Whole Reasoning, LNAI 1771, pp. 55-98, 2000
© Springer-Verlag Berlin Heidelberg 2000

in the sense of chapter 5. To handle this kind of containment we introduce the notion of *module*. A module o_1 of a composite object o_2 is a composite object itself that contains parts of o_2 and no others. Modules can be seen as parts (in a broader sense) of a composite object that are not named. We define modules formally and use them as a basis together with the part-of relation of chapter 5, for defining *compositional inclusion*. Compositional inclusion is another transitive relation with part-of intuition and can be seen as an approximation of the basic part-of relation of [Sim87, AFGP96, Var96]. We also define a compositional inclusion hierarchy which extends the part-of hierarchy of chapter 5.

The chapter is organized as follows. In section 6.2 we introduce new constructs that allow for the representation of ordering information in the definition of concepts and individuals, and we provide some support for inheritance via part-whole relations. In section 6.3 we introduce the notions of *module* and compositional inclusion for individuals together with a compositional inclusion hierarchy for individuals. Section 6.4 describes a compositional inclusion hierarchy for concepts. The main purpose of this hierarchy is to be used as a search framework for the specialized inferences for part-of. The inferences are described in sections 6.5 (*composes*), 6.6 (*assembly*) and 6.7 (*completion*).

6.2 Extended Language

6.2.1 Terminological Knowledge

The language defined in chapter 5 allows for differentiation between different kinds of parts by using different part names. Thus we can have both item parts and pallet parts in the definition of parcels. However, we have no way of differentiating between different instances of the same part name. If a truck load contains different deliveries each for a different client, we cannot, in the definition of truck load, differentiate these from each other. However, this seems to be necessary in several applications, in particular to support ordering of parts at the individual level. In this example the order of the different deliveries is important when loading the truck.[1] We introduce the ability to specify which is delivery 1, which delivery 2, and so on. We extend the language by allowing a number to be attached to the part name in some instances. The ordering of these numbers is used to induce an order on the associated parts. To allow this ordering to extend over all the parts of a composite in a uniform way, we also introduce the notion of an order constraint between two different kinds of parts. This is written as in

---

[1] In a document management application the need for ordering information is even more obvious. It is not acceptable for the sections of a document to appear in random order.

(**order-constraint**[2] *original-p copy-p*). This indicates that in the ordering of parts, *original-p* comes before *copy-p*. If there are several original parts (in the case this would be allowed by the definition), indicated as *original-p:1*, *original-p:2* and so on, then these will be ordered by ordering number, and all come before any *copy-p*. In the remainder we say that if a part name is followed by an ordering number, the part name is qualified.[3]

In a way similar to inheritance via is-a, inheritance via part-of can be useful. For instance, in our example domain we may define a delivery containing parcels. The weight of the delivery can then be computed as the sum of the weights of all the parcels that are part of the delivery. We introduce constructs in the language that give us the ability to do a limited form of propagation of information via part-of. The constructs allow us to infer attribute values of parts based on those of wholes, or vice versa, or attribute values of parts, based on those of other parts. Attributes are roles which can have exactly one filler. The first construct we introduce is **same-filler**[4] which is similar to *same-as* in CLASSIC, but with restricted path length. It allows us to state, for instance, in the definition of a parcel such things as (**same-filler** *card-p.card-number pallet-p.pallet-number*), indicating that the card number attribute of a card part has the same value as the pallet number attribute of the pallet part. We also introduce the **aggregate**[5] construct which allows us to aggregate a set of attribute values for a particular kind of part and declare these to be role fillers of a particular role within the composite object. Thus (**aggregate** *location-p location-supervisor location-supervisors*) in the definition of a pick space indicates that the value of the role *location-supervisors* for the pick space is an aggregate of the *location-supervisor* attribute in each of the location parts of the pick space.

The final extension is to allow a user to state that particular individuals are modules of other individuals or sets of individuals. This allows for a modular instantiation of composite individuals. First we can define the less complex composite individuals and then we can use them as wholes to instantiate more complex composite individuals. We do not discuss this any further here as we introduce the notion of module in section 6.3.

Syntax. The syntax of the language is defined in figure 6.1. The notions of terminological axioms and Tbox are the same as in chapter 5.

In figures 6.2, 6.3 and 6.4 we redefine some of the concepts for the distribution company domain. For instance, the definition of parcel now contains three **same-filler** constructs as well. The first requirement states that the

---

[2] This construct may be seen as a variant of the generalized value restriction in [Han92].

[3] In the syntax of the language this corresponds to $<q\text{-}part>$.

[4] This construct may be seen as a restricted variant of the role value map (e.g. [BS85]). The paths of the role value map are restricted to part-attribute paths.

[5] This construct may be seen as a restricted variant of the role value map. The first path is of the form q-part.attribute, while the second path is a role. At the end of the paths we do not have equality, but a sub-set relation.

<concept-descr> ::=
    ⊤
    | ⊥
    | *<concept-name>*
    | (**and** *<concept-descr>*$^+$)
    | (**all** *<role-name>* *<concept-descr>*)
    | (**atleast** *<positive-integer>* *<role-name>*)
    | (**atmost** *<non-negative-integer>* *<role-name>*)
    | (**fills** *<role-name>* *<individual-name>*$^+$)
    | (**allp** *<q-part>* *<concept-descr>*)
    | (**atleastp** *<positive-integer>* *<part-name-name>*)
    | (**atmostp** *<non-negative-integer>* *<part-name-name>*)
    | (**part-fills** *<part-name-name>* *<individual-name>*$^+$)
    | (**module-fills** *<individual-name>*$^+$)
    | (**pp-constraint** *<role-name>* *<q-part>* *<q-part>*)
    | (**order-constraint** *q-part q-part*)
    | (**same-filler** *part-attr-path part-attr-path*)
    | (**aggregate** *q-part attribute-name role-name*)

<concept-name> ::=	*<symbol>*
<individual-name> ::=	*<symbol>*
<role-name> ::=	*<symbol>*
<attribute-name> ::=	*<symbol>*
<part-name-name> ::=	*<symbol>*
<q-part> ::=	*<part-name-name>*
	| *<part-name-name:positive-number>*
<part-attr-path> ::=	*<attribute-name>* | *<q-part.attribute-name>*

Fig. 6.1. Syntax of an extended description logic for composite objects.

values of the item numbers of the item parts are all the same as the value of the item number of the parcel. The second requirement states that the value of the item number of the card part is the same as the value of the item number of the parcel. The third requirement states that the card number attribute of the card part has the same value as the pallet number attribute of the pallet part of the parcel. We have also added some new concepts that exemplify the new constructs. For instance, a pick space is something that contains different pick locations. We have inheritance of values for location supervisors using the **aggregate** construct via the location parts. We have also defined a delivery document that contains three parts: the original document and two carbon copies. We employ the constraint that the original document has to come before the carbon copies.

item $\dot{\le}$
          (**and** (**atleast** *1 item-number*)
                    (**atmost** *1 item-number*))

pallet $\dot{\le}$
          (**and** (**atleast** *1 pallet-number*)
                    (**atmost** *1 pallet-number*))

parcel-card $\doteq$
          (**and** (**atleast** *1 card-number*)
                    (**atmost** *1 card-number*)
                    (**atleast** *1 item-number*)
                    (**atmost** *1 item-number*)
                    (**atleast** *1 pick-location-number*)
                    (**atmost** *1 pick-location-number*)
                    (**atleast** *1 quantity*)
                    (**atmost** *1 quantity*))

parcel $\doteq$
          (**and** (**atleast** *1 item-number*)
                    (**atmost** *1 item-number*)
                    (**atleastp** *1 card-p*)
                    (**atmostp** *1 card-p*)
                    (**allp** *card-p parcel-card*)
                    (**atleastp** *1 pallet-p*)
                    (**atmostp** *1 pallet-p*)
                    (**allp** *pallet-p pallet*)
                    (**allp** *item-p item*)
                    (**same-filler** *item-p.item-number item-number*)
                    (**same-filler** *card-p.item-number item-number*)
                    (**same-filler** *card-p.card-number pallet-p.pallet-number*))

Fig. 6.2. Concept definitions in a distribution company domain - 1.

pick-location $\doteq$
   (**and** (**atleast** *1 capacity*)
      (**atmost** *1 capacity*)
      (**atleast** *1 location-number*)
      (**atmost** *1 location-number*)
      (**atleast** *1 location-supervisor*)
      (**atmost** *1 location-supervisor*))

pick-space $\doteq$
   (**and** (**atleast** *1 supervisor*)
      (**atmost** *1 supervisor*)
      (**allp** *location-p pick-location*)
      (**aggregate** *location-p location-supervisor location-supervisors*))

Fig. 6.3. Concept definitions in a distribution company domain - 2.

delivery-document $\doteq$
   (**and** (**atleastp** *1 original-p*)
      (**atmostp** *1 original-p*)
      (**atleastp** *2 copy-p*)
      (**atmostp** *2 copy-p*)
      (**allp** *original-p original-document*)
      (**allp** *copy-p copy-document*)
      (**order-constraint** *original-p copy-p*))

delivery $\doteq$
   (**and** (**atleast** *1 client*)
      (**atmost** *1 client*)
      (**atleast** *1 document*)
      (**atmost** *1 document*)
      (**all** *document delivery-document*)
      (**atmostp** *60 parcel-p*)
      (**allp** *parcel-p parcel*)
      (**allp** *loose-item-p item*))

truck-load $\doteq$
   (**and** (**atleastp** *1 delivery-p*)
      (**allp** *delivery-p delivery*))

Fig. 6.4. Concept definitions in a distribution company domain - 3.

Semantics. An interpretation of the language consists of a tuple $< \mathcal{D}, \ll , \varepsilon >$, where $\mathcal{D}$ is the domain, $\ll$ a mapping that associates to each object in the domain a partial order over the domain, and ε the extension function. The extension function ε maps part name names and role names into sub-sets of $\mathcal{D} \times \mathcal{D}$, concept names into sub-sets of $\mathcal{D}$ and individual names into elements of $\mathcal{D}$ such that $\varepsilon[i_1] \neq \varepsilon[i_2]$ whenever $i_1 \neq i_2$. The partial orders associated with $\ll$ are used to represent the order of the parts of composite objects. The partial order associated to object x in the domain is denoted by $\ll (x)$. We assume that in a domain of an interpretation the assumptions in section 3.2 about parts hold. The semantics for the different constructs are shown in figure 6.5. The semantics for the **and, all, atleast, atmost, fills, atleastp, atmostp, part-fills** are the same as for the language presented in chapter 5. For part names the **allp** and **pp-constraint** have the same semantics as those given in chapter 5, but they can now also contain qualified part names. Their semantics in this case are the natural extensions.

$$\varepsilon[\top] = \mathcal{D}$$
$$\varepsilon[\bot] = \emptyset$$
$$\varepsilon[(\textbf{and } A \ B)] = \varepsilon[A] \cap \varepsilon[B]$$
$$\varepsilon[(\textbf{all } r \ A)] = \{ \ x \in \mathcal{D} \mid \forall \ y \in \mathcal{D}: <x,y> \in \varepsilon[r] \to y \in \varepsilon[A]\}$$
$$\varepsilon[(\textbf{atleast } m \ r)] = \{ \ x \in \mathcal{D} \mid \sharp \ \{ \ y \in \mathcal{D} \mid <x,y> \in \varepsilon[r]\} \geq m \ \}$$
$$\varepsilon[(\textbf{atmost } m \ r)] = \{ \ x \in \mathcal{D} \mid \sharp \ \{ \ y \in \mathcal{D} \mid <x,y> \in \varepsilon[r]\} \leq m \ \}$$
$$\varepsilon[(\textbf{fills } r \ i_1 \ ... \ i_m)] = \{ \ x \in \mathcal{D} \mid <x,\varepsilon[i_1]> \in \varepsilon[r] \wedge ... \wedge <x,\varepsilon[i_m]> \in \varepsilon[r] \ \}$$
$$\varepsilon[(\textbf{allp } p \ A)] = \{ \ x \in \mathcal{D} \mid \forall \ y \in \mathcal{D}: y \lhd_p x \to y \in \varepsilon[A]\}$$
$$\varepsilon[(\textbf{atleastp } m \ n)] = \{ \ x \in \mathcal{D} \mid \sharp \ \{ \ y \in \mathcal{D} \mid y \lhd_n x \ \} \geq m \ \}$$
$$\varepsilon[(\textbf{atmostp } m \ n)] = \{ \ x \in \mathcal{D} \mid \sharp \ \{ \ y \in \mathcal{D} \mid y \lhd_n x \ \} \leq m \ \}$$
$$\varepsilon[(\textbf{part-fills } n \ i_1 \ ... \ i_m)] = \{ \ x \in \mathcal{D} \mid \varepsilon[i_1] \lhd_n x \wedge ... \wedge \varepsilon[i_m] \lhd_n x \ \}$$
$$\varepsilon[(\textbf{module-fills } i_1 \ ... \ i_m)] = \{ \ x \in \mathcal{D} \mid \varepsilon[i_1] \lhd_{\textbf{mod}} x \wedge ... \wedge \varepsilon[i_m] \lhd_{\textbf{mod}} x \ \}$$
$$\varepsilon[(\textbf{pp-constraint } r \ p_1 \ p_2)] = \{ \ x \in \mathcal{D} \mid \forall \ y_1,y_2 \in \mathcal{D}:$$
$$(y_1 \lhd_{p_1} x \wedge y_2 \lhd_{p_2} x) \to <y_1,y_2> \in \varepsilon[r]\}$$
$$\varepsilon[(\textbf{order-constraint } p_1 \ p_2)] = \{ \ x \in \mathcal{D} \mid \forall \ y_1,y_2 \in \mathcal{D}:$$
$$(y_1 \lhd_{p_1} x \wedge y_2 \lhd_{p_2} x) \to y_1 \ll(x) \ y_2 \ \}$$
$$\varepsilon[(\textbf{same-filler } p_1.a_1 \ p_2.a_2)] = \{ \ x \in \mathcal{D} \mid a_1(p_1(x)) = a_2(p_2(x)) \ \}$$
$$\varepsilon[(\textbf{aggregate } p \ a \ r)] = \{ \ x \in \mathcal{D} \mid \forall \ y,z \in \mathcal{D}:$$
$$(y \lhd_p x \wedge <y,z> \in \varepsilon[a]) \to <x,z> \in \varepsilon[r]\}$$

Fig. 6.5. Semantics of an extended description logic for composite objects.

An interpretation $< \mathcal{D}, \ll, \varepsilon >$ is a *model* for a Tbox if for all $A \stackrel{.}{\leq} C$ in the Tbox $\varepsilon[A] \subseteq \varepsilon[C]$ and for all $A \stackrel{.}{=} C$ in the Tbox $\varepsilon[A] = \varepsilon[C]$.

Subsumption. The notion of subsumption is extended in the obvious way. A subsumes B, written $B \Rightarrow A$, iff $\varepsilon[B] \subseteq \varepsilon[A]$ for every interpretation $<\mathcal{D},\ll,\varepsilon>$. Subsumption between concepts can also be defined with respect to a Tbox by requiring that the interpretations in the definition are models of the Tbox. With respect to parts we obtain the semantics that if A subsumes B, then B may have additional kinds of parts, more known part or module fillers, or more specialized parts or qualified parts than A, and the constraints (**pp-constraints** as well as **order-constraints**) between the parts and qualified parts of B may be stronger than those between the parts and qualified parts of A. The possible numbers of direct parts with a particular part name defined in B are all in the interval of possible numbers of direct parts with the same part name defined in A. Also the relationship between the composition and the parts and qualified parts may be stronger in B than in A (via the **same-filler** and **aggregate** constructs).

Structural subsumption rules for the part of the language involving part-of are given in figure 6.6. They are the same for the **atleastp**, **atmostp** and **part-fills** constructs as in the framework in chapter 5. The rule for the **allp** construct is similar to the rule in chapter 5 but deals also with qualified part names. Finally, the rules for the other constructs state that constraints for qualified part names are not as restricted as constraints for part names. A similar situation exists for the normalization rules. The rules of chapter 5 still hold, but in the case of the **allp** construct we also deal with qualified part names. The other rules deal with consistency checking, reflexivity of identity of part-attribute paths and the traversing of part-attribute paths. Normalization rules can be found in figures 6.7 and 6.8. The most interesting new inferences occur in the combinant inference rules in figures 6.9 and 6.10. The combinant inference rules deal with properties of the order relation, properties of the identity of part-attribute paths, traversing of the part-attribute paths and different kinds of interactions between the different constructs.

Decidability. It follows from a result by Schmidt-Schauss [Schm89] that the **same-filler** construct as defined here leads to undecidability for subsumption. The undecidability proof is based on a reduction of the word problem for groups to the subsumption problem in a suitable description logic.[6]

For practical purposes, however, we do not really have a problem. We note that in practice for most applications it should be easy to determine a maximum number of parts for a concept.[7] (For instance, in our distribution example a delivery contains at most 60 parcel parts.) Therefore, we could restrict the use of the **same-filler** construct to part-attribute paths that are *attributes* or of the form *part-name-name:pos-number.attribute-name*. We then have the same situation as *same-as* in CLASSIC that only allows paths where all the roles in a path are attributes. We could still have (**same-filler** *n.a ap*) as an abbreviation for (**and** (**same-filler** *n:1.a ap*) ... (**same-filler** *n:max.a ap*)) where *max* is the maximum number of *n*-parts for that concept. In practice this would mean that we maintain the syntactical restriction that we can only use (**same-filler** *n.a ap*) in the case where we also have an **atmostp** construct for part name n in the definition of the concept.

---

[6] We are indebted to Werner Nutt and Martin Buchheit for pointing out how to use the undecidability result in [Schm89] for our language.

[7] Actually we would only need to give a maximum number of parts with respect to the part names for the concepts that have a **same-filler** construct involving those part names in their definition.

Specializing the range of a part name leads to a more specialized concept.

$$\frac{\vdash\ C_1\ \Rightarrow\ C_2}{\vdash\ (\textbf{allp}\ p\ C_1)\ \Rightarrow\ (\textbf{allp}\ p\ C_2)}$$

Higher lower bounds are more restrictive.

$$\frac{m_1\ <\ m_2}{\vdash\ (\textbf{atleastp}\ m_2\ n)\ \Rightarrow\ (\textbf{atleastp}\ m_1\ n)}$$

Higher upper bounds are less restrictive.

$$\frac{m_1\ <\ m_2}{\vdash\ (\textbf{atmostp}\ m_1\ n)\ \Rightarrow\ (\textbf{atmostp}\ m_2\ n)}$$

Requiring a larger set of part fillers is more restrictive.

$$\frac{\{ii\}\ \subseteq\ \{jj\}}{\vdash\ (\textbf{part}-\textbf{fills}\ n\ jj)\ \Rightarrow\ (\textbf{part}-\textbf{fills}\ n\ ii)}$$

Constraints for qualified part names are not as restrictive as constraints for part names - **pp-constraint**.

$\vdash (\textbf{pp-constraint}\ r\ n\ p) \Rightarrow (\textbf{pp-constraint}\ r\ n{:}m\ p)$

$\vdash (\textbf{pp-constraint}\ r\ p\ n) \Rightarrow (\textbf{pp-constraint}\ r\ p\ n{:}m)$

$\vdash (\textbf{pp-constraint}\ r\ n_1\ n_2) \Rightarrow (\textbf{pp-constraint}\ r\ n_1{:}m_1\ n_2{:}m_2)$

Constraints for qualified part names are not as restrictive as constraints for part names - **order-constraint**.

$\vdash (\textbf{order-constraint}\ n\ p) \Rightarrow (\textbf{order-constraint}\ n{:}m\ p)$

$\vdash (\textbf{order-constraint}\ p\ n) \Rightarrow (\textbf{order-constraint}\ p\ n{:}m)$

$\vdash (\textbf{order-constraint}\ n_1\ n_2) \Rightarrow (\textbf{order-constraint}\ n_1{:}m_1\ n_2{:}m_2)$

Constraints for qualified part names are not as restrictive as constraints for part names - **same-filler**.

$\vdash (\textbf{same-filler}\ ap\ n.a) \Rightarrow (\textbf{same-filler}\ ap\ n{:}m.a)$

$\vdash (\textbf{same-filler}\ n.a\ ap) \Rightarrow (\textbf{same-filler}\ n{:}m.a\ ap)$

$\vdash (\textbf{same-filler}\ n_1.a_1\ n_2.a_2) \Rightarrow (\textbf{same-filler}\ n_1{:}m_1.a_1\ n_2{:}m_2.a_2)$

Constraints for qualified part names are not as restrictive as constraints for part names - **aggregate**.

$\vdash (\textbf{aggregate}\ n\ a\ r) \Rightarrow (\textbf{aggregate}\ n{:}m\ a\ r)$

Fig. 6.6. Structural subsumption rules for an extended description logic for composite objects.

and *is distributive over* **allp**.

$\vdash$ (**and** (**allp** n C_1) (**allp** n C_2)) $\equiv$ (**allp** n (**and** C_1 C_2))

$\vdash$ (**and** (**allp** n C_1) (**allp** $n{:}m$ C_2)) $\equiv$ (**and** (**allp** n C_1) (**allp** $n{:}m$ (**and** C_1 C_2)))

and *of* **part-fills** *is like union.*

$\vdash$ (**and** (**part-fills** n ii) (**part-fills** n jj)) $\equiv$ (**part-fills** n $ii \cup jj$)

If you cannot have parts, then all parts must belong to the empty set.

$\vdash$ (**allp** n $\perp$) $\equiv$ (**atmostp** 0 n)

If the parts can be anything, then this is not really a constraint.

$\vdash$ (**allp** n $\top$) $\equiv$ $\top$

Inconsistent upper and lower bounds.

$$\frac{m_1 < m_2}{\vdash \ (\textbf{and } (\textbf{atmostp } m_1 \ n) \ (\textbf{atleastp } m_2 \ n)) \ \equiv \ \perp}$$

No parts of any type can come before themselves.

$\vdash$ (**order-constraint** n n) $\equiv$ (**atmostp** 0 n)

$\vdash$ (**order-constraint** $n{:}m$ n) $\equiv$ (**atmostp** $m{-}1$ n)

$\vdash$ (**order-constraint** n $n{:}m$) $\equiv$ (**atmostp** $m{-}1$ n)

Qualified part names and the order.

$$\frac{\vdash \ m_1 < m_2}{\vdash \ (\textbf{order} - \textbf{constraint } n : m_1 \ n : m_2) \ \equiv \ \top}$$

$$\frac{\vdash \ m_1 \leq m_2}{\vdash \ (\textbf{order} - \textbf{constraint } n : m_2 \ n : m_1) \ \equiv \ (\textbf{atmostp } m_2 - 1 \ n)}$$

Reflexivity of identity of part-attribute paths.

$\vdash$ (**same-filler** a a) $\equiv$ $\top$

$\vdash$ (**same-filler** $n{:}m.a$ $n{:}m.a$) $\equiv$ $\top$

Symmetry of identity of part-attribute paths.

$\vdash$ (**same-filler** ap_1 ap_2) $\equiv$ (**same-filler** ap_2 ap_1)

Traversing of part-attribute paths.

$\vdash$ (**same-filler** $n{:}m.a_1$ $n{:}m.a_2$) $\equiv$ (**allp** $n{:}m$ (**same-filler** a_1 a_2))

Fig. 6.7. Normalization rules for an extended description logic for composite objects - 1.

Information about parts which cannot exist is redundant.

$$\frac{\vdash\ m_1\ <\ m_2}{\vdash\ (\textbf{and}\ (\textbf{atmostp}\ m_1\ n)\ (\textbf{allp}\ n:m_2\ C))\ \equiv\ (\textbf{atmostp}\ m_1\ n)}$$

$$\frac{\vdash\ m_1\ <\ m_2}{\vdash\ (\textbf{and}\ (\textbf{atmostp}\ m_1\ n)\ (\textbf{pp}-\textbf{constraint}\ r\ n:m_2\ p))\ \equiv\ (\textbf{atmostp}\ m_1\ n)}$$

$$\frac{\vdash\ m_1\ <\ m_2}{\vdash\ (\textbf{and}\ (\textbf{atmostp}\ m_1\ n)\ (\textbf{pp}-\textbf{constraint}\ r\ p\ n:m_2))\ \equiv\ (\textbf{atmostp}\ m_1\ n)}$$

$$\frac{\vdash\ m_1\ <\ m_2}{\vdash\ (\textbf{and}\ (\textbf{atmostp}\ m_1\ n)\ (\textbf{order}-\textbf{constraint}\ n:m_2\ p))\ \equiv\ (\textbf{atmostp}\ m_1\ n)}$$

$$\frac{\vdash\ m_1\ <\ m_2}{\vdash\ (\textbf{and}\ (\textbf{atmostp}\ m_1\ n)\ (\textbf{order}-\textbf{constraint}\ p\ n:m_2))\ \equiv\ (\textbf{atmostp}\ m_1\ n)}$$

$$\frac{\vdash\ m_1\ <\ m_2}{\vdash\ (\textbf{and}\ (\textbf{atmostp}\ m_1\ n)\ (\textbf{same}-\textbf{filler}\ n:m_2.a\ ap))\ \equiv\ (\textbf{atmostp}\ m_1\ n)}$$

$$\frac{\vdash\ m_1\ <\ m_2}{\vdash\ (\textbf{and}\ (\textbf{atmostp}\ m_1\ n)\ (\textbf{same}-\textbf{filler}\ ap\ n:m_2.a))\ \equiv\ (\textbf{atmostp}\ m_1\ n)}$$

$$\frac{\vdash\ m_1\ <\ m_2}{\vdash\ (\textbf{and}\ (\textbf{atmostp}\ m_1\ n)\ (\textbf{aggregate}\ n:m_2\ a\ r))\ \equiv\ (\textbf{atmostp}\ m_1\ n)}$$

Fig. 6.8. Normalization rules for an extended description logic for composite objects - 2.

6.2.2 Assertional Knowledge

The assertional language is extended with a construct to be able to make statements about the order relation over the individuals. We write $i_1 \ll (i)$ i_2 if $\varepsilon[i_1] \ll (\varepsilon[i])\ \varepsilon[i_2]$ in every interpretation. The syntax of the assertional language is presented in figure 6.11. The statement $i :: C$ for a concept description C means that $\varepsilon[i] \in \varepsilon[C]$ and the statement $i :: (\textbf{before}\ i_1\ ...$ $i_m\ \textbf{in}\ i')$ means that $\varepsilon[i] \ll (\varepsilon[i'])\ \varepsilon[i_1]$ and ... and $\varepsilon[i] \ll (\varepsilon[i'])\ \varepsilon[i_m]$. The concept and order statements can be combined with the **and** constructor that denotes the intersection operation. In figure 6.12 we define a truck-load individual with three given delivery parts. For the delivery parts we have also some information. For instance, we have the ordering information that d_1 comes before d_2 and d_2 comes before d_3.

We say that an interpretation $< \mathcal{D}, \ll, \varepsilon >$ is a *model* for an Abox A if $\varepsilon[i] \in \varepsilon[C]$ for every assertional statement $i :: C$ in the Abox A. A knowledge base is defined as a tuple $< T, A >$ where T is a Tbox and A an Abox. An interpretation is a model for a knowledge base $< T, A >$ if it is a model for T and a model for A. Subsumption can be defined with respect to a knowledge base by requiring that the interpretations in the definition of subsumption are models of the knowledge base.

Knowing a sub-set of the set of part fillers provides a lower bound on the number of part fillers.

$$\frac{size(\{ii\}) \ = \ m}{\vdash \ (\textbf{part} - \textbf{fills} \ n \ ii) \ \Rightarrow \ (\textbf{atleastp} \ m \ n)}$$

Transitivity of the order.

$\vdash$ (**and** (**order-constraint** p_1 p_2) (**order-constraint** p_2 p_3))
$\Rightarrow$ (**order-constraint** p_1 p_3)

Transitivity of identity of part-attribute paths.

$\vdash$ (**and** (**same-filler** ap_1 ap_2) (**same-filler** ap_2 ap_3))
$\Rightarrow$ (**same-filler** ap_1 ap_3)

Traversing of part-attribute paths.

$\vdash$ (**same-filler** $n.a_1$ $n.a_2$) $\Rightarrow$ (**allp** n (**same-filler** a_1 a_2))

Domain restrictions and part-attribute paths.

$\vdash$ (**and** (**same-filler** a_1 a_2) (**all** a_1 C)) $\Rightarrow$ (**all** a_2 C)

$\vdash$ (**and** (**same-filler** a_1 $p.a_2$) (**all** a_1 C)) $\Rightarrow$ (**allp** p (**all** a_2 C))

$\vdash$ (**and** (**same-filler** $p.a_1$ a_2) (**allp** p (**all** a_1 C))) $\Rightarrow$ (**all** a_2 C)

$\vdash$ (**and** (**same-filler** $p_1.a_1$ $p_2.a_2$) (**allp** p_1 (**all** a_1 C))) $\Rightarrow$ (**allp** p_2 (**all** a_2 C))

Domain restrictions and aggregates.

$\vdash$ (**and** (**aggregate** p a r) (**all** r C)) $\Rightarrow$ (**allp** p (**all** a C))

Fig. 6.9. Combinant inferences for an extended description logic for composite objects - 1.

Constraints and roles.

⊢ (**and** (**pp-constraint** $r\ p_1\ p_2$) (**atleastp** $1\ p_1$) (**allp** p_1 (**atmost** $m\ r$)))
⇒ (**atmostp** $m\ p_2$)

⊢ (**and** (**pp-constraint** $r\ p_1\ p_2$) (**atleastp** $1\ p_1$) (**allp** p_1 (**all** $r\ C$)))
⇒ (**allp** p_2 C)

⊢ (**and** (**pp-constraint** $r\ p_1\ p_2$) (**atleastp** $m\ p_2$))
⇒ (**allp** p_1 (**atleast** $m\ r$))

⊢ (**and** (**pp-constraint** $r\ p_1\ p_2$) (**part-fills** $p_2\ i_1...i_k$))
⇒ (**allp** p_1 (**fills** $r\ i_1...i_k$))

Aggregates and part-attribute paths.

⊢ (**and** (**aggregate** $p_1\ a_1\ r$) (**same-filler** $p_1.a_1\ p_2.a_2$)) ⇒ (**aggregate** $p_2\ a_2\ r$)

⊢ (**and** (**aggregate** $n{:}m\ a_1\ r$) (**same-filler** $n.a_1\ p.a_2$)) ⇒ (**aggregate** $n\ a_1\ r$)

Aggregates and attributes.

⊢ (**and** (**aggregate** $n\ a\ r$) (**atmost** $1\ r$)) ⇒ (**same-filler** $n.a\ n.a$)

Fig. 6.10. Combinant inferences for an extended description logic for composite objects - 2.

<*assertional-statement*> ::=
    <*individual-name*> :: <*assert-descr*>
<*assert-descr*> ::=
    <*concept-descr*>
    | (**before** <*individual-name*>+ **in** <*individual-name*>)
    | (**and** <*assert-descr*>+)

Fig. 6.11. Assertional language.

tr ::
          (**and** *truck-load*
                (**part-fills** *delivery-p* $d_1\ d_2\ d_3$))

d_1 ::
          (**and** (**before** d_2 **in** *tr*)
                (**fills** *client* cl_1))

d_2 ::
          (**and** (**before** d_3 **in** *tr*)
                (**fills** *client* cl_2))

Fig. 6.12. A truck load individual.

The recognition algorithm for individuals has to be extended to deal with the new constructs and with the ordering information. In the case where the definitions involve qualified part names we want to investigate whether a part comes at a certain place in the order. To know that an individual i_1 is the mth n-part of an individual i we would have to know that the part name n is closed for i, we would have to be able to deduce the order between the n-parts of i from the information in the knowledge base (e.g. by having assertional statements involving the **before** construct), and there would have to be exactly m-1 of the n-parts of i that are before i_1 in the order for individuals. As in the previous chapter we know that an individual i belongs to (**pp-constraint** r p_1 p_2) if it is told to be so, can be inferred from the told information, or when all its p_1-parts have all its p_2-parts as r-fillers. The latter can only be checked in the case where we know all the p_1-parts and p_2-parts of i. A similar condition holds for the **order-constraint** construct. In this case the part fillers must be in the correct order with respect to each other. Recognition of the **same-filler** construct may be based on the recognition of *same-as* in CLASSIC. We have to follow the paths and check that we arrive at the same individuals. Finally, for an individual i to belong to (**aggregate** p a r) it has to be told to be so, inferred from the told information or we have to check that all individuals that are attribute fillers for a in the p-parts of i are also r-fillers for i. The latter can only be checked if we know all the p-parts of i.

The system also has to check that the ordering information is consistent. In particular, it should be checked that no cycles occur. Further, if we know that an individual i_1 is the m_1th n-part of individual i and i_2 is the m_2th n-part of i with $m_1 < m_2$, then i_1 must come before i_2 in the order. The system also has to represent the transitivity of the ordering.

A number of propagations have to be performed. For instance if (**pp-constraint** r p_1 p_2) occurs in the description of an individual, we have to find all its part-fillers for part names p_1 and p_2 and add the p_2-parts as r-fillers to the p_1-parts. We have to perform a similar propagation for **order-constraints**. For the **same-filler** construct we have to traverse the part-attribute paths and instantiate attribute fillers at the ends if necessary. If (**aggregate** p a r) occurs in the description of an individual, we have to find all the a-fillers of its p-parts and add them as r-fillers to the individual. In figures 6.13 and 6.14 we show the rules for reasoning about individuals that are specific for this language and that involve the part-of relation.

6.3 Compositional Inclusion for Individuals

6.3.1 Modules and Compositional Inclusion

In our applications we found that one convenient way to instantiate composite individuals in the knowledge base is to instantiate the less complex

Qualified parts are parts.

$$\frac{kb \ \vdash \ x \ \vartriangleleft_{n:m} \ y}{kb \ \vdash \ x \ \vartriangleleft_n \ y}$$

Qualified parts and order.

$$\frac{kb \ \vdash \ x \ \vartriangleleft_{n:m_1} \ z, \ kb \ \vdash \ y \ \vartriangleleft_{n:m_2} \ z, \ m_1 \ < \ m_2}{kb \ \vdash \ x \ \ll (z) \ y}$$

Transitivity of order.

$$\frac{kb \ \vdash \ x \ \ll (v) \ y, \ kb \ \vdash \ y \ \ll (v) \ z}{kb \ \vdash \ x \ \ll (v) \ z}$$

Number of parts.

$$\frac{kb \ \vdash \ \sharp \{x \ | \ x \ \vartriangleleft_n \ y\} = m}{kb \ \vdash \ y \ \rightarrow \ (\textbf{atleastp} \ m \ n)}$$

Constraints for qualified parts.

$$\frac{kb \ \vdash \ x \ \vartriangleleft_{n_1:m_1} \ y, \ kb \ \vdash \ z \ \vartriangleleft_{n_2:m_2} \ y, \ kb \ \vdash \ r(x,z)}{kb \ \vdash \ y \ \rightarrow \ (\textbf{pp} - \textbf{constraint} \ r \ n_1 : m_1 \ n_2 : m_2)}$$

$$\frac{kb \ \vdash \ x \ \vartriangleleft_{n_1:m_1} \ y, \ kb \ \vdash \ z \ \vartriangleleft_{n_2:m_2} \ y, \ kb \ \vdash \ x \ \ll (y) \ z}{kb \ \vdash \ y \ \rightarrow \ (\textbf{order} - \textbf{constraint} \ n_1 : m_1 \ n_2 : m_2)}$$

$$\frac{kb \ \vdash \ x \ \vartriangleleft_{n_1:m_1} \ y, \ kb \ \vdash \ z \ \vartriangleleft_{n_2:m_2} \ y, \ kb \ \vdash \ a_1(x,v), \ kb \ \vdash \ a_2(z,v)}{kb \ \vdash \ y \ \rightarrow \ (\textbf{same} - \textbf{filler} \ n_1 : m_1.a_1 \ n_2 : m_2.a_2)}$$

$$\frac{kb \ \vdash \ x \ \vartriangleleft_{n:m} \ y, \ kb \ \vdash \ a_1(x,v), \ kb \ \vdash \ a_2(y,v)}{kb \ \vdash \ y \ \rightarrow \ (\textbf{same} - \textbf{filler} \ n : m.a_1 \ a_2)}$$

Fig. 6.13. Reasoning about individuals in an extended description logic for composite objects - 1.

Propagation rules.

$$\frac{kb \;\vdash\; x \;\lhd_p\; y, \; kb \;\vdash\; y \;\rightarrow\; (\textbf{allp } p \; C)}{kb \;\vdash\; x \;\rightarrow\; C}$$

$$\frac{kb \;\vdash\; x_1 \;\lhd_{p_1}\; y, \; kb \;\vdash\; x_2 \;\lhd_{p_2}\; y \;, \; kb \;\vdash\; y \;\rightarrow\; (\textbf{pp} - \textbf{constraint } r \;\; p_1 \; p_2)}{kb \;\vdash\; r(x_1, x_2)}$$

$$\frac{kb \;\vdash\; x_1 \;\lhd_{p_1}\; y, \; kb \;\vdash\; x_2 \;\lhd_{p_2}\; y \;, \; kb \;\vdash\; y \;\rightarrow\; (\textbf{order} - \textbf{constraint } p1 \; p2)}{kb \;\vdash\; x_1 \;\ll (y) \; x_2}$$

$$\frac{kb \;\vdash\; x \;\lhd_p\; y, \; kb \;\vdash\; a2(y,v), \; kb \;\vdash\; y \;\rightarrow\; (\textbf{same} - \textbf{filler } p.a1 \; a2)}{kb \;\vdash\; a1(x,v)}$$

$$\frac{kb \;\vdash\; x \;\lhd_p\; y, \; kb \;\vdash\; a1(x,v), \; kb \;\vdash\; y \;\rightarrow\; (\textbf{same} - \textbf{filler } p.a1 \; a2)}{kb \;\vdash\; a2(y,v)}$$

$$\frac{kb \vdash x_1 \lhd_{p1} y, kb \vdash x_2 \lhd_{p2} y, kb \vdash a2(x_2,v), kb \vdash y \rightarrow (\textbf{same} - \textbf{filler } p1.a1 \; p2.a2)}{kb \;\vdash\; a1(x_1,v)}$$

$$\frac{kb \vdash x_1 \lhd_{p1} y, kb \vdash x_2 \lhd_{p2} y, kb \vdash a1(x_1,v), kb \vdash y \rightarrow (\textbf{same} - \textbf{filler } p1.a1 \; p2.a2)}{kb \;\vdash\; a2(x_2,v)}$$

$$\frac{kb \;\vdash\; x \;\lhd_p\; y, \; kb \;\vdash\; a(x,v), \; kb \;\vdash\; y \;\rightarrow\; (\textbf{aggregate } p \; a \; r)}{kb \;\vdash\; r(y,v)}$$

Fig. 6.14. Reasoning about individuals in an extended description logic for composite objects - 2.

composite individuals first and then use them to instantiate the more complex individuals. For instance, to make a delivery ready for a particular client one may collect a number of parcels from the pick location at the same time and use these parcels together with other goods to assemble the delivery. These less complex composite individuals are contained in the more complex individuals and therefore we could consider them to be parts of the more complex individuals in the general sense of part-of. However, they are not parts in the sense of direct parts or parts as introduced in chapter 5. To model this new kind of relation with part-of intuition we introduce the notion of *module*. Thus the notion of module formalizes a notion of containment which is based on, but is not the same as, the part-of relation we defined before. A module can be used as a building block to build together with other objects a more complex composition. Essentially, a module of a composite object is an object which contains a collection of direct parts of the composition and no others. The module is, thus, itself a composite object.

Definition 6.3.1. *Let x and y be composite objects.*
y is a **module** *of x, (notation: $y \lhd_{\mathbf{mod}} x$) iff*
$(\forall z,n : z \lhd_n y \rightarrow z \lhd_n x) \land (\exists z,n_1 : (z \lhd_{n_1} x \land \forall n: \neg(z \lhd_n y)))$

The following properties are easily provable [Lam96].

- $\forall$ x,y,z: $(x \lhd_n y \land y \lhd_{\mathbf{mod}} z) \rightarrow x \lhd_n z$
- $\forall$ x: $\neg(x \lhd_{\mathbf{mod}} x)$
- $\forall$ x,y,z: $(x \lhd_{\mathbf{mod}} y \land y \lhd_{\mathbf{mod}} z) \rightarrow x \lhd_{\mathbf{mod}} z$

We observe that given the assumption that there can be no parts between a composite object and its direct parts (chapter 3), it is not possible for an object x to be at the same time a part and a module of another object y. It is, however, possible for an object to be a part of one object and a module of another object.

We say that an object *builds* another object if it is a direct part or a module of that individual. The builds relation is then used as a basis for the relation *compositionally includes*, which represents a relation with part-of intuition that includes the part-of relation defined in chapter 5 as well as modules. It can be shown that compositional inclusion for objects is a strict partial order [Lam96].

Definition 6.3.2. *y builds x (notation $y \mathbin{\widehat{\lhd}} x$) iff*
$(\exists n: y \lhd_n x) \lor y \lhd_{\mathbf{mod}} x$

Definition 6.3.3. *x compositionally includes y*
(notation $x \mathbin{\widehat{\rhd}^*} y$) iff $(y,x) \in Anc(builds)$
where $Anc(builds)$ is the transitive closure of *builds*.

6.3.2 Modules and Compositional Inclusion for Individuals

As we did before for the notions of direct part and part, we introduce the notions of module, builds and composite inclusion for individuals based on their counterparts for objects.

Definition 6.3.4. *A composite individual i_1 is a **module** of composite individual i_2 with respect to knowledge base $< T, A >$ (notation $i_1 \ \lhd_{\mathbf{mod}} {}_{<T,A>} i_2$)*[8] *iff $\varepsilon[i_1] \ \lhd_{\mathbf{mod}} \varepsilon[i_2]$ for every model $<\mathcal{D}, \ll, \varepsilon>$ of $< T, A >$.*

*An individual i_1 **builds** an individual i_2 with respect to knowledge base $< T, A >$ (notation $i_1 \ \widehat{\lhd} {}_{<T,A>} i_2$) iff $\varepsilon[i_1] \ \widehat{\lhd} \ \varepsilon[i_2]$ for every model $<\mathcal{D}, \ll, \varepsilon>$ of $< T, A >$.*

*An individual i_1 **compositionally includes** an individual i_2 with respect to knowledge base $< T, A >$ (notation $i_1 \ \widehat{\rhd}^* {}_{<T,A>} i_2$) iff $\varepsilon[i_1] \ \widehat{\rhd}^* \ \varepsilon[i_2]$ for every model $<\mathcal{D}, \ll, \varepsilon>$ of $< T, A >$.*

We can state in the description logic language that particular individuals are modules of another individual or set of individuals. This can be accomplished by using the **module-fills** construct in the definition of an individual and a concept respectively.

The structural subsumption and normalization rules for **module-fills** are analogues of the rules for **part-fills**. To recognize that an individual has another individual as module, this has to be told information, inferred from the told information or all the parts of the second individual must be parts of the first individual and the first individual must have more parts. The latter can only be checked if we know all the parts of the second individual. However, this would require the notion of performing a closure over all the part names at the same time. This is not available in the current system. We may instead provide a user function that assumes a closed-world assumption at the moment the function is called. The user should, however, be aware of this fact. The system should also reflect the information that $\lhd_{\mathbf{mod}}$ is transitive and that direct parts of modules of a composite individual are also direct parts of that composite individual. The different rules concerning modules are given in figure 6.15.

Compositional inclusion for individuals is a strict partial order. The hierarchy based on compositional inclusion extends the hierarchy based on part-of and can be used in a similar way. Except for traversal via direct part relations as in the part-of hierarchy, the compositional inclusion hierarchy also allows traversal via modules. A system supporting a compositional inclusion hierarchy for individuals needs to check that the model for part-of is satisfied. In particular, we need to check that the hierarchy does not contain any cycles.

---

[8] We sometimes also write $i_1 \ \lhd_{\mathbf{mod}} i_2$ in $< T, A >$. When it is clear which knowledge base we are using, we often do not mention the knowledge base in the symbols for modules, builds and compositional inclusion.

Structural Subsumption Rule.

Requiring a larger set of module fillers is more restrictive.

$$\frac{\{ii\} \subseteq \{jj\}}{\vdash \ (\mathbf{module - fills}\ jj)\ \Rightarrow\ (\mathbf{module - fills}\ ii)}$$

Normalization Rule.

and *of* **module-fills** *is like union.*

$\vdash (\mathbf{and}\ (\mathbf{module\text{-}fills}\ ii)\ (\mathbf{module\text{-}fills}\ jj)) \equiv (\mathbf{module\text{-}fills}\ ii \cup jj)$

Reasoning about Individuals.

Parts and modules.

$$\frac{kb\ \vdash\ x\ \lhd_n\ y,\ kb\ \vdash\ y\ \lhd_{\mathrm{mod}}\ z}{kb\ \vdash\ x\ \lhd_n\ z}$$

Transitivity of $\lhd_{\mathrm{mod}}$.

$$\frac{kb\ \vdash\ x\ \lhd_{\mathrm{mod}}\ y,\ kb\ \vdash\ y\ \lhd_{\mathrm{mod}}\ z}{kb\ \vdash\ x\ \lhd_{\mathrm{mod}}\ z}$$

Fig. 6.15. Rules for modules.

6.4 Compositional Inclusion for Concepts

In this section we introduce a compositional inclusion hierarchy for concepts. Similar to the case of individuals, we define here first what it means for a concept to be a direct part of another concept, then what it means for a concept to be a module of another concept and finally, we use these two notions to define compositional inclusion. The compositional inclusion hierarchy for concepts should not be considered as describing an ontological dependency between concepts. For instance, following our definition the concept *item* is compositionally included in the concept *parcel*. However, it is not clear that there is an ontological relation between these two concepts as such. Rather, the compositional inclusion hierarchy for concepts should be seen as a tool that can be used to answer queries and can be used in more complex reasoning tasks such as the ones we define in the following sections. The intuition for the hierarchy can be described as follows. To build an individual belonging to concept C, good candidates as building blocks are individuals belonging to concepts that are compositionally included in C. We discuss this more in the next chapter.

For convenience we introduce the following notation. If (**pp-constraint** r p_1 p_2) occurs[9] in the normalized definition[10] of C, then we write $C_{p_1 r p_2}$. Similarly, if (**order-constraint** p_1 p_2) occurs in the normalized definition of C, then we write $C_{p_1 \ll p_2}$. If (**same-filler** ap_1 ap_2) occurs in the normalized definition of C, then we write $C_{ap_1 = ap_2}$ and if (**aggregate** p a r) occurs in the normalized definition of C, then we write $C_{agg(p.a)=r}$. If (**part-fills** n i) occurs in the normalized definition of C, then we write $i \lhd_n C$ and if (**module-fills** i) occurs in the normalized definition of C, then we write $i \lhd_{\mathbf{mod}} C$.

We also need the *arity* of a part name for a concept.

Definition 6.4.1. *The arity $N(n,C)$ of part name n for concept C is defined as follows:*

*if (**atleastp** l n) and (**atmostp** u n) occur in the normalized definition of C then $N(n,C) = [l,u]$*

*if (**atleastp** l n) but no **atmostp**-construct involving n occurs in the normalized definition of C then $N(n,C) = [l,\infty[$*

*if (**atmostp** u n) but no **atleastp**-construct involving n occurs in the normalized definition of C then $N(n,C) = [0,u]$*

*if no **atleastp**-construct and no **atmostp**-construct occur in the normalized definition of C, but (**allp** n C') for some concept C' occurs, then $N(n,C) = [0,\infty[$*

otherwise $N(n,C)$ is not defined.

Intuitively, a concept C_1 is a direct part of another concept C_2 if individuals belonging to C_1 can be parts of individuals belonging to C_2. A concept C_1 is a module of another concept C_2 if individuals belonging to C_1 are composite individuals themselves which can be used together with other individuals to compose individuals belonging to C_2. The definitions that we give for these notions are based on the definitions of the concepts and subsumption relations.

Definition 6.4.2. *A is a **defined p-part** of B (notation: $A \lhd_p^d B$) iff* (**allp** p A) *occurs in the normalized definition of B.*

Definition 6.4.3. *A is a **direct part with name** p of B (notation: $A \lhd_p B$) iff $\exists$ A': $(A' \lhd_p^d B) \wedge (A \Rightarrow A')$*

---

[9] Occurring in the definition means on the highest level, not nested. For instance, let A be defined as (**and** (**pp-constraint** r p_1 p_2) (**allp** p_3 (**pp-constraint** r' p_4 p_5))) then $C_{p_1 r p_2}$, but not $C_{p_4 r' p_5}$.

[10] For an explanation of the normalization procedure see e.g. [Neb90b]. As an example let A be defined as (**and** B C) with B being defined as (**and** (**allp** n D) (**atmostp** 3 n)) and C being defined as (**and** (**allp** n E) (**atleastp** 1 n)) and D and E being not further defined concepts, then the normalized definition of A is (**and** (**allp** n (**and** D E)) (**atleastp** 1 n) (**atmostp** 3 n)).

Definition 6.4.4. *A is a **module** of B (notation: $A \lhd_{\mathbf{mod}} B$) iff the following conditions hold:*

(i) $\forall\, n,l_1,u_1\colon N(n,A) = [l_1,u_1] \to (\exists\, l_2,u_2\colon N(n,B) = [l_2,u_2] \land u_1 \le u_2)$

(ii) $(\exists\, n\colon N(n,A)$ *is not defined* $\land\ N(n,B)$ *is defined)*
$\lor\ (\exists\, n,l_1,u_1,l_2,u_2\colon N(n,A) = [l_1,u_1] \land N(n,B) = [l_2,u_2] \land u_1 < u_2)$

(iii) $\forall\, n,\, C\ \colon C \lhd_n^d A \to C \lhd_n B$

(iv) $\forall\, n_1,\, n_2,\, r\ \colon (B_{n_1}r_{n_2} \land N(n_1,A)$ *is defined*
$\land\ N(n_2,A)$ *is defined)* $\to A_{n_1}r_{n_2}$

(v) $\forall\, n_1,\, n_2\ \colon (B_{n_1}\ll_{n_2} \land N(n_1,A)$ *is defined*
$\land\ N(n_2,A)$ *is defined)* $\to A_{n_1}\ll_{n_2}$

In order for A to be a *module* for B we require (i), that the part names with a defined arity in A also have a defined arity in B with the maximum numbers of parts for each such part name being at least as many for B as for A; (ii) that B has more kinds of parts with a defined arity than A or that there is a part name such that B can have more parts of that part name than A; (iii) that the domains for part names in A are included in the domains of those part names for B; (iv-v) that the constraints defined between part names existing in A (**pp-constraints** and **order-constraints**) are at least as strong for A as for B.

In figure 6.16 we define an *item-parcel-group* as something that contains at most ten parcels and each of the parcels contains the same kind of goods. Such a group of parcels may be the maximum capacity of parcels that a forklift-truck of a particular type can retrieve from a pick location at one time. The concept *item-parcel-group* is then a module of the concept *delivery*.

item-parcel-group $\doteq$
> (**and** (**atleast** *1 item-number*)
>   (**atmost** *1 item-number*)
>   (**atmostp** *10 parcel-p*)
>   (**allp** *parcel-p parcel*)
>   (**same-filler** *parcel-p.item-number parcel-p.item-number*)

Fig. 6.16. A group of parcels.

Observe that the definition of module does not involve qualified part names. The reason is that the m_1th n-part in a module can become the m_2th n-part in the composition (with $m_1 \ne m_2$) and thus constraints for the mth n-part in the composition may not be relevant for the mth n-part in the module. For instance, the second parcel part of an item parcel group may well be the twenty-second parcel part in a delivery of which the item parcel group is a module. Thus a constraint involving the second parcel part in the item parcel group is not relevant to the second parcel part in the delivery. The definition does not involve the **same-filler** and **aggregate** constructs either. These constructs connect role or attribute fillers for an individual with attribute fillers for their parts. However, as the modules and compositions belong to different concepts, the roles and attributes defined for one of them may not be relevant for the other.

We say that a concept *builds* another concept if it is a direct part or a module of that concept.

Definition 6.4.5. *A builds B (notation: A $\widehat{\lhd}$ B) iff*
($\exists$ p: A $\lhd_p$ B) $\vee$ (A $\lhd_{\mathbf{mod}}$ B)

The relation of *compositional inclusion* which is defined as the transitive closure of the inverse of builds is then the basis for the compositional inclusion hierarchy for concepts. This relation is a strict partial order [Lam96].

Definition 6.4.6. *B* **compositionally includes** *A*
(written B $\widehat{\rhd}^*$ A) iff (A,B) $\in$ Anc(builds)
where *Anc(builds)* is the transitive closure of *builds*.

Compositional inclusion is clearly a central relationship for discussing and reasoning about relationships between parts and compositions. If, given an individual, we wanted to consider what types of compositions it could be 'part of', we would look at the concepts which compositionally include the concept the individual belongs to. If we wanted to see what types of parts may be used to build an individual belonging to a composite concept A, we would look at the concepts compositionally included in A.

6.5 Composes

The inferences for a description logic system for composite objects we propose in this chapter are all about the building of composite objects. In each case some individuals are given. These individuals are to be used as direct parts or modules of a composite object that has to be of a particular type. For instance, some parcels, item parcel groups and loose items may be used to create a delivery. One inference, compositional extension, allows us to let the system automatically build new composite individuals given a knowledge base. Another inference, completion, tells us which kind of parts and constraints are still missing to build a new composite individual of a particular kind. In this section we define an inference that allows us to check whether a set of individuals can be used as parts and modules of a composite individual belonging to a specific type. For instance, we can check whether we can use a particular pallet and goods to build a parcel. The candidate parts and modules have to satisfy the requirements which are dictated by the definition of the composite concept, including the constraints between the parts. We introduce the relation *composes* that relates a pair representing the candidate individuals and a concept defined in the Tbox. The first argument of the pair represents the individuals that are to be used as direct parts. They are given as a set of <individual,part name> pairs. The second argument represents the individuals that are to be used as modules. Given a particular knowledge base, the composes relation holds if the parts and modules satisfy the requirements in the definition of the concept.

Before defining the composes relation we introduce a number of useful notions. First, we define the number of direct parts for a particular part name for an individual in a knowledge base. This number is an interval reflecting all possible numbers of direct parts in the different models of the knowledge base.

Definition 6.5.1. *For an individual i and part name n, defined in the knowledge base $< T, A >$, we define $N(n,i) = [Min, Max]$ where*
$$Min = min_{(<D, \ll, \varepsilon> \ model \ of \ <T,A>)} \sharp \{y \in D \mid y \vartriangleleft_n \varepsilon[i]\}$$
and $Max = max_{(<D, \ll, \varepsilon> \ model \ of \ <T,A>)} \sharp \{y \in D \mid y \vartriangleleft_n \varepsilon[i]\}$

If we have no information about n-parts of individual i then $N(n,i) = [0, \infty[$. In other cases the interval may be smaller. For instance, if we know that i belongs to a concept for which the definition includes (**atleastp** 3 n) and (**atmostp** 5 n) then the interval is included[11] in [3,5].

We want to use individuals both as direct parts and as modules. Therefore it is convenient to define the notion of direct part with respect to a pair of sets with the first set containing direct parts and the second set modules.

Definition 6.5.2. *Let α be a set of pairs $< i, n >$ where i is an individual and n is a part name, and let β be a set of individuals. Assume all individuals and part names are defined in the knowledge base $< T, A >$. Then an individual i is an n-part of $< \alpha, \beta >$ in $< T, A >$ (notation: $i \vartriangleleft_n < \alpha, \beta >)$[12] iff $(< i, n > \in \alpha) \vee (\exists i_1 : i_1 \in \beta \wedge i \vartriangleleft_n i_1)$*

The definition states that an individual is a direct part of the pair of sets if it is told to be so, i.e. by having this information in the first set or if we have a module for which the individual is a direct part. We also introduce a similar definition for the mth n-part of this pair of sets.

Definition 6.5.3. *Let α be a set of pairs $< i, n >$ where i is an individual and n is a part name, and let β be a set of individuals. Assume all individuals and part names are defined in the knowledge base $< T, A >$. Then, if $\ll_o$ orders all n-parts of $< \alpha, \beta >$ with respect to each other, we say that an individual i is the mth n-part in $< \alpha, \beta >$ with respect to $\ll_o$ in $< T, A >$, (notation: $i \vartriangleleft_{n:m} < \alpha, \beta >)$ iff $(i \vartriangleleft_n < \alpha, \beta >) \wedge (\sharp \{i_1 \mid i_1 \vartriangleleft_n < \alpha, \beta > \wedge i_1 \ll_o i\} = m\text{-}1)$*

---

[11] We may have some other information restricting the interval even further.

[12] When it is clear which knowledge base we are using, we do not refer to the knowledge base in the notation. This remark holds as well for the other definitions in this section.

We also define what it means for an individual to be a module for the pair of sets.

Definition 6.5.4. *Let α be a set of pairs $< i, n >$ where i is an individual and n is a part name, and let β be a set of individuals. Assume all individuals and part names are defined in the knowledge base $< T, A >$. Then a composite individual i is a module of $< \alpha, \beta >$ in $< T, A >$ (notation: $i \lhd_{\mathbf{mod}} < \alpha, \beta >$) iff $(\forall\ i', n : i' \lhd_n i \rightarrow i' \lhd_n < \alpha, \beta >)$*
$\wedge\ (\exists\ i', n_1 : (i' \lhd_{n_1} < \alpha, \beta > \wedge \forall\ n : \neg(i' \lhd_n i)))$

When we are using the individuals in α and β as parts and modules for an individual belonging to a particular concept, various constraints have to be satisfied. The first constraint is that if every individual belonging to that concept must have a particular individual as direct part, then this individual must be used (by being in α or by being a direct part of an individual in β).

Definition 6.5.5. *Let α be a set of pairs $< i, n >$ where i is an individual and n is a part name, and let β be a set of individuals. Let C be a concept. Assume all individuals, part names and concept are defined in the knowledge base $< T, A >$. Then we say that $< \alpha, \beta >$ satisfies the part fillers constraints with respect to C in $< T, A >$ iff $\forall i, n : i \lhd_n C \rightarrow i \lhd_n < \alpha, \beta >$*

A similar constraint holds for module fillers. If every individual belonging to the concept must have a particular individual as module, then we must recognize the parts of that particular individual among the individuals in α or the parts of the individuals in β. However, there should also be more parts in $< \alpha, \beta >$.

Definition 6.5.6. *Let α be a set of pairs $< i, n >$ where i is an individual and n is a part name, and let β be a set of individuals. Let C be a concept. Assume all individuals, part names and concept are defined in the knowledge base $< T, A >$. Then we say that $< \alpha, \beta >$ satisfies the module fillers constraints with respect to C in $< T, A >$ iff $\forall\ i : i \lhd_{\mathbf{mod}} C \rightarrow i \lhd_{\mathbf{mod}} < \alpha, \beta >$*

When we assemble a collection of individuals into a composite individual of a particular kind, then we want to make sure that the parts belong to the required domain. We define formally the notion of *conforming parts*.

Definition 6.5.7. *Let α be a set of pairs $< i, n >$ where i is an individual and n is a part name, and let β be a set of individuals. Let C be a concept. Assume all individuals, part names and concept are defined in the knowledge base $< T, A >$. Then we say that $< \alpha, \beta >$ has conforming parts with respect to C in $< T, A >$ iff $\forall p, C' : C' \lhd_p^d C \rightarrow (\forall i : i \lhd_p < \alpha, \beta > \rightarrow$*
$\forall < D, \ll, \varepsilon > models\ of < T, A >: \varepsilon[i] \in \varepsilon[C'])$

To be able to assemble a collection of individuals into a composite individual of a particular kind, we also have to check whether the different constraints are satisfied. For the **pp-constraints** we have to check that the parts are in the required relations to each other.

Definition 6.5.8. *Let α be a set of pairs $< i, n >$ where i is an individual and n is a part name, and let β be a set of individuals. Let C be a concept. Assume all individuals, part names and concept are defined in the knowledge base $< T, A >$. Then we say that $< \alpha, \beta >$ satisfies the role constraints between parts with respect to C in $< T, A >$ iff $\forall p_1, p_2, r : C_{p_1} r_{p_2} \rightarrow$*
$(\forall i_1, i_2 : (i_1 \lhd_{p_1} < \alpha, \beta > \ \wedge \ i_2 \lhd_{p_2} < \alpha, \beta >) \rightarrow$
$\forall < D, \ll, \varepsilon > models \ of < T, A >:< \varepsilon[i_1], \varepsilon[i_2] >\in \varepsilon[r])$

For the **order-constraints** we have to check that the parts have the required order.

Definition 6.5.9. *Let α be a set of pairs $< i, n >$ where i is an individual and n is a part name, and let β be a set of individuals. Let $\ll_o$ be a partial order over the individuals in α and the direct parts of the individuals in β. Let C be a concept. Assume all individuals, part names and concept are defined in the knowledge base $< T, A >$. Then we say that $< \alpha, \beta >$ satisfies the order constraints with respect to C and $\ll_o$ in $< T, A >$ iff $\forall p_1, p_2 : C_{p_1} \ll_{p_2} \rightarrow$*
$(\forall i_1, i_2 : (i_1 \lhd_{p_1} < \alpha, \beta > \ \wedge \ i_2 \lhd_{p_2} < \alpha, \beta >) \rightarrow i_1 \ll_o i_2)$

For the path equality constraints we have to make sure that following the different part-attribute paths yields the same result. However, as we only have the direct parts and modules and the concept to which the assembled individual has to belong, we only need to check the part-attribute paths involving part names. The part-attribute paths without part names are attributes of the whole and there actually may not be an instantiation of the whole in the knowledge base. For instance, if (**same-filler** $p_1.a_1 \ p_2.a_2$) occurs in the concept definition, then we have to check that following any $p_1.a_1$ path and any $p_2.a_2$ path gives the same result. However, if (**same-filler** $n_1.a_1 \ a_2$) occurs in the concept definition, we need only to check that following any $n_1.a_1$ path gives the same result.

Definition 6.5.10. *Let α be a set of pairs $< i, n >$ where i is an individual and n is a part name, and let β be a set of individuals. Let C be a concept. Assume all individuals, part names and concept are defined in the knowledge base $< T, A >$. Then we say that $< \alpha, \beta >$ satisfies the path equality constraints with respect to C in $< T, A >$ iff the following conditions hold:*
(i) $\forall p_1, p_2, a_1, a_2 : C_{p_1.a_1} =_{p_2.a_2} \rightarrow$
$((\forall i_1, i_2 : (i_1 \lhd_{p_1} < \alpha, \beta > \wedge i_2 \lhd_{p_2} < \alpha, \beta >) \rightarrow$
$\forall < D, \ll, \varepsilon > models \ of < T, A >: \varepsilon[a_1](\varepsilon[i_1]) = \varepsilon[a_2](\varepsilon[i_2]))$
$\wedge (\forall i_1, i_2 : (i_1 \lhd_{p_1} < \alpha, \beta > \wedge i_2 \lhd_{p_1} < \alpha, \beta >) \rightarrow$
$\forall < D, \ll, \varepsilon > models \ of < T, A >: \varepsilon[a_1](\varepsilon[i_1]) = \varepsilon[a_1](\varepsilon[i_2]))$
$\wedge (\forall i_1, i_2 : (i_1 \lhd_{p_2} < \alpha, \beta > \wedge i_2 \lhd_{p_2} < \alpha, \beta >) \rightarrow$
$\forall < D, \ll, \varepsilon > models \ of < T, A >: \varepsilon[a_2](\varepsilon[i_1]) = \varepsilon[a_2](\varepsilon[i_2])))$
(ii) $\forall n, a_1, a_2 : C_{n.a_1} =_{a_2} \rightarrow$
$(\forall i_1, i_2 : (i_1 \lhd_n < \alpha, \beta > \wedge i_2 \lhd_n < \alpha, \beta >) \rightarrow$
$\forall < D, \ll, \varepsilon > models \ of < T, A >: \varepsilon[a_1](\varepsilon[i_1]) = \varepsilon[a_1](\varepsilon[i_2]))$

(iii) $\forall n, a_1, a_2 : C_{a_1} =_{n.a_2} \rightarrow$
$(\forall i_1, i_2 : (i_1 \lhd_n < \alpha, \beta > \wedge\ i_2 \lhd_n < \alpha, \beta >) \rightarrow$
$\forall < D, \ll, \varepsilon >\ models\ of\ < T, A >: \varepsilon[a_2](\varepsilon[i_1]) = \varepsilon[a_2](\varepsilon[i_2]))$

When we are aggregating the fillers of attributes in parts to a role in the composite individual, we have to make sure that the number of fillers is not higher than the upper number restriction for the role.

Definition 6.5.11. *Let α be a set of pairs $< i, n >$ where i is an individual and n is a part name, and let β be a set of individuals. Let C be a concept. Assume all individuals, part names and concept are defined in the knowledge base $< T, A >$. Then we say that $< \alpha, \beta >$ satisfies the aggregate constraints with respect to C in $< T, A >$ iff $\forall p, a, r, m$: $(C_{agg(p.a)=r} \wedge (\textbf{atmost } m\ r)$ occurs in the definition of $C) \rightarrow \forall < D, \ll, \varepsilon >$ models of $< T, A >: \sharp\{x \in D \mid i \lhd_p < \alpha, \beta > \wedge\ \varepsilon[a](\varepsilon[i]) = x\} \leq m$*

We have now all the necessary definitions to easily define the notion of *composes*. This notion checks the requirements which a set of direct parts and a set of modules must satisfy to be able to assemble these direct parts and modules into a composite individual. We assume that an individual does not appear more than once in the sets of direct parts and modules.

Definition 6.5.12. *Let α be a set of pairs $< i, n >$ where i is an individual and n is a part name, and let β be a set of individuals such that all individuals in α, β, and the direct parts of individuals in β are different. Let $\ll_o$ be a partial order over the individuals in α and the direct parts of the individuals in β. Let C be a concept. Assume all individuals, part names and concept are defined in the knowledge base $< T, A >$. Then, $(< \alpha, \beta >, \ll_o)$ **composes** C with respect to $< T, A >$ iff the following conditions hold:*
(i) $< \alpha, \beta >$ satisfies the part fillers constraints with respect to C in $< T, A >$
(ii) $< \alpha, \beta >$ satisfies the module fillers constraints with respect to C in $< T, A >$
(iii) $< \alpha, \beta >$ has conforming parts with respect to C in $< T, A >$
(iv) $\forall i, n : i \lhd_n < \alpha, \beta > \rightarrow N(n, C)$ is defined
(v) $\forall n : (\sharp\{i \mid < i, n > \in \alpha\} +^* \Sigma_{i \in \beta} N(n, i)) \subseteq N(n, C)$
(vi) $< \alpha, \beta >$ satisfies the role constraints between parts with respect to C in $< T, A >$
(vii) $< \alpha, \beta >$ satisfies the order constraints with respect to C and $\ll_o$ in $< T, A >$
(viii) $< \alpha, \beta >$ satisfies the path equality constraints with respect to C in $< T, A >$
(ix) $< \alpha, \beta >$ satisfies the aggregate constraints with respect to C in $< T, A >$
(x) $\sharp \alpha + \sharp \beta \geq 2$

If α is a set of pairs $< i, n >$ containing individuals which are to be direct parts in the composition and β a set of individuals which are to be modules of the composition, then we say that $(< \alpha, \beta >, \ll_o)$ **composes** C

with respect to a knowledge base $< T, A >$ iff (i-ii) all parts and modules of the concept are also parts and modules in $< \alpha, \beta >$; (iii) all direct parts in α and indirectly in β belong to the concept required for that part by the definition of the concept being composed; (iv) every member of α and every direct part of every member in β are motivated by the occurrence of a part name in the definition of the concept being composed; (v) the number of parts of a given part name in the set of composing individuals is an allowed number of parts for that part name following the concept definition;[13] (vi-ix) the constraints between part names required by the definition of the concept being composed hold between the composing individuals; and finally (x) at least two individuals are needed to compose a concept.

When no partial order is given, but only parts and modules, we define composes as follows.

Definition 6.5.13. *Let α be a set of pairs $< i, n >$ where i is an individual and n is a part name, and let β be a set of individuals such that all individuals in α, β, and the direct parts of individuals in β are different. Let C be a concept. Assume all individuals, part names and concept are defined in the knowledge base $< T, A >$. Then, $< \alpha, \beta >$ composes C with respect to $< T, A >$ iff there exists a partial order $\ll_o$ over the individuals in α and the direct parts of the individuals in β such that $(< \alpha, \beta >, \ll_o)$ composes C with respect to $< T, A >$.*

Consider a knowledge base $< T, A >$ where T contains the definitions of concepts in the distribution company domain as defined in this chapter and A is as in figure 6.17. Then we have that $<\{ < pl, pallet\text{-}p >, < i_1, item\text{-}p >, < i_2, item\text{-}p >, < i_3, item\text{-}p >, < i_4, item\text{-}p >, < c, card\text{-}p > \}, \emptyset>$ composes *parcel* with respect to $< T, A >$. We also have that $<\{ < p, parcel\text{-}p >, < i_5, loose\text{-}item\text{-}p > \}, \{ ipg \}>$ composes *delivery* with respect to $< T, A >$.

6.6 Assembly

In this section we propose an inference that allows us to let the system automatically create new composite individuals given the existence of individuals that can be used as parts and modules. We first define compositional assembly, that represents the facts that necessarily need to be added to a knowledge base to create a new composite individual of a certain type with certain individuals as its parts and modules. Then, we define the notion of compositional extension that allows to infer new composite individuals automatically. We present an algorithm that computes a compositional extension. For the case where different alternatives exist, we propose a preference relation.

---

[13] The sum in (v) should be interpreted as follows: $[Min_1, Max_1] + [Min_2, Max_2] = [Min_1 + Min_2, Max_1 + Max_2]$ and $x +^* [Min, Max] = [Min + x, Max + x]$.

pl ::

> (**and** *pallet*
>   (**fills** *pallet-number pn*))

i_1 ::

> (**and** *item*
>   (**fills** *item-number in*))

i_2 ::

> (**and** *item*
>   (**fills** *item-number in*))

i_3 ::

> (**and** *item*
>   (**fills** *item-number in*))

i_4 ::

> (**and** *item*
>   (**fills** *item-number in*))

i_5 ::

> (**and** *item*
>   (**fills** *item-number in*))

c ::

> (**and** *parcel-card*
>   (**fills** *card-number pn*)
>   (**fills** *item-number in*))

ipg ::

> (**and** *item-parcel-group*
>   (**fills** *item-number in*)
>   (**part-fills** *parcel-p p_1 p_2 p_3*))

p :: *parcel*

Fig. 6.17. Composing individuals.

6.6.1 Compositional Assembly

To realize a composition which did not exist in a knowledge base before, using individuals in the knowledge base as parts and modules, we extend the Abox of the knowledge base with a number of assertional statements. These statements state to which concept the new individual necessarily must belong, which are its necessary parts and modules and in which relations the individual participates.

We define *compositional assembly* to be a mapping from a tuple in the composes relationship plus a new identifier and an order relation, to a set of assertional statements, thus allowing a composition to be realized.

Definition 6.6.1. *If* $\alpha = \{< i_{1j}, n_j >\}_{j=1}^k, \beta = \{i_{2j}\}_{j=1}^l,$ *and* $(< \alpha, \beta >, \ll_o)$ *composes* C *with respect to knowledge base* $< T, A >$ *and* i *is a new identifier not yet occurring in* $< T, A >$ *then* $Assembly(< \alpha, \beta >, C, \ll_o, i) = $
$\{ i :: C,$
$i :: ($**part-fills** $n_1\ i_{11}),..., i :: ($**part-fills** $n_k\ i_{1k}),$
$i :: ($**module-fills** $i_{21}),..., i :: ($**module-fills** $i_{2l})\}$
$\cup \{ i' :: ($**before** i'' **in** $i) \mid < i', i'' >\in\ \ll_o \}$
$\cup \{ i :: ($**fills** $a\ i') \mid$
$\exists p, a' : (C_a =_{p.a'} \vee C_{p.a'} =_a) \wedge (\forall i'' : i'' \lhd_p < \alpha, \beta > \rightarrow a'(i'') = i')\ \}$
$\cup \{ i :: ($**fills** $r\ i') \mid$
$\exists p, a : (C_{agg(p.a)=r} \wedge (\exists i'' : i'' \lhd_p < \alpha, \beta > \wedge a(i'') = i'))\ \}$

The Abox sentences in $Assembly(< \alpha, \beta >, C, \ll_o, i)$ represent the following facts. The new individual belongs to the concept C. The individuals in α are parts of the new individual with the assigned part names. The individuals in β are modules of the new individual. The order between the parts of the new individual is defined by $\ll_o$. Finally, the new individual receives role fillers for the attributes involved in a **same-filler** construct in the definition of C and for the roles involved in an **aggregate** construct in the definition of C.

6.6.2 Compositional Extension

As a first step we make the assumption that it is only reasonable to infer a new composition in those cases where the composition is able to exclusively own its parts. This assumption seems justified in many practical cases. For instance, it is not possible to create a new delivery using parts of an already existing delivery. However, we do not want to exclude sharing of parts if it is the user's wish to do so. Thus our Abox language allows a user to state explicitly that parts are shared, but we do not infer composites which are obliged to share their parts.[14] We define the notion of an assembly being

---

[14] Of course, parts are shared between a composition and its own modules. This kind of sharing does not disqualify compositional inference.

disallowed in those cases where it would result in failure of the instantiated individual to exclusively own its parts.

Definition 6.6.2. *Assembly* $(< \alpha, \beta >, C, \ll_o, i)$ *is* **disallowed** *in* $< T, A >$
iff the following conditions hold:
(i) $(< \alpha, \beta >, \ll_o)$ *composes* C *with respect to* $< T, A >$
(ii) $\exists i_1, i_2, n_1, n_2 :$
$(i_1 \lhd_{n_1} < \alpha, \beta > \lor i_1 \lhd_{\mathbf{mod}} < \alpha, \beta >)$
$\land((i_1 \lhd_{n_2} i_2 \ in \ < T, A >) \lor (i_1 \lhd_{\mathbf{mod}} i_2 \ in \ < T, A >))$
$\land \neg(i \lhd_{\mathbf{mod}} i_2 \ in \ < T, A \ \cup \ Assembly(< \alpha, \beta >, C, \ll_o, i) >)$
$\land \neg(i_2 \lhd_{\mathbf{mod}} i \ in \ < T, A \ \cup \ Assembly(< \alpha, \beta >, C, \ll_o, i) >))$

Thus a disallowed assembly with respect to a knowledge base is one which (i) can be composed in the knowledge base but would result in (ii) one of the parts or modules of the new individual being a part or module of another separate individual.

A *compositional extension*, where no further inferences can be made regarding the existence of compositions, is then defined as follows:

Definition 6.6.3. *A knowledge base* $< T, A' >$ *is a* **compositional extension** *of a knowledge base* $< T, A >$
iff it is a minimal knowledge base that satisfies the following conditions:
(i) $A \subseteq A'$
(ii) $< \alpha, \beta >$ *composes* C *with respect to* $< T, A' > \rightarrow$
$\exists i, \ll_o : ((Assembly(< \alpha, \beta >, C, \ll_o, i) \subseteq A')$
$\lor (Assembly(< \alpha, \beta >, C, \ll_o, i) \ is \ disallowed \ in \ < T, A' >))$
(iii) $\forall i : (i \ is \ defined \ in \ < T, A' > \ \land \ i \ is \ not \ defined \ in \ < T, A >) \rightarrow$
$(\exists \alpha, \beta, \ll_o, C : Assembly(< \alpha, \beta >, C, \ll_o, i) \subseteq A')$
(iv) $\forall i_1, i_2, i_3, n_1, n_2 : ((i_1 \lhd_{n_1} i_2 \ in \ < T, A' >) \land (i_1 \lhd_{n_2} i_3 \ in \ < T, A' >)) \rightarrow$
$((i_3 \lhd_{\mathbf{mod}} i_2 \ in \ < T, A' >) \lor (i_2 \lhd_{\mathbf{mod}} i_3 \ in \ < T, A' >)$
$\lor ((i_1 \lhd_{n_1} i_2 \ in \ < T, A >) \land (i_1 \lhd_{n_2} i_3 \ in \ < T, A >)))$
(v) $\forall i_1, i_2, i_3, n : (i_1 \lhd_n i_2 \ in \ < T, A' > \ \land \ i_1 \lhd_{\mathbf{mod}} i_3 \ in \ < T, A' >) \rightarrow$
$(i_1 \lhd_n i_2 \ in \ < T, A > \ \land \ i_1 \lhd_{\mathbf{mod}} i_3 \ in \ < T, A >)$

Thus (i) the original Abox is always contained in the Abox of a *compositional extension*, (ii) if it is possible to find individuals (parts and modules) to compose a concept, then they will be used to instantiate an individual of that concept in the compositional extension, unless this would result in a disallowed sharing of parts (i.e. non-module-wise sharing), (iii) all new individuals have originated from an assembly (iv-v) any sharing of parts between individuals is either a result of a situation given in the original knowledge base, or of sharing between a module and a 'larger' composition using that module. A compositional extension is then a knowledge base where we can build no more compositions.

6.6.3 Algorithm

The outline of an algorithm for finding a compositional extension is as follows (see figure 6.18).

Let $< T, A >$ be the original knowledge base. The set *Used* is the set of the individuals which have been used already to compose other individuals. The final value for $< T, A' >$ is a compositional extension. *Preprocess* initializes the variables we use and instantiates intermediate modules using the individuals in $< T, A >$. *Used* is initialized to be the set of individuals in $< T, A >$ that already participate in a composition. A' is initialized to A. The *instantiate-intermediate-modules* step makes sure that when we instantiate an individual we also instantiate as many as possible of its potential modules and add these intermediate modules to *Used*.

```
begin
   Preprocess(A, Used, A');
   repeat
     if possible then
       begin
       choose α, β, C, ≪₀ such that
           (i) α = {<i₁₁,n₁>,...,<i₁ₖ,nₖ> } such that
           each i₁r is defined in A',
           (ii) β = { i₂₁,...,i₂ₘ } such that
           each i₂ₛ is defined in A',
           (iii) (< α,β >,≪₀) composes C with respect to < T, A' >,
           (iv) none of the i₁r in α is in Used,
           (v) none of the i₂ₛ in β is in Used;
       instantiate-intermediate-modules(α,β,< T, A' >);
       generate-unique-individual-name(i);
       A' ← A' ∪ Assembly(< α,β >,C,≪₀,i);
       Used ← Used ∪ { i₁₁,...,i₁ₖ } ∪ { i₂₁,...,i₂ₘ }
       end
     else break
     endif
   endrepeat
end
```

Fig. 6.18. Algorithm for compositional extensions.

It is in the process of choosing a suitable α, β and C, that the compositional inclusion hierarchy helps structure the search space. A non-used individual can first be placed with respect to the compositional inclusion hierarchy. Each of the concepts which compositionally includes the concept representing the given individual are then candidates for the C parameter in composes.

If there is some part lacking[15] in each concept that is built by the concept representing the given individual, then that individual cannot be used in any composes. Similarly, if there is some part lacking in each concept that builds a particular concept, then neither that concept, nor any concept which compositionally includes that concept can be formed.

The compositional inclusion hierarchy can also be used to facilitate instantiation of the intermediate modules. The search for such an intermediate module is limited to individuals belonging to concepts which are compositionally included by the C under consideration and which themselves can be composed by a combination of elements in the candidate α or β.

It can be shown that the algorithm terminates and that the final value for $< T, A' >$ is a compositional extension [Lam96].

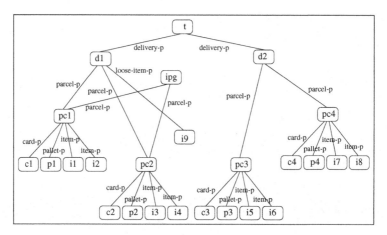

Fig. 6.19. Individuals in a compositional extension.

We illustrate a simplified view of the algorithm. Assume that we have a knowledge base $< T, A >$ where T defines the concepts in figures 6.2, 6.3, 6.4 and 6.16 and where A defines four pallets p_j (for $j = 1 .. 4$), nine items i_j (for $j = 1 .. 9$), and four parcel cards c_j (for $j = 1 .. 4$). We assume that we have the appropriate relationships that allow for the assemblies that we instantiate. Preprocessing sets A' to A and $Used = \emptyset$. If we first take the parcel card c_1, we can match it to the concept *parcel-card*. A concept that is built by *parcel-card* is the concept *parcel* and we investigate this as a candidate for composes. We may find that $< \{<c_1, card-p>, <p_1, pallet-p>, <i_1, item-p>, <i_2, item-p>\}, \emptyset >$ composes *parcel*. There are no possible intermediate modules and we instantiate a parcel pc_1. *Used* contains now

---

[15] Lacking means that such an individual is not available and we are not able to compose such an individual.

c_1, p_1, i_1 and i_2. Let us assume we can instantiate similar parcels pc_2, pc_3, and pc_4 using the other parcel cards, pallets and some of the items. *Used* would then contain all c_j, all p_j, and the i_j for $j = 1 \mathbin{..} 8$. As *parcel* is compositionally included in *delivery*, we can try to compose a delivery. We may find that $< \{<pc_1, parcel\text{-}p>, <pc_2, parcel\text{-}p>, <i_9, loose\text{-}item\text{-}p>\}, \emptyset >$ composes *delivery*. Checking for intermediate modules tells us that we can instantiate an item parcel group *ipg* using the two parcels. We also instantiate a delivery individual d_1. The individuals pc_1, pc_2, i_9 and *ipg* are added to *Used*. We assume that the other two parcels can also be used to instantiate a delivery d_2. There are no intermediate modules. Then the only non-used individuals are d_1 and d_2. These may be used to instantiate a truck load t. Finally, this is the only non-used individual and thus we cannot assemble any more. The compositional extension defines, then, the individuals in the original knowledge base and the new individuals pc_1, pc_2, pc_3, pc_4, *ipg*, d_1, d_2 and t (see figure 6.19).

6.6.4 Preference Relation for Compositional Extension

In cases where it is possible to use parts for building different composites, there are a number of compositional extensions. We wish to define preferences which, in the absence of application-specific preferences, we believe reasonable to be applied when inferring composites from parts. We have identified two such general-purpose preferences. We state these briefly, informally, then define them formally and give examples to clarify our intuitions.

1. Inferred composite individuals should make use of given information at the most specific level possible.
2. When inferring composite individuals on the basis of their parts, we should infer as little additional information as possible.

The application of these preferences will result in what we call *credulous compositional extensions*.[16]

In the compositional extensions which we generate, we have a number of new individuals (originating from an assembly). In order to be able to compare extensions we need to define the notion of equivalent individuals, which are the same except for differences in their names.

Definition 6.6.4. *Given an original knowledge base* $< T, A >$, *compositional extensions* Σ_1 *and* Σ_2 *of* $< T, A >$, *an individual* i_1 *defined in* Σ_1 *and an individual* i_2 *defined in* Σ_2, *then we define* **same**$(i_1, i_2, \Sigma_1, \Sigma_2)$ *as follows:*
1) If i_1 *is defined in* $A \lor i_2$ *is defined in* A
then $(same(i_1, i_2, \Sigma_1, \Sigma_2)$ *iff* $i_1 = i_2)$

---

[16] The analogy is to credulous extensions in defeasible inheritance, where these represent extensions where some relatively indisputable preferences (specificity in the inheritance case) have been applied, but there is still potential for multiple extensions.

2) If i_1 is not defined in $A \wedge i_2$ is not defined in A
then (same($i_1, i_2, \Sigma_1, \Sigma_2$) iff [17] the following conditions hold:
(i) $\forall C$ defined in T : $(\forall < D, \ll, \varepsilon >$ model of Σ_1 : $\varepsilon[i_1] \in \varepsilon[C]) \leftrightarrow$
$(\forall < D, \ll, \varepsilon >$ model of Σ_2 : $\varepsilon[i_2] \in \varepsilon[C])$
(ii)$(\alpha_1 = \{< a, n >| a \vartriangleleft_n {}_{\Sigma_1} i_1\} \wedge \alpha_2 = \{< b, n >| b \vartriangleleft_n {}_{\Sigma_2} i_2\}) \rightarrow$
$\exists f : \alpha_1 \rightarrow \alpha_2$:
  $((a)f : \alpha_1 \rightarrow \alpha_2$ is $1 - 1$
  $\wedge (b)\forall a, b, n_1, n_2 : f(< a, n_1 >) = < b, n_2 > \rightarrow n_1 = n_2$
  $\wedge (c)\forall a_1, a_2, b_1, b_2, n_1, n_2, : (f(< a_1, n_1 >) = < b_1, n_1 >$
   $\wedge \ f(< a_2, n_2 >) = < b_2, n_2 > \wedge a_1 \ll_{\Sigma_1} (i_1) \ a_2) \rightarrow b_1 \ll_{\Sigma_2} (i_2) \ b_2$
  $\wedge (d)\forall a, b, n_1 : f(< a, n_1 >) = < b, n_1 > \rightarrow$ same$(a, b, \Sigma_1, \Sigma_2))$

This definition states that an individual in the original knowledge base can only be the same as itself and an individual inferred by compositional inferencing (i.e. which did not exist in the original knowledge base) can only be the same as another inferred individual. In the latter case we require (i) that they belong to the same concepts, and (ii) there is a (a) one-to-one (c) order preserving mapping between the parts of the individuals, that (b) maps parts with the same part name to each other such that (d) corresponding parts are the same according to this definition - i.e. non-inferred parts are identical, while inferred parts are identical except for the name.

In order to capture preferences between individuals which are not equivalent, we define two further relations. The first of these is one which we call *more specific with respect to parts*. The intuition motivating this definition is that if we are going to infer an individual on the basis of the existence of the parts, we prefer to infer an individual belonging to a concept which makes use of the specific nature of the parts or the constraints between them. For example, if we have an Australian pallet, a parcel card and a collection of items, then we would prefer to infer an Australian parcel to inferring a parcel although both would be correct. We define this relation as follows:

Definition 6.6.5. *Let $\Sigma_1 = < T, A_1 >$ and $\Sigma_2 = < T, A_2 >$. An individual i_1 defined in knowledge base Σ_1 is* **more specific with respect to parts** *than an individual i_2 defined in knowledge base Σ_2 (notation:*
$\mathbf{s_T}(i_1, i_2, \Sigma_1, \Sigma_2))$ iff $\exists C1, C2$:
(i) $C1$ is a most specific concept defined in T such that
$\forall < D, \ll, \varepsilon >$ models of Σ_1 : $\varepsilon[i_1] \in \varepsilon[C1]$
(ii) $C2$ is a most specific concept defined in T such that
$\forall < D, \ll, \varepsilon >$ models of Σ_2 : $\varepsilon[i_2] \in \varepsilon[C2]$
(iii) $C1 \Rightarrow C2$
(iv) $\forall$ n: $N(n, C1)$ is defined $\leftrightarrow N(n, C2)$ is defined
(v) (a) $(\exists p, B, B' : ((B \ \vartriangleleft_p^d \ C1) \wedge (B' \ \vartriangleleft_p^d \ C2) \wedge B \Rightarrow B' \wedge \neg(B' \Rightarrow B)))$
  $\vee$ (b)$(\exists n_1, n_2, r : C1_{n_1} r_{n_2} \wedge \neg \ C2_{n_1} r_{n_2})$
  $\vee$ (c)$(\exists n_1, n_2 : C1_{n_1} \ll_{n_2} \wedge \neg \ C2_{n_1} \ll_{n_2})$

---

[17] The symbol $\ll_{\Sigma_1}$ denotes the order for individuals in Σ_1.

$\vee\ (d)(\exists p, a_1, a_2 : C1_{p.a_1} =_{a_2} \wedge\neg\ C2_{p.a_1} =_{a_2})$
$\quad\vee\ (\exists p, a_1, a_2 : C1_{a_1} =_{p.a_2} \wedge\neg\ C2_{a_1} =_{p.a_2})$
$\quad\vee\ (\exists p_1, p_2, a_1, a_2 : C1_{p_1 a_1} =_{p_2.a_2} \wedge\neg\ C2_{p_1 a_1} =_{p_2.a_2})$
$\quad\vee\ (e)(\exists p, a, r : C1_{agg(p.a)=r} \wedge\neg\ C2_{agg(p.a)=r})$

This definition specifies that for i_1 to be more specific with respect to parts than i_2, there must exist most specific concepts, $C1$ for i_1 and $C2$ for i_2, (i,ii) such that (iii) $C1$ is more specific than $C2$, (iv) both concepts define the same part names (and because of (iii) the allowed number of parts for a part name in $C1$ is included in the allowed number of parts for that part name in $C2$, the domains for the part names in $C1$ are included in the domains of those part names in $C2$, and the constraints for parts in $C1$ are stronger than the constraints in $C2$), and (v) (a) there is a part name or qualified part name which has a strictly more specific domain in $C1$ than in $C2$ or (b-e) there is a constraint between part names which appears in the definition of $C1$ but not in the definition of $C2$.

In the above case our intuition is that we prefer to compose the more specific individual, because it is making use of a more specific part or constraint between parts. However, when specificity is based on aspects other than specificity of parts, we intuitively prefer to infer individuals which are as general as possible. For example, if we have a collection of parcels and a collection of items, then we would prefer to infer a delivery to inferring a delivery to a foreign client. Intuitively, there is no reason to infer the extra property of the delivery that it goes to a foreign client. We thus define the relationship *more general without specific parts* which actually means more general, providing that there is not already a relationship more specific with respect to parts.

Definition 6.6.6. *Let* $\Sigma_1 = <T, A_1>$ *and* $\Sigma_2 = <T, A_2>$. *An individual* i_1 *defined in knowledge base* Σ_1 *is* **more general without specific parts** *than an individual* i_2 *defined in knowledge base* Σ_2, *(notation:* $\mathbf{g_T}(i_1, i_2, \Sigma_1, \Sigma_2)$) *iff the following conditions hold:*
(i) $\neg\ \mathbf{s_T}(i_2, i_1, \Sigma_2, \Sigma_1)$
(ii) $(\alpha_1 = \{<a, n>|\ a \lhd_n\ _{\Sigma_1} i_1\} \wedge \alpha_2 = \{<b, n>|\ b \lhd_n\ _{\Sigma_2} i_2\}) \rightarrow$
$\exists f : \alpha_1 \rightarrow \alpha_2 : (f$ *is a* $1-1$ *mapping*
$\wedge (\forall a, b, n_1, n_2 : f(<a, n_1>) =<b, n_2> \rightarrow n_1 = n_2)$
$\wedge (\forall a, b, n : f(<a, n>) =<b, n> \rightarrow$
$(\forall C\ defined\ in\ T : (\forall <D, \ll, \varepsilon>\ models\ of\ \Sigma_1 : \varepsilon[a] \in \varepsilon[C]) \leftrightarrow$
$(\forall <D, \ll, \varepsilon>\ models\ of\ \Sigma_2 : \varepsilon[b] \in \varepsilon[C])))$
$\wedge (\forall a_1, a_2, b_1, b_2, n_1, n_2 : (f(<a_1, n_1>) =<b_1, n_1>$
$\wedge f(<a_2, n_2>) =<b_2, n_2> \wedge a_1 \ll_{\Sigma_1} (i_1)\ a_2) \rightarrow b_1 \ll_{\Sigma_2} (i_2)\ b_2))$
(iii)$(\forall C\ defined\ in\ T : (\forall <D, \ll, \varepsilon>\ models\ of\ \Sigma_1 : \varepsilon[i_1] \in \varepsilon[C]) \rightarrow$
$(\forall <D, \ll, \varepsilon>\ models\ of\ \Sigma_2 : \varepsilon[i_2] \in \varepsilon[C]))$
$\wedge (\exists C\ defined\ in\ T : (\forall <D, \ll, \varepsilon>\ models\ of\ \Sigma_2 : \varepsilon[i_2] \in \varepsilon[C] \wedge$
$\neg((\forall <D, \ll, \varepsilon>\ models\ of\ \Sigma_1 : \varepsilon[i_1] \in \varepsilon[C])))$

Thus for i_1 to be more general without specific parts than i_2, (i) i_2 may not be more specific with respect to parts than i_1, (ii) the parts in i_1 and i_2 must belong to the same concepts, and (iii) i_1 must be strictly more general than i_2.

We are now ready to define a preference relation over extensions, based on the relations between individuals.

Definition 6.6.7. *Given an original knowledge base* $< T, A >$, *composition- al extensions* Σ_1 *and* Σ_2 *of* $< T, A >$, *then* Σ_2 *is preferred over* Σ_1 *(notation:* $\Sigma_2 \propto_{1T} \Sigma_1$) *iff*
$\exists I_1, I_{11}, I_{12}, I_2, I_{21}, I_{22}$ *sets of individuals which satisfy the following conditions:*
(i) $I_1 = \{i \mid i \text{ is defined in } \Sigma_1\} \wedge I_2 = \{i \mid i \text{ is defined in } \Sigma_2\}$
$\wedge\, I_{11} \bigcup I_{12} = I_1 \wedge I_{11} \cap I_{12} = \emptyset \wedge I_{21} \bigcup I_{22} = I_2 \wedge I_{21} \cap I_{22} = \emptyset$
(ii) $\exists$ *mapping* $f : I_1 \rightarrow I_2$:
$\quad$ *((a)* $f : I_{11} \rightarrow I_{21}$ *is 1-1*
$\quad \wedge$ *(b)*$f : I_{12} \rightarrow I_{22}$ *is 1-1*
$\quad \wedge$ *(c)*$\forall i \in I_{11} : same(i, f(i), \Sigma_1, \Sigma_2)$
$\quad \wedge$ *(d)*$(\forall i \in I_{12} : (d1)\, \mathbf{s_T}(f(i), i, \Sigma_2, \Sigma_1) \vee (d2)\, \mathbf{g_T}(f(i), i, \Sigma_2, \Sigma_1)$
$\quad \quad \vee (d3)\, \exists i' \in I_{12} : (i \widehat{\triangleright}^*{}_{\Sigma_1} i' \wedge (\mathbf{s_T}(f(i'), i', \Sigma_2, \Sigma_1) \vee \mathbf{g_T}(f(i'), i', \Sigma_2, \Sigma_1))))$
$\quad \wedge$ *(e)*$(\forall i, i' \in I_1 : i \widehat{\triangleright}^*{}_{\Sigma_1} i' \leftrightarrow f(i) \widehat{\triangleright}^*{}_{\Sigma_2} f(i')))$

This definition states that we compare two extensions by partitioning the sets of defined individuals in each extension into two disjoint parts, (i). The individuals in the first of these partitions can be mapped directly to *same* individuals in the corresponding partition of the other extension, (a,c). In the remaining partition, in order for Σ_2 to be preferred over Σ_1, there must be a 1-1 mapping, (b), between the individuals in the second partition of each extension such that (d), each individual in Σ_2 is preferred to its correspond- ing individual in Σ_1 by a (d1) $\mathbf{s_T}$ or (d2) $\mathbf{g_T}$ preference; or (d3), there is a $\mathbf{s_T}$ or $\mathbf{g_T}$ preference between compositionally included individuals. The intuition for the latter case is that the earlier decisions in the building process are the most important. If we make a 'wrong' choice earlier on, then we cannot trust preferences based on individuals built from these less preferred build- ing blocks. Finally, (e), the mapping requires that for composite individuals compositionally included individuals are mapped to compositionally included individuals of the corresponding individual in the other extension. It can be shown that this preference relation is transitive [Lam96].

We present the following brief example to illustrate the preference pro- cedure. Assume that we have an original knowledge base $< T, A >$ where T defines the concepts in figures 6.2, 6.3, 6.4 and 6.20,[18] and where A defines an

---

[18] Observe that an Australian delivery does not necessarily have to be a foreign delivery. The client may be an intermediate company in the same country that later ships the goods to Australia.

Australian-pallet $\dot{\leq}$
    pallet

Australian-parcel $\dot{=}$
        (**and** *parcel*
            (**allp** *pallet-p Australian-pallet*)

Australian-delivery $\dot{=}$
        (**and** *delivery*)
            (**allp** *parcel-p Australian-parcel*))

foreign-delivery $\dot{=}$
        (**and** *delivery*)
            (**all** *client foreign-client*))

Fig. 6.20. Concept definitions in a distribution company domain - 4.

Australian pallet ap, the items i_1, i_2, i_3, i_4, and i_5, and a parcel card c. We assume that we have the appropriate relations that allow for the assemblies that we instantiate. Let Σ_1 be a compositional extension which introduces a new individual apc which is an Australian parcel (with parts ap, i_1, i_2, i_3, i_4, and c) and an individual fd which is a foreign delivery (with parts i_5 and apc). Let Σ_2 be a compositional extension which introduces a new individual pc which is a parcel (with parts ap, i_1, i_2, i_3, i_4, and c) and an individual d which is a delivery (with parts i_5 and pc). Then we have the following:

Σ_2		Σ_1
ap	same(ap,ap,Σ_2,Σ_1)	ap
c	same(c,c,Σ_2,Σ_2)	c
i_5	same($i_5,i_5,\Sigma_2,\Sigma_1$)	i_5
i_1	same($i_1,i_1,\Sigma_2,\Sigma_1$)	i_1
i_2	same($i_2,i_2,\Sigma_2,\Sigma_1$)	i_2
i_3	same($i_3,i_3,\Sigma_2,\Sigma_1$)	i_3
i_4	same($i_4,i_4,\Sigma_2,\Sigma_1$)	i_4
i_5	same($i_5,i_5,\Sigma_2,\Sigma_1$)	i_5
pc	$\mathbf{s_T}(apc,pc,\Sigma_1,\Sigma_2)$	apc
d	$\mathbf{g_T}(d,fd,\Sigma_1,\Sigma_2)$	fd

We have then an $\mathbf{s_T}$ preference between the parcels favoring Σ_1 and a $\mathbf{g_T}$ preference between the deliveries favoring Σ_2. However, the $\mathbf{g_T}$ preference is allowed to be overridden due to the fact that the parcels are compositionally included in the deliveries. Thus Σ_1 is preferred to Σ_2.

Given this preference relation, we can define the notion of *credulous compositional extension*. A credulous compositional extension is a preferred compositional extension. It is possible to show that there always exists at least one credulous compositional extension [Lam96].

Definition 6.6.8. *A compositional extension Σ of $< T, A >$ is a* **credulous compositional extension** *of $< T, A >$ iff*
$$\forall \Sigma' : (\Sigma' \text{ is a compositional extension of } < T, A > \wedge \Sigma' \propto_{1T} \Sigma) \rightarrow \Sigma \propto_{1T} \Sigma'$$

For the example above, let Σ be a compositional extension which introduces a new individual apc which is an Australian parcel (with parts ap, i_1, i_2, i_3, i_4, and c) and an individual ad which is an Australian delivery (with parts i_5 and apc). Then Σ is a credulous compositional extension.

Although credulous compositional extensions may allow significant pruning in the space of all possible compositional extensions, there are still many cases where we have multiple credulous compositional extensions. In an implementation we may want to have a way of capturing the information that is common to all credulous compositional extensions. To this purpose the notion of *skeptical compositional inclusion* can be introduced [PL94]. A skeptical compositional inclusion then infers compositions only when no ambiguity remains.

6.7 Completion

The inference we propose in this section allows us to infer information about missing parts. We define the inference by introducing the notion of completion. We present an algorithm that finds a completion in the case where we know that a completion exists. For the case where different alternatives exist, we propose a preference relation.

6.7.1 Completion

A common way of instantiating composite objects is by using a template. The composite object is created according to a concept description, but its parts still have to be instantiated. What is important in this method is the fact that at all times we want to be able to find out what parts are still missing, given that some parts may become instantiated. The information we need is of which kind these missing parts necessarily should be, and what the necessary relationships should be among these parts and between these parts and the already available parts. At the same time we do not want unmotivated new parts. The notion of *completion* allows us to express this information need formally.

Definition 6.7.1. *Let $\alpha = \{< i_{1j}, n_j >\}_{j=1}^{k}$ and $\beta = \{i_{2l}\}_{l=1}^{m}$ such that all i_{1j} and i_{2l} are individuals and all n_j are part names. Let C be a concept.*

*Assume that all individuals, part names and concept are defined in knowledge base Σ. Then a **completion** of $(<\alpha,\beta>,C)$ with respect to Σ is a pair $<\Sigma',\alpha_{\Sigma'}>$ such that $\alpha_{\Sigma'}$ is a set of pairs $\{<i_{3r},n_r>\}_{r=1}^s$ with all i_{3r} different individuals and all n_r part names defined in Σ' and Σ' is a minimal knowledge base which satisfies the following conditions:*

(i) $\Sigma \subseteq \Sigma'$,

(ii) $\forall\, i\colon ((i$ is defined in $\Sigma' \wedge i$ is not defined in $\Sigma) \leftrightarrow (\exists\, n\colon <i,n> \in \alpha_{\Sigma'}))$

(iii) $<\alpha \cup \alpha_{\Sigma'},\beta>$ composes C with respect to Σ'

A completion is essentially a knowledge base that represents a proposal for a generation of the missing parts and thus a possible way to 'complete' the composition. The first condition says that the new knowledge base contains the original knowledge base. Following condition (ii), $\alpha_{\Sigma'}$ contains all the new individuals and no original individuals. Condition (iii) ensures us that we can compose the concept using α, β and the new individuals and that all the new individuals are actually used in the composing.

Observe that it may be necessary to involve original individuals in new relationships. For instance, in the case where (**pp-constraint** *is-boss-of leader-p member-p*) has to be satisfied, as for a standard work group, it is natural to introduce the *is-boss-of*-relationship between an original leader part and an individual which is to be a new member part. However, by requiring that a completion is the smallest possible knowledge base, we do not introduce unmotivated new relationships.

6.7.2 Algorithm

For some Σ, α, β and C there may not exist a completion. This can, for example, occur if some constraints between the given parts are not satisfied. It is also possible that $<\Sigma,\emptyset>$ is the only completion, as in the case where $<\alpha,\beta>$ *composes* C with respect to Σ. In this case Σ is the smallest knowledge base satisfying the conditions and no new individuals or relationships need to be introduced. There may also be many possible completions. We show here an algorithm that finds a completion in the case where there exists a completion.

The outline of this algorithm is as follows (see figure 6.21). Let Σ be the original knowledge base and let also α, β and C be given.

Check-initial-individual-set checks the following:

(i) if $i \lhd_n <\alpha,\beta>$ then $N(n,C)$ must be defined

(ii) if $N(n,C) = [l,u]$ then $\sharp\{i \mid i \lhd_n <\alpha,\beta>\} \le u$

If one of these constraints is not satisfied then there can be no completion which uses all the individuals in $<\alpha,\beta>$ to compose the given concept.

Preprocess initializes the variables we use. α_1 is initialized to α. Σ' is initialized to Σ. $\ll_o$ is initialized to $\emptyset$. The final value for $<\Sigma',\alpha_1 \backslash \alpha>$ is a completion if there exists one.

begin
  if not check-initial-individual-set(Δ,α,β,C)
  then return("no completion")
  Preprocess$(\Sigma,\Sigma',\alpha,\alpha_1,\ll_o)$
  repeat
    if $(<\alpha_1,\beta>,\ll_o)$ composes C with respect to Σ'
    then return$(<\Sigma',\alpha_1\backslash\alpha>)$
    if not add-constraints$(\Sigma',\alpha_1,\beta,C,\ll_o)$ **then** backtrack
    if number of parts is in the allowed range for each part name
    then if add-qualified-constraints$(\Sigma',\alpha_1,\beta,C)$ **then** return$(<\Sigma',\alpha_1\backslash\alpha>)$
    if not add-individual$(\Sigma',\alpha_1,\beta,C,\ll_o)$ **then** backtrack
  endrepeat
  return("no completion")
end

Fig. 6.21. Algorithm for completions.

For the following constraints, if they are not satisfied, we try to add Abox sentences in *add-constraints* to make sure they do satisfy the constraints.
(i) $<\alpha_1,\beta>$ satisfies the part fillers constraints.
(ii) $<\alpha_1,\beta>$ satisfies the module fillers constraints.
(iii) $<\alpha_1,\beta>$ has conforming parts for the part names.
(iv) $<\alpha_1,\beta>$ satisfies the order constraints for the part names.
(v) $<\alpha_1,\beta>$ satisfies the path equality constraints for the part names.
(vi) $<\alpha_1,\beta>$ satisfies the aggregate constraints for the part names.
Adding Abox sentences is possible if the new Abox is not inconsistent. This is not always the case. For instance, if we require that n_1-parts come before n_2-parts and we have an n_2-part coming before an n_1-part, then adding the constraint would give rise to a problem. The function returns the value false in the case where we cannot consistently add the sentences to satisfy the constraints. When these constraints cannot be satisfied, we cannot compose with the current set of individuals, order and the current Abox. Therefore, we revise our choices by backtracking. Observe that qualified part names are not taken into consideration. The reason is that there may be missing parts and thus we cannot know in which place the given parts will occur in a composition.

If the (non-qualified) constraints for composes are satisfied, and the number of direct parts in $<\alpha_1,\beta>$ is in the desired interval for every part name, we try to satisfy the constraints for qualified part names in *add-qualified-constraints*. In the case where we manage to satisfy these constraints too, we know that we can compose and the function returns the value true. Otherwise, we may have to add new individuals.

When adding an individual as a direct part we have to make sure that the part name is defined and that the total number of direct parts for that part name does not exceed the maximum allowed number. We have a choice as to where in the order of individuals we put the new individual. (This order influences the possibility of satisfying the **order-constraint**s.) Adding individuals could be achieved in the following way.

1. If there is a part name that requires an individual, then add an individual for that part name.

We apply 2 if no further application of 1 is possible.

2. If there is a part name which can have more individuals and the maximum number of direct parts for that part name is finite, then add an individual for that part name.

If 2 is no longer applicable, we backtrack on 2 until we have finished all possible combinations of allowed numbers of parts for the part names with a finite upper bound, while keeping the other parts as is.

3. If there is a part name which can have more individuals (without an upper bound), add an individual for that part name. Try all combinations with that individual and the possible combinations of allowed numbers of direct parts for the part names with a finite upper bound, while keeping the other parts as is.

If all these combinations have been tried, then add a new individual. If there are several such part names, make sure all part names are tried first with one added individual and no others, then combinations of two added individuals and so on.

We illustrate a simplified view of the algorithm. Assume that we have a knowledge base $< T, A >$ where T includes the definitions presented in figure 6.2 and A defines the items i_1, i_2, i_3, and i_4, with the same item number and a parcel card c all with the same item number. Assume that we want to find a completion of ($< \{ < i_1,item\text{-}p >, < i_2,item\text{-}p >, < i_3,item\text{-}p >, < i_4,item\text{-}p >, < c,card\text{-}p > \}, \emptyset >$, *parcel*) with respect to $< T, A >$. *Check-initial-individual-set* returns true as for all given parts the part names are defined and there are not too many parts for those part names with respect to the definition of *parcel*. Preprocessing sets Σ' to $< T, A >$, α_1 to $\{<i_1,item\text{-}p>, <i_2,item\text{-}p>, <i_3,item\text{-}p>, <i_4 item\text{-}p>, <c,card\text{-}p>\}$ and $\ll_o$ to $\emptyset$. We cannot compose *parcel* yet, so we call *add-constraints*. This has no effect on the knowledge base and the function returns true. The number of parts is not in the allowed range (for the part name *pallet-p*) and thus we try to add an individual. As we still need a pallet part, we add $<p,pallet\text{-}p>$ to α_1. We still cannot compose *parcel*. *Add-constraints* adds the fact that p has to belong to *pallet* and that the *pallet-number* filler for p is the same as the *card-number* filler for c. The *add-qualified-constraints* statement does not change the knowledge base but returns true. We have found a completion.

6.7.3 Preference Relation for Completion

For the case where several completions exist we define a preference relation between different completions where we prefer to have as general as possible new individuals for the different part names (while still having them compose the concept) and as 'few' as possible new individuals.

To define this preference formally we need two relations between individuals in different knowledge bases. The first relation is the *same* relation as defined in section 6.6.4. Individuals in the original knowledge base can only be the same as themselves and a new individual can only be the same as another new individual. In the latter case we require that they belong to the same concepts, that there is an order-preserving one-to-one mapping between the parts of the individuals, and that corresponding parts are the same. The second relation compares individuals with respect to generality.

Definition 6.7.2. *Given an original knowledge base* $< T, A >$ *and completions* $<\Sigma_1, \alpha_{\Sigma_1}>$ *and* $<\Sigma_2, \alpha_{\Sigma_2}>$, *an individual* i_1 *defined in* Σ_1 *and an individual* i_2 *defined in* Σ_2, *then* $\mathbf{gen_T}(i_1, i_2, \Sigma_1, \Sigma_2)$ *iff the following conditions hold:*
(i) $(\forall C$ *defined in* $T : (\forall < D, \ll, \varepsilon >$ *models of* $\Sigma_1 : \varepsilon[i_1] \in \varepsilon[C])$
$\rightarrow (\forall < D, \ll, \varepsilon >$ *models of* $\Sigma_2 : \varepsilon[i_2] \in \varepsilon[C]))$
(ii) $(\exists C$ *defined in* $T : (\forall < D, \ll, \varepsilon >$ *models of* $\Sigma_2 : \varepsilon[i_2] \in \varepsilon[C]) \wedge$
$\neg((\forall < D, \ll, \varepsilon >$ *models of* $\Sigma_1 : \varepsilon[i_1] \in \varepsilon[C])))$

The definition states that an individual i_1 is more general than another individual i_2 if (i) i_2 belongs to all the concepts i_1 belongs to, but (ii) i_2 also belongs to concepts i_1 does not belong to. We can now define a preference relation between two completions.

Definition 6.7.3. *Given an original knowledge base* $< T, A >$ *and completions* $<\Sigma_1, \alpha_{\Sigma_1}>$ *and* $<\Sigma_2, \alpha_{\Sigma_2}>$. *Then completion* $<\Sigma_1, \alpha_{\Sigma_1}>$ *is preferred over completion* $<\Sigma_2, \alpha_{\Sigma_2}>$ *(notation:* $<\Sigma_1, \alpha_{\Sigma_1}> \propto_{2T} <\Sigma_2, \alpha_{\Sigma_2}>$) *iff*
$\exists I_1, I_2 : I_1 = \{i \mid i$ *is defined in* $\Sigma_1\} \wedge I_2 = \{i \mid i$ *is defined in* $\Sigma_2\}$
$\wedge \exists$ *function* $f : I_1 \rightarrow I_2$:
(i) f *is injective*
(ii) $\forall i: i$ *is defined in* $< T, A > \rightarrow f(i) = i$
(iii) $\forall i: (i$ *is defined in* $\Sigma_1 \wedge i$ *is not defined in* $< T, A >)$
$\rightarrow (< i, n > \in \alpha_{\Sigma_1} \rightarrow < f(i), n > \in \alpha_{\Sigma_2})$
(iv) $\forall i: (i$ *is defined in* $\Sigma_1 \wedge i$ *is not defined in* $< T, A >)$
$\rightarrow (same(i, f(i), \Sigma_1, \Sigma_2) \vee gen_T(i, f(i), \Sigma_1, \Sigma_2))$

The first condition for the function ensures that Σ_2 has at least as many individuals as Σ_1. Following the second condition the original individuals are mapped to each other. The third condition assures us that new individuals which are to be n-parts in Σ_1 are mapped to new individuals which are n-parts in Σ_2, i.e. we compare new individuals in the completions only if they have the same part name. Finally, the individuals in Σ_1 are the same or more general than their counterparts in Σ_2. It can be proven that this preference relation for completions is transitive [Lam96].

We present the following brief example to illustrate the preference procedure. Assume that we have a knowledge base $< T, A >$ where T contains the concept definitions in figures 6.2 and 6.20 and A defines the items i_1, i_2, i_3, and i_4, and a parcel card c all with the same item number. Then there are different completions of $(< \{ < i_1, item\text{-}p >, < i_2, item\text{-}p >, < i_3, item\text{-}p >, < i_4, item\text{-}p >, < c, card\text{-}p > \}, \emptyset >, parcel)$ with respect to the knowledge base. Let $<\Sigma_1, \alpha_{\Sigma_1}>$ be a completion which introduces a new individual, ap, which is an Australian pallet. Let $<\Sigma_2, \alpha_{\Sigma_2}>$ be a completion which introduces a new individual, p, which is a pallet. This results in the following:

Σ_2		Σ_1
i_1	$same(i_1, i_1, \Sigma_2, \Sigma_1)$	i_1
i_2	$same(i_2, i_2, \Sigma_2, \Sigma_1)$	i_2
i_3	$same(i_3, i_3, \Sigma_2, \Sigma_1)$	i_3
i_4	$same(i_4, i_4, \Sigma_2, \Sigma_1)$	i_4
c	$same(c, c, \Sigma_2, \Sigma_1)$	c
p	$gen_T(p, ap, \Sigma_2, \Sigma_1)$	ap

What is achieved, then, is a gen_T preference between the parcels favoring $<\Sigma_2, \alpha_{\Sigma_2}>$ over $<\Sigma_1, \alpha_{\Sigma_1}>$. Thus we prefer adding a pallet to adding an Australian pallet.

The notion of *credulous completion* represents preferred completions.

Definition 6.7.4. *A completion* $<\Sigma, \alpha_\Sigma>$ *of* $< T, A >$ *is a* **credulous completion** *of* $< T, A >$ *iff*
$$\forall \Sigma', \alpha_{\Sigma'} : (< \Sigma', \alpha_{\Sigma'} > \text{ is a completion of } < T, A >$$
$$\wedge < \Sigma', \alpha_{\Sigma'} > \propto_{2T} < \Sigma, \alpha_\Sigma >) \rightarrow < \Sigma, \alpha_\Sigma > \propto_{2T} < \Sigma', \alpha_{\Sigma'} >$$

It can be shown that for a given knowledge base, if there exists a completion, then there exists also a credulous completion [Lam96]. In the previous example $<\Sigma_2, \alpha_{\Sigma_2}>$ is a credulous completion.

6.8 Summary

We have extended the representational capabilities of the description logic in the previous chapter in several ways. We allow the user to define an order on the parts of a composite (qualified part names, **order-constraint, before**). Further, we allow for inheritance information using **same-filler** and **aggregate**.

We introduced a compositional inclusion hierarchy for individuals that includes the part-of hierarchy presented in the previous chapter. Compositional inclusion is based on the notions of direct part and modules. We also defined a compositional inclusion hierarchy that can be used to structure the search space of concepts when search involves part-of.

To cope with the new expressivity, the standard inferences had to be extended. We also defined new inferences which allow us to use the specific nature of part-of. These inferences do not make sense for ordinary roles. The inferences all have to do with the building of composite individuals given a collection of individuals that can be used as direct parts and modules. The new inferences allow us to check whether the requirements for building are satisfied, to generate new compositions, and to find out what kinds of parts are missing. In the latter cases when multiple results could be obtained, we defined a preference relation. The preference relations should be seen as examples to show how preferences can be defined. The practical usefulness of the preferences as defined here should be tested in applications.

In chapters 5 and 6 we defined a description logic for composite objects. In the next chapter we discuss some aspects of our framework and compare it to other proposals.

7. Comparison of the Framework with Other Approaches

In this chapter we compare some aspects of our description logic for composite objects as introduced in chapters 5 and 6 to other approaches dealing with part-of in description logics. These other approaches were introduced in chapter 4. We discuss the underlying model for part-of, the description logic language, subsumption, specialized inferences and hierarchies for part-of for individuals and concepts.

7.1 Model for Part-of

Few approaches discuss their underlying part-of model. In [SP94a] the physical part-of relation is modeled. The model introduces a directly contains relation and derives the contains relation. A composite object cannot be part of itself. Each part has to be connected to another part. However, as in the description logic part-whole roles are used, the underlying model is not obvious in the language. In [Fra93] part-of is a partial order and special quantifiers are introduced with respect to part-of. In [Sat98] a model for part-of and a taxonomy for part-whole relations is given.

In contrast to these approaches, we introduced in chapter 3 direct part relations that have names as the basis of our model. From these relations we have then derived the notion of part-of. This part-of is a strict partial order. The assumptions we make also assure us of the fact that the intended meaning of direct parts is preserved. In chapter 6 we defined the notion of modules and derived the notion of compositional inclusion. This allows us to represent different kinds of part-whole relations while still retaining the flexibility to reason about a more basic transitive part-of relation.

7.2 Part-of in the Description Logic

Many of the approaches allow us to represent only one part-of relation. This is usually reflected in the language by the occurrence of a predefined role representing part-of. The approach in [Sat95] distinguishes six categories of part-whole relations and introduces predefined roles for them. In the approach

P. Lambrix: Part-Whole Reasoning, LNAI 1771, pp. 99-102, 2000
© Springer-Verlag Berlin Heidelberg 2000

in [SP94a] as well as in our own approach different kinds of part-whole relations can be introduced by user-defined part names. We believe that the latter approach provides a user with greater flexibility and expressivity. An advantage of predefined roles may be that sometimes more specialized inferences can be built into the system. For instance, part-of may be transitive for some kinds of part-whole relations and this may be supported directly by the system.

Also with respect to the constructs of the language our approach is similar to [SP94a]. The language we defined in chapter 5 contains the same constructs as [SP94a] except for the fact that we do not have inverses of part names, but we do have the **pp-constraint** construct. In our extended language as presented in chapter 6 we have introduced constructs that are variants of generalized value restriction and role value map. Another approach that allows special constructs for part-of in the language is [Fra93] where special quantifiers are introduced.

The other approaches use predefined roles and do not introduce specialized constructs for part-of. In these approaches the representational capabilities which are needed are discussed and then standard constructs are used to model this. For instance, in [Sat95] a highly expressive language is needed including primitive concept negation, inverses of roles, role conjunction, role disjunction, role composition and transitive closure of roles.

7.3 Subsumption Relationships

In our framework the subsumption relationships are computed via natural extensions of the procedures of a standard description logic. The interaction between is-a and part-of with respect to subsumption is achieved through the subsumption relationships concerning the new constructs.

We do not support the interaction between is-a and part-of as in [JP89, Ber94]. We cannot conclude from the fact that nephrons are part of kidneys that a nephron-disease is a kidney-disease. However, the fact that this property does not hold in general and thus allowing for this subsumption relationship requires taking into account the specific relation between the part and the whole is discussed in [JP89, Ber94]. In [JP89] this is done by allowing a user to state 'indirect transitivity' of a concept via a role. In [Ber94] part-sensitive subsumption is proposed to complement the classical subsumption. In the latter case, however, as there is only one part-of relation, all different kinds of part-whole relations are treated in the same way. It is not possible to have classical subsumption for some part-whole relations and part-sensitive subsumption for other part-whole relations.

7.4 Specialized Inferences

One of the strong points of our approach is that we give part-of not only a first class status with respect to representation, but we also consider different inferences that are targeted to part-of. Other approaches extend the representational capability and the standard inferences of description logics, but do not introduce specialized inferences for part-of. In chapter 5 we have added functionality to a description logic system to traverse a part-of hierarchy for individuals. In chapter 6 we have introduced inferences that are based on the notion of building composite objects. These inferences make use of the specialized nature of part-of and do not make sense for ordinary roles in general. We consider it important for a system supporting composite objects to also support reasoning about part-of.

7.5 Part-of Hierarchy for Individuals

Interestingly enough, only the approach in [SP94a] and our own approach consider a part-of hierarchy for individuals. A part-of hierarchy can be used to answer such queries as to which composites does a particular individual belong. In both approaches it is possible to state in the language that a particular individual is part of another individual. Other approaches seem to concentrate on introducing part-of at the concept level.

7.6 Compositional Inclusion Hierarchy for Concepts

The compositional inclusion hierarchy we define for concepts is used in the algorithms for compositional extension and completion. The intuition behind the hierarchy is that if $C_1 \mathbin{\widehat{\triangleright}}^* C_2$ then C_2 individuals may be used to build C_1 individuals. For example, by requiring that the title parts of a document are strings, it follows that *document* $\mathbin{\widehat{\triangleright}}^*$ *string*. One may argue that a part-of hierarchy for concepts should reflect an ontological relation [AFGP96]. In this case *string* should not be included in *document* as there is no ontological relation between these concepts as such.

One way to distinguish between different kinds of parts is to introduce the notions of essential, possible and impossible parts for a concept. A concept C_1 is an essential part of a concept C_2 if every C_2 individual has to have a C_1 individual as part.[1] A concept C_1 is a possible part of a concept C_2 if every C_2 individual may have a C_1 individual as part.[2] A concept C_1 cannot

---

[1] This is similar to the *contains* relation between concepts as defined in [SP94b].

[2] This is similar to the *may contain* relation between concepts as defined in [SP94b].

possibly be part of a concept C_2 if no C_2 individual may have a C_1 individual as part.

To be able to compute these different relations, given the definitions of the concepts we could do the following. Essential parts occur in the definition of a concept in an **allp** restriction for a part name and there is also an **atleastp** restriction asserting that there must be a least one part for the part name. The concepts that are not essential, but that occur in an **allp** construct, are possible parts. However, given the open-world assumption in description logics, other concepts can also be possible parts, but there is no way of knowing them. Impossible parts seem to be unexpressible in the language we propose.

In [SP94b] a *contains* and *may contain* relation between concepts are defined in a similar way to the essential and possible parts. The authors also define an *is part of* and *may be part of* relation as follows. A concept C_1 is (may be) part of concept C_2 if every C_1 individual is (may be) part of a C_2 individual. However, it is not clear how these relations can be inferred given the definitions of the concepts.

As our compositional inclusion hierarchy is mainly to be seen as a tool for the building of new individuals, the hierarchy should reflect reasonable candidates for this building, i.e. individuals belonging to a concept that is compositionally included in another concept are reasonable candidates for building an individual of the second concept. Reasonable candidates are individuals belonging to essential parts and possible parts that are mentioned in the definition of the composite concept. We have also included the concepts that are more specialized than the essential and possible parts. Although it is not always the case that these more specialized individuals can be used,[3] in many cases it appears that they are good candidates.

---

[3] For instance, in the case where a standard family is defined as containing offspring parts that must be children, the concept child and the more specific concepts are compositionally included in the concept standard family. However, children that are orphans are not included in a standard family. We thank Erik Sandewall for this example.

Well, Dear Reader, You have arrived at a point where You have learned a language to talk to a machine about part-of. In the rest of this work You gain experience with the language by going through a number of application areas where the language has been found to be useful. In the first area we take an existing system where the need for support for part-of is recognized. We use our language to re-model the specific domain of the application and show that our approach provides a number of advantages. In the second area we model documents which have a structure that can naturally be modeled using part-of. We show how our language provides support for the representation of documents and instantiation and management of document knowledge-bases. We also show how we extend the query capabilities with respect to a document knowledge-base by supporting part-of. Finally, we sketch how our language can be used to let the machine You talk to learn composite concepts.

Part III

Application Areas

8. Domain Modeling in an Agent-Oriented Application

8.1 Motivation

In this chapter we investigate the use of a description logic for composite objects for modeling an agent's conceptualization of the world and its beliefs about the current world state in a particular application. This application involves automating the monitoring of the Reaction Control System (RCS) of NASA's space shuttle. The application has been modeled before and an implementation exists using the agent-oriented system dMARS (distributed Multi Agent Reasoning System) from the Australian Artificial Intelligence Institute, an updated version of PRS (Procedural Reasoning System) [GI89, IGR92]. Although it was recognized that part-of played an important role in the application, the existing implementation did not provide any support for representing and inferencing with part-of. The use of our description logic for composite objects has provided a number of advantages.

An increasing number of complex applications are being built using agent-oriented systems. 'Agents' in this context are autonomous software modules, able to react rationally, in a robust way, in a complex and dynamic world. An important part of an agent model is the *belief database* (see figure 8.1[1]) which models the beliefs of a particular agent regarding the world. The actions of the agent are determined by a combination of the *goals* of the agent, and the agent's beliefs about the state of the world. For example, if an agent has a goal to get to the airport as cheaply as possible, it may choose to take the train. However, if it believes there is a train strike, it will not choose this particular way of achieving its goal. Actions are often organized into *plans* which are complex structures of actions at varying levels of abstraction. Plans typically include information regarding what is expected to be true in order for the plan to be applicable. An agent recognizes a plan as being applicable or not, depending on its beliefs about what is true in the world. When an agent has decided to perform a plan, the plan is put into the *intention structure.*

In this work we replace the belief database of a dMARS agent in the RCS application with a description logic system. We found that the belief database of the existing implementation contains many part-whole relations. Most of these part-whole relations are modeled using a PART-OF relation,

---

[1] The figure is taken from [GI90].

P. Lambrix: Part-Whole Reasoning, LNAI 1771, pp. 107-119, 2000
© Springer-Verlag Berlin Heidelberg 2000

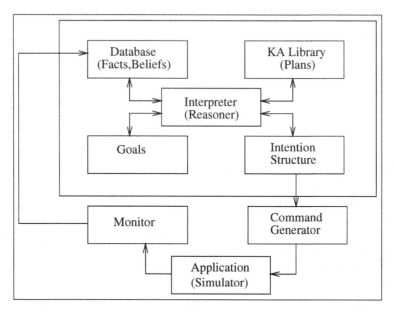

Fig. 8.1. PRS system structure.

while others received more specific names. In some cases the part-of relation between two objects is modeled using different relations. Also the plans that use the information in the belief database contain many queries involving the structure of the domain. However, although it is recognized that part-of plays an important part in the application, there is no specialized way to represent and reason about part-of.

The description logic system that we have used for this application is the system described in chapter 5, extended to include capabilities for representing and reasoning about modules. Our choice of application gives us the advantage that we have an application where the need for representing and reasoning with part-of is recognized as being important. Further, we have an existing implementation to compare our system with. We have modeled the RCS domain using our description logic system and have rewritten several of the plans to use our description logic system instead of the belief database.

We have found that using a description logic for composite objects has a number of advantages. For instance, the support for part-of leads to a more natural model of the domain and the modeling and instantiation of composites can be done in a convenient modular fashion. There are also other advantages. For instance, our approach allows for the reasoning processes regarding the state that the world is in to be separated out from reasoning processes regarding what goals the agent most wishes to achieve and how. It also allows for consistency checking when building the agent's model of the world, and in addition ensures that certain kinds of logical consequences occur automatically, rather than needing to be encoded into results of plans.

In the following sections we describe dMARS (section 8.2) and the Reaction Control System application (section 8.3). In section 8.4 we describe how we modeled the RCS application in our description logic system. We discuss the advantages and disadvantages that the combination of the agent-oriented system and the description logic system gave for the RCS application in section 8.5.

8.2 dMARS

PRS [GI89, IGR92] and dMARS are situated reasoning systems that were built to satisfy most of the behavioral properties that one expects a reasoning system suited to real-time applications to have. Essential properties in this context (based on [LCSKR88]) are:

- asynchronous event handling,
- guaranteed reaction and response times,
- procedural representation of knowledge, such that maintenance and manual procedures can be represented in situation-specific procedures,
- handling of multiple problems,
- reactive and goal-directed behavior,
- focus of attention, to be able to complete tasks in real time,
- reflective reasoning, to be able to change focus,
- continuous embedded operation,
- handling of incomplete or inaccurate data.

Each dMARS agent consists of the following components: a database of current beliefs or facts about the world, a set of current goals to be realized, a set of plans describing how a sequence of actions may achieve a given goal or forming a reaction to a particular situation, and an intention structure containing a set of plans that have been chosen for eventual execution. An inference mechanism selects appropriate plans on the basis of the agent's beliefs and goals, and places these selected plans in the intention structure and executes them. The system interacts with its environment through its database by acquiring new beliefs and through the actions it performs.

The belief database typically contains both static and dynamic information. The static information describes the structural model of the domain, such as what (types of) objects there are, and how they are related. The dynamic information consists of variables which are modified as the world changes or is believed to have changed. An agent typically believes the world has changed (and updates its belief database), when it takes some action designed to produce change in the world, or when it is notified (by some other agent) that something has happened.

Plans consist of a body, which describes the different steps in the procedure, and an invocation consisting of a triggering part and a context condition part. The triggering part describes the events that must occur for the plan to be executed. These can be the acquisition of a new goal or some change in the belief database. The context condition describes conditions which must be satisfied in the belief database. The set of plans in an application not only contains specific knowledge about the application domain, but also meta-level plans containing information about how the beliefs, goals and intentions are to be manipulated. An example of such a meta-level plan is a plan that chooses a plan from a set of plans. The dMARS decides which plans are applicable by matching beliefs and goals with invocation conditions by unification.

For a deeper discussion on how the inference mechanism selects the applicable plans, manages them in the intention structure and decides on execution we refer to [GI89, IG89, IGR92].

8.3 Reaction Control System

The problem domain which we have worked on is the Reaction Control System of NASA's space shuttle. A space shuttle has three RCSs, two aft and one forward. An RCS provides propulsive forces from a collection of jet thrusters to control the attitude of the space shuttle. The RCS modules contain a collection of jets, a fuel tank, an oxidizer tank, two helium tanks, feedlines, manifolds and other supporting equipment. Each RCS module receives all commands via the space shuttle flight software. The various valves in an RCS module are controlled from a panel of switches and talkbacks. The talkbacks provide feedback on the position of their associated valves. The aim of the RCS application is to automate the malfunction procedures for the RCS.

Each RCS is managed by two dMARS agents. The Interface agent handles all information concerning transducer readings, valve switches and valve talkbacks. The belief database for this agent contains the domain model including the knowledge about transducer readings and switch and talkback positions. It has no knowledge about pressures as these have to be deduced from the transducer readings. The plans are typically about calculating pressures, switch movements and malfunction detection. The Controller agent takes a high-level view of the application. The belief database is similar to the database of the Interface agent, but contains information about pressures rather than about specific transducer readings. This information is obtained by asking the Interface agent. The plans contain the high-level malfunction procedures as they appear in the shuttle's malfunction handling manuals.

For more information about how the RCS application is modeled in the existing dMARS application we refer to [GI89, IG89, GI90, IGR92].

8.4 Modeling the Belief Knowledge Base

As a framework for the modeling of this application we used a description logic with the following constructors: **and**, **all**, **atleast**, **atmost**, **fills**, **one-of**, **allp**, **atleastp**, **atmostp**, **part-fills**, **pp-constraint**, and a variant of **module-fills**. We did not use information about the order of the parts. With respect to modules we found that it was useful to allow for the part names to change from the module to the composite it is a module of. For instance, in a helium tank assembly the different part names may be *tank-p*, *valve-p* and so on, while in the definition of propellant system the same parts may be called *he-tank-p*, *he-valve-p* and so on, to distinguish them from other parts. Then, following the definition in chapter 6, a helium tank assembly cannot be a module of a propellant system. To allow for this fact we define the notion of *module with part name changes*.

Definition 8.4.1. *Let x and y be composite individuals.*
y is a **module** *of x with part names changes n_{11} to n_{12}, ..., n_{m1} to n_{m2},*
(notation: $y \lhd_{\mathbf{mod} \{n_{11} \to n_{12}, ..., n_{m1} \to n_{m2}\}} x$)
iff the following conditions hold:
(i) $\forall \, z, j \in \{1, ..., m\} : z \lhd_{n_{j1}} y \to z \lhd_{n_{j2}} x$
(ii) $\forall \, z, n \notin \{n_{11}, ..., n_{m1}\} : z \lhd_n y \to z \lhd_n x$
(iii) $\exists \, z, n_1 : (z \lhd_{n_1} x \land \forall \, n : \neg(z \lhd_n y))$

The definition for modules with part name changes for individuals is the natural extension of the definition in chapter 6. We extend the syntax of the language to also include the following as a concept description:
(**module-fills** $<individual\text{-}name>^+$ $<part\text{-}name\text{-}change>^+$) where
$<part\text{-}name\text{-}change> ::= <part\text{-}name\text{-}name> \to <part\text{-}name\text{-}name>$. However, part name changes are not required to occur. The semantics for the construct is then:

$$\varepsilon[(\mathbf{module\text{-}fills} \; i_1 \; ... \; i_m \; n_{11} \to n_{12} \; ... \; n_{k1} \to n_{k2})] =$$
$$\{ \, x \in \mathcal{D} \mid \varepsilon[i_1] \; \lhd_{\mathbf{mod} \{n_{11} \to n_{12}, ..., n_{k1} \to n_{k2}\}} x \land ...$$
$$\land \, \varepsilon[i_m] \; \lhd_{\mathbf{mod} \{n_{11} \to n_{12}, ..., n_{k1} \to n_{k2}\}} x \, \}$$

The syntax and semantics of the other constructs are as defined in chapter 6 with the exception that q-parts are replaced by part-name-names.

In modeling the RCS system we have used both the model as it is in the existing dMARS, and the NASA manual [Bus87] describing the RCS of the space shuttle and its operation, which was the original source document for the application.

We have modeled concepts such as jets, tanks, valves, switches and the necessary instances of these concepts. The resulting knowledge base contains 44 concepts and 153 individuals with 38 different part-of relations and 23 other relations. There are between one and sixteen individuals for each concept. This model closely follows the original source document.

In the previous model several new relations existed that did not occur in the original description of the application. These were mainly added for efficiency reasons, in order to skip some unification steps. They usually involve individuals in different sub-systems that have similar functions or individuals where one individual operates the other. An example of the latter is the case of valves, switches and talkbacks that are connected. In the previous model new relations (such as associated-switch) were introduced between these individuals. In our system these extra relations are not needed. We can simply traverse the part-of hierarchy for the composite object to find the relevant individual(s). For instance, in the previous model a valve was always connected to its corresponding switch, by a relation associated-switch. We can find the correct switch without the introduced relation associated-switch, simply by accessing the switch that is part of the same composite individual as the valve.

In the case where additional relations may be desirable for extra efficiency we have used the **pp-constraint** construct to automatically introduce these relations between the different individuals. In the case of valves, switches and talkbacks, for instance, we introduced the concept of valve-switch-talkback-system. The definition of this concept contains the **pp-constraint** that the valves and the talkback must be in the associated-switch relation with the switch. Each collection of connected valves, switches and talkbacks make up one such valve-switch-talkback-system. When a valve-switch-talkback-system is instantiated with the specific individuals, the description logic system makes sure that the associated-switch relations are also maintained.

When adding the various individual components of the system we found that the notion of modules allowed for a convenient "bottom-up" building of objects. We were able to first instantiate the "smallest" composite individuals, such as a connection, and then use the **module-fills** construct to include these in more complex composite individuals, such as an assembly (see figure 8.3), whereupon the constraints are checked automatically and values are propagated. In the example in figure 8.3 the parts of the modules are propagated to fu-prop-tk-assembly and the constraints are checked. For instance, it is checked that there is at most one tank part and at most two valve parts.

In addition to modeling the world within the description logic system, it was necessary for us to rewrite the system plans, in order to query the description logic knowledge-base regarding the state of the world rather than performing unification on the dMARS representation of the world state. This was relatively straightforward and in some cases resulted in a conceptual simplification of the plans produced. A significant number of the queries needed relied on the representation of individuals as composite entities made up of parts, thus justifying our choice of the extended description logic rather than the simpler unmodified CLASSIC system. The following types of queries appeared in the plans and were all frequently used.

propellant-tank-assembly $\stackrel{.}{\leq}$
        (**and**   (**atleastp** 1 *tank-part*)
                (**atmostp** 1 *tank-part*)
                (**allp** *tank-part propellant-tank*)
                (**atleastp** 2 *p-sensor-part*)
                (**atmostp** 2 *p-sensor-part*)
                (**allp** *p-sensor-part p-xdcr*)
                (**atleastp** 2 *leg-part*)
                (**atmostp** 2 *leg-part*)
                (**allp** *leg-part leg*)
                (**atleastp** 2 *valve-part*)
                (**atmostp** 2 *valve-part*)
                (**allp** *valve-part propellant-tank-isol-valve*))

Fig. 8.2. A propellant-tank-assembly.

fu-prop-tk-assembly ::
        (**and**   *propellant-tank-assembly*
                (**module-fills** *fu-12-connection*)
                (**module-fills** *fu-345-connection*)
                (**part-fills** *p-sensor-part frcs-fu-tk-p-xdcr frcs-fu-tk-out-p-xdcr*))

fu-12-connection ::
        (**and**   *prop-tank-connection*
                (**part-fills** *tank-part frcs-fu-tk*)
                (**part-fills** *valve-part frcs-fu-tk-isol-12-valve*)
                (**part-fills** *leg-part frcs-fu-tk-12-leg*))

fu-345-connection ::
        (**and**   *prop-tank-connection*
                (**part-fills** *tank-part frcs-fu-tk*)
                (**part-fills** *valve-part frcs-fu-tk-isol-345-valve*)
                (**part-fills** *leg-part frcs-fu-tk-345-leg*))

Fig. 8.3. A propellant-tank-assembly individual.

- Is individual i' part of individual i ?
- Is individual i' part of an individual belonging to C ?
- Is there an individual belonging to C that is part of individual i ?
- Get all individuals that are part of individual i.
- Get all individuals of which individual i' is a part.
- Get all individuals that belong to concept C and are part of individual i.
- Get all individuals that belong to concept C and of which individual i' is a part.

It is also worth noting that we often require only one query, whereas the previous dMARS model typically had to perform the query in several unification steps introducing intermediary variables. One reason for this is the fact that our system allows us to state complex queries regarding the part-of relation (see 'Functions involving the part-of hierarchy for individuals' in appendix A).

We found that the checking of the context condition in the dMARS plans can often be split into two conceptually separate phases. In the first phase the actual context condition is checked, i.e. the requirements that have to hold for this plan to be instantiated. The second part of the context conditions then instantiates different variables that are not part of the plan instantiation requirements but for which a plan has to be instantiated for each possible binding.

An example of this is a plan for updating the reading of the quantity in a tank with bad pvt-status by using its associated helium tank. Instead of having nine clauses, binding five different variables, some of which are only intermediate variables for passing between clauses, we were able to simply form two queries - the first ascertaining whether the invocation condition for the plan was met (the given tank is a propellant tank with bad pvt-status and is included in a propellant system for which the other-propellant-system also has a tank with bad pvt-status) and the second to ascertain which individual helium tank is included in the same propellant system as the original tank. It was also possible to define the body of this plan without the use of additional variables.

In the process of building the knowledge base, some mistakes were found in the original database on which we were working.[2] A number of these errors would have been automatically detected, or more easily noticed, using a description logic for composite objects. Examples of types of errors detected include:

- information appearing twice - a description logic system detects the fact that the information already exists, and does not add the redundant fact.
- typing mistakes in some relation names, resulting in the relations being undefined - a description logic system issues a warning when it creates the new (mistyped) entity.

---

[2] Here we used the database as in [GI90]. Newer versions of the database exist.

– mismatch between concepts in plans and concepts in the database - a description logic system detects an error.
– some connection relations were missing - the description logic system can check this by using a system function to check whether all (part-of) relations are closed, i.e. whether all necessary relations are completely instantiated.
– some of the extra relations were missing - the way that we modeled this, these are automatically created by the description logic system, because they are defined as being necessary for all individuals of the given type.

Although the errors were either corrected in a later version, or were unimportant for the correct functioning of the system, it is clearly beneficial to have support which minimizes such problems.

8.5 Advantages and Disadvantages

The approach that we have taken of extracting the belief database of a rational agent and using a description logic knowledge-base for modeling this aspect of the agent leads to a number of advantages. There is greater support for conceptual modeling, and the description logic system is able to aid in verification and consistency checking. These are important when initially building the knowledge base, and become even more important during maintenance, as the system is changed possibly by people who do not have as thorough an understanding of the whole as the original designers.

A potential disadvantage of our approach (and the only property of d-MARS (section 8.2) that may be affected negatively) is the possible reduced efficiency and responsiveness resulting from the added communication between systems. Testing to date indicates, however, that this may not be a problem. We now explore in more detail both the advantages and disadvantages of our approach.

8.5.1 Advantages

The use of a description logic system allows us to represent knowledge about concepts in one place, from where it is inherited by specific individuals belonging to that concept. This support for modeling the types of entities in the domain, separate from the individuals, is similar to the support of object-oriented languages for modeling types. The essential difference is the added logical inferencing and automatic classification. In the approach we have used there is also additional support for composite objects, which was essential to this domain.

The use of concept definitions allows for the expression of 'generic' knowledge and general constraints. For instance, as shown in figure 8.2, a propellant-tank-assembly always has exactly two valve parts and these parts must always be propellant tank isolation valves. The concept hierarchy allows for inheriting information. There are several different sub-types of valves, but all inherit the properties of the general valve type. This inheritance allows for modularity and for a minimum of facts. For instance, in the previous implementation the knowledge engineer had to specifically assert for every individual propellant tank isolation valve an extra fact saying that it is also a valve. Now this information is inherited, by virtue of the fact that propellant tank isolation valves are a sub-type of valve. Sometimes such facts were inadvertently missed, whereas now this is not possible.

Our model of the application is closer to the description in the NASA manual than the previous implementation. For instance, some relations such as connection relations which seem to be symmetric in nature were implemented in the previous model as asymmetric relations. The reason for this was to make unification more efficient by avoiding paths that would lead to certain fail. What was actually missing in these situations was type information that would allow the system to avoid such paths. In our model the type information is included in a natural way so that we could model the symmetric relations more intuitively. As mentioned before, our model allows for a convenient bottom-up instantiating of composite objects. Some levels in the part-of hierarchy which existed in the NASA manual did not exist in the previous model. These levels were usually levels representing modules in our part-of hierarchy.

In the previous implementation there was information in the database regarding what types an individual object belonged to. However, this information was simply an attribute. The system had no ability to ensure that an object exhibited the characteristics of the type, or to recognize an object as belonging to a given type on the basis of its description.

A clear advantage of using a description logic system is the constant automatic consistency checking. Previously, all consistency checking had to be done manually, and as the system increased in size, various errors arose. The description logic system uses the concept definitions and the statements about individuals to constantly check the consistency of the knowledge base. For instance, when asserting the properties of the fuel propellant tank assembly shown in figure 8.3, the system does not allow frcs-fu-tk-p-xdcr to be a pressure sensor part of fu-prop-tk-assembly if this would cause an inconsistency, for instance if the properties required of this part were inconsistent with the properties required of pressure transducers, the concept to which frcs-fu-tk-p-xdcr belongs.

If a given fact does cause an inconsistency, the system issues a warning and does not update the knowledge base. The knowledge engineer can then examine the cause of the problem, and modify either the knowledge base or the new fact.

Another useful aspect of the description logic system is the automatic calculation of the logical consequences of a new fact. A simple example of this is the case where the facts that switch A and valve B are parts of a particular valve-switch-talkback-system are introduced. This results in a new fact being inferred, namely that there is an associated switch relation between switch A and valve B (as this is required in the concept definition of a valve-switch-talkback-system). The database of the previous implementation did, in fact, contain inconsistencies resulting from missing facts of this kind.

In this application the capabilities of dynamically updating of the knowledge base and the automatic calculation of the logical consequences in the knowledge base were mainly used during modeling rather than at runtime. Propagation occurred, for instance, using the constraints between parts or when domain restrictions for roles and part names were applied. Although it has not been used so far in this application, it seems reasonable to assume that the ability to detect information which causes an inconsistency in the knowledge base at runtime would also be useful. It could alert an agent to a situation which needed further investigation, or be used as a filter for noisy data.

Another useful feature for consistency checking is the ability in CLASSIC to define disjoint groupings of concepts such that no individual can belong to any pair of concepts in the group. The system then makes sure that no information is added to the knowledge base that would make an individual belong to disjoint concepts. This facility was useful in the modeling of the system in a number of places, such as the case where we needed to distinguish between different kinds of tanks.

There are also other facilities that allow for verifying the model. For instance, it is easy to check whether all individuals have the properties they are supposed to have. A particularly useful item of functionality was the ability to check whether a given relation for an individual was completely instantiated. This enabled us to detect some omissions in the database which had existed in the previous implementation.

Although it is important to ensure that the knowledge base does not become inconsistent, it is equally important to be able to reason with incomplete data. The use of a description logic system has added to this ability, as in a description logic system (unlike many other logic-based systems) not all information about an individual has to be available.

The new system provides the ability to not only represent and reason about the is-a relation, but also about part-of. In a natural model of the RCS application the part-of relation plays an important role in the description of the system. As we have already mentioned, many of the queries in the plans of the application relied on the composite nature of objects. In our system there is support for part-of by allowing the distinction between part-whole relations and other relations, and among different kinds of part-whole relations, by allowing domain restrictions and number restrictions, and by allowing for constraints between parts. The previous implementation contained significant information about part-of, but this could not be represented in a standard manner. For instance, the relation between a system and its oxidizer sub-system was represented by 'part-of' and 'oxidizer-subsystem'. The first relation was used in plans when any sub-system could be used in the unification process, while the other relation required the sub-system to be the oxidizer sub-system. In our model we used the part name 'oxidizer-subsystem' which by definition then has the part-of intuition. In a situation where different sub-systems could be used, we can use the description logic system functions to find all possible sub-systems.

8.5.2 Disadvantages

The major concern regarding possible disadvantages of this approach has to do with possible decreases in efficiency and responsiveness. Given that dMARS currently fully integrates agent beliefs within the total system, there is no communication overhead, as there is in our approach.

We have analyzed the behavior of the previous implementation and found that most of the queries regarding beliefs are generated during the computation of the set of applicable plans. Queries are often generated for plans that turn out not to be applicable, as well as for the plans which succeed. Complex context conditions with many potential solutions may generate large numbers of queries. We have examined the plans that generate the most queries as a result of complex context conditions and it appears that we can reduce the number of queries using a description logic system rather than unification. While this is positive in terms of communication overhead, the description logic queries may be complex and empirical testing is needed to ascertain the effect on efficiency.

We note that after writing the plans all the queries to the description logic system are known. Therefore all the concepts that occur in the queries can be defined and classified in advance and thus no time-consuming classification of these concepts has to take place at run-time.

We have tested individual sequences of plans and the resulting queries, and the behavior of the system is interactive in real time. This leads us to hope that further testing will reveal that there is no (or insignificant) loss of efficiency using this approach. Even if efficiency were to be affected negatively, we would argue that the use of a description logic system is beneficial during the knowledge engineering phase, and can be removed if necessary at runtime.

One of the important properties of dMARS is the guaranteed reaction and response time. When plans take too long to execute, or when important competing issues arise, plans can be interrupted. We would like to maintain this responsiveness by being able to interrupt the description logic system processing at any time as well. The problem with this is the danger that the knowledge base could be left in an inconsistent state. However, querying the description logic system does not alter the consistency and thus it should be possible to interrupt queries without extra overhead. During an update of the knowledge base individuals are reclassified and information is propagated.

Thus a mechanism needs to be developed to allow recovery if an interrupt occurs during an update. This is not a significant issue for this application, as the nature of the updating is such that there is little propagation, and thus little opportunity for interrupting and leaving the knowledge base in an inconsistent state.

8.6 Conclusion

In this chapter we have demonstrated how a description logic system can be used to provide support for implementing the belief sub-system of a rational agent, and we have indicated some of the concrete advantages found in using this approach. Several of the advantages were obtained by using a description logic system where knowledge about the part-of relation could be expressed.

We saw that a natural model of the application needed the part-of relation. This is obvious when we notice that the model actually contains 38 different part-whole relations. The fact that the model is closer to the original source document than the existing dMARS model comes mainly from the fact that we used part-of. For instance, we did not need to introduce different part-of relations between the same two individuals. From a logical point of view we did not need to introduce the extra relations that were introduced in the existing dMARS model as traversing the part-of hierarchy gives us the same information. When these extra relations were desirable for efficiency reasons, we used the **pp-constraint** construct to automatically maintain these relations. Using this approach we were able to correct some mistakes found in the existing database. The **module-fills** construct allowed for a bottom-up instantiation of composite individuals, where more complex individuals were instantiated using less complex individuals. We saw that the notion of module was also present in the original source document, but had disappeared in the existing dMARS model. Many of the queries used in the plans involved part-of. Therefore it was natural to use a system where knowledge about part-of can be expressed in a natural way. The user functions of our description logic system also enabled an easy way of traversing the part-of hierarchy.

9. Document Management

9.1 Motivation

Document structure is one of the important characteristics of a document, as are content and graphical characteristics. For instance, a document may be composed of a title and some sections where each section in its turn is composed of a title and paragraphs. Research in recent years shows that it is advantageous to be able to use the structure of a document in the representation of the documents in document bases (e.g. [BRG88, AFQ89, GZC89, KLMN90, MRT91, LZS95]), thereby creating *structured documents*. Further, international standards such as SGML (e.g. [Gol90]) and ODA (e.g. [IOS87]) have been developed requiring documents to be defined in terms of a structure of parts.

The natural hierarchical structure of documents lends itself well to a document representation based on composite objects. For instance, a document may be represented by an object containing sections where each section is represented by an object with particular properties and characteristics in its own right. An advantage of a composite object model for documents, is the fact that it supports reusability of document components. For instance, sections may be shared between different documents. The approach also allows for the development of special tools for assisting the authors of documents. For instance, a table of contents may be created automatically by a program that visits the different component objects and gathers their titles. The ability to query a document base is also important. The composite object model allows for queries involving structured as well as unstructured information.[1]

In this chapter we examine the usefulness of introducing a description logic for composite objects for use in a project document management system based on the requirements of the application. In this application system support is required for such things as definition of document types, classification and checking of documents for completeness with respect to definition, inheritance of attributes between parts and wholes, and declaration and management of part-of relationships. The requirements that we consider here, are based on documentation describing current manual routines at a local company [Åke94].

---

[1] This is the topic of chapter 11.

P. Lambrix: Part-Whole Reasoning, LNAI 1771, pp. 121-129, 2000
© Springer-Verlag Berlin Heidelberg 2000

On analysis of the document templates provided to us we have determined requirements for the terminological and assertional components of the description logic. We discuss these requirements and their influence on the expressivity of the description logic in section 9.2. We have also identified a number of queries and inferences related to part-of which users would like to make to the system. We discuss them in section 9.3. We also discuss how the system can be used to make the inferences and answer the queries desired by users.

9.2 Modeling the Document Management Domain

Early in our analysis of the templates used for document management we found that it was important to be able to distinguish between different kinds of parts. Different kinds of parts can have different properties. For instance, it is natural to distinguish between the properties of the title of a document and the properties of the sections. For this purpose we use part names as defined in chapter 5. Further, we need the **allp**, **atleastp** and **atmostp** constructs to define domain and number restrictions. For instance, (**allp** *title-p string*) in the definition of a document means that all the title parts of the document are strings while (**atleastp** *3 section-p*), indicates that there are at least 3 section parts.

In this application order information is particularly important. For a document, for instance, it is not acceptable for its sections to appear in random order. We need the ability to specify which is section 1, which section 2, and so on. As we saw in chapter 6, we can do this by using qualified part names. The **order-constraint** construct allows us to state restrictions such as (**order-constraint** *section-p reference-p*). This indicates that in the ordering of parts, the section parts come before the reference parts.

Finally, we require in the language the ability to express inheritance information via part-whole relations. We use the **same-filler** and **aggregate** constructs. This allows us to state that the project name attribute of a document part has the same value as the project name attribute of the folder it belongs to by having (**same-filler** *project-name document-p.project-name*) in the definition of the folder. This gives us the ability to require that all documents in a folder concern the same project. The system does not allow a document to be entered into a folder with another project name or to have documents with different project names in the same folder. Having (**aggregate** *document-p supervisor supervisors*) in the definition of a folder indicates that the value of the supervisors role for the folder is an aggregate of the supervisor attribute in each of the document parts of the folder. Thus every document supervisor (represented by the supervisor attribute in the document representation) is included in the list of folder supervisors (represented by the supervisors role in the folder representation).

This language then allows us to make definitions such as those shown in figure 9.1. In our application project documentation consists of eight different folders, each describing a different step in the life-cycle of the project. Each such folder contains a number of documents which are sometimes organized in sub-folders. In figure 9.1 we present a simplified example of a folder and the documents it can contain. In the example a document usually has exactly three section parts of which the first is an introduction, the second contains the definitions and the third section the actual content and methods used. Further, it usually also has exactly one author. We define a standard document as a document that has exactly this structure and property (see figure 9.2).

In figure 9.3 we show a particular document with its parts. The language for assertional knowledge allows the same constructs as the language for terminological knowledge extended with the **before** construct. This construct is used to state information about the order of particular individuals.

The document knowledge-base consists, then, of terminological axioms containing information about the different types of documentation, folders and documents. The assertional component contains information about the actual projects and their documents. The information about the different types can be used as templates for the actual instantiation of documents. For instance, upon creation of a new document the system may show the user a template in which the different fields represent the different properties (such as the project name or the authors) and the structure (as in the case of a standard document where the template may show exactly three section parts to be instantiated) of the document.

The fact that we can dynamically add and retract information from individuals in a description logic system makes it possible to store partial information about specific documents and update the document knowledge-base later on. This facility is useful, for instance, when new information becomes available or when we want to update or correct some information. Every time information is added to or retracted from the document knowledge-base, integrity checking is automatically performed. The description logic system does not allow data to be entered that would make the knowledge base inconsistent. For instance, as seen before, when a new document is created in a particular folder, the project name associated to the document has to be the same as the project name associated to the folder. If the project name is the same for both, then the system accepts the information. If the project names are different, the system does not enter the new information into the knowledge base and warns the user. In the case where the project name attribute is instantiated in the folder but not in the document, or vice versa, the system instantiates the missing attribute value with the project name.

At all times it is possible to retrieve all information about a concept or individual from the knowledge base using the system's user functions. The

documentation $\doteq$
>   (**and** (**atleast** *1 supervisors*)
>   (**atleast** *1 project-name*)
>   (**atmost** *1 project-name*)
>   (**atleastp** *8 folder-p*)
>   (**atmostp** *8 folder-p*)
>   (**allp** *folder-p folder*)
>   (**same-filler** *project-name folder-p.project-name*))

folder $\doteq$
>   (**and** (**atleast** *1 supervisors*)
>   (**atleast** *1 project-name*)
>   (**atmost** *1 project-name*)
>   (**atleastp** *2 document-p*)
>   (**allp** *document-p document*)
>   (**same-filler** *project-name document-p.project-name*)
>   (**aggregate** *document-p supervisor supervisors*))

document $\doteq$
>   (**and** (**atleast** *1 project-name*)
>   (**atmost** *1 project-name*)
>   (**atleast** *1 supervisor*)
>   (**atmost** *1 supervisor*)
>   (**atleastp** *1 title-p*)
>   (**atmostp** *1 title-p*)
>   (**allp** *title-p string*)
>   (**atleastp** *3 section-p*)
>   (**allp** *section-p section*)
>   (**allp** *section-p:1 introduction*)
>   (**allp** *reference-p reference*)
>   (**order-constraint** *title-p section-p*)
>   (**order-constraint** *section-p reference-p*))

Fig. 9.1. A project documentation description - definitions.

standard-document $\doteq$
  (**and** (**atleast** *1 project-name*)
       (**atmost** *1 project-name*)
       (**atleast** *1 supervisor*)
       (**atmost** *1 supervisor*)
       (**atleast** *1 author*)
       (**atmost** *1 author*)
       (**atleastp** *1 title-p*)
       (**atmostp** *1 title-p*)
       (**allp** *title-p string*)
       (**atleastp** *3 section-p*)
       (**atmostp** *3 section-p*)
       (**allp** *section-p section*)
       (**allp** *section-p:1 introduction*)
       (**allp** *section-p:2 definition*)
       (**allp** *section-p:3 method*)
       (**allp** *reference-p reference*)
       (**order-constraint** *title-p section-p*)
       (**order-constraint** *section-p reference-p*))

Fig. 9.2. A standard document.

d ::
       (**and** *document*
            (**part-fills** *title-p t*)
            (**part-fills** *section-p s_1 s_2 s_3*)
            (**fills** *project-name dl-project*)
            (**fills** *supervisor John*))

t ::
       (**and** *string*
            (**before** *s_1* **in** *d*))

s_1 ::
       (**and** *introduction*
            (**before** *s_2* **in** *d*))

s_2 ::
       (**and** *section*
            (**before** *s_3* **in** *d*))

s_3 ::
       section

Fig. 9.3. A document individual and its parts.

information in the document knowledge-base can then be used in a number of ways. This we discuss in the next section.

9.3 Useful Queries and Inferences

In addition to examining what the application needed from the language in order to be able to describe its constructs, we have also examined what questions users wish to ask, as well as what inferences are useful in this application and have relevance to the notion of part-of or composite objects. In this section we discuss five tasks for a description logic system for document management that are interesting from this point of view. The first two tasks provide support for the writing of documents in different ways. The third task allows us to traverse the structure of the documentation. The fourth task is the recognition of individuals, which is a standard operation in description logics. The last task allows for information retrieval from a document knowledge-base.

9.3.1 Top-Down Instantiation of Documents

A common way of writing documents is by using a template. A document individual is then created following the document concept description, but its parts still have to be instantiated. In this method it is important that we at all times are able to find out what parts are still missing from the document, given that some parts have already been written. The information we need is of what kind these missing parts necessarily should be, and what the necessary relationships should be among these parts, and between these parts and the already available parts. We do not want to introduce unmotivated new parts either.

This information can be obtained by using the notion of completion as defined in chapter 6. Assume that we have an initial knowledge base $< T, A >$, that the document has to belong to concept C and that the available parts and modules are given in the sets α and β. Then a completion of $(< \alpha, \beta >, C)$ with respect to $< T, A >$ represents a proposal for an instantiation of the missing parts.

For instance, given the fact that we want to create a standard document having as its parts an already existing introduction section and a definition section, then a possible completion is one that defines a method section and a title to be parts of the document. The completion also contains the information that the title must be a string and come before the introduction section and that the method section must come after the definition section.

The completion does not instantiate a new composite (a document in this example). If the user wants to instantiate a new composite, the assembly function can be used.

9.3.2 Bottom-Up Instantiation of Documents

In the creation of a document the supervisor for the document may wish
to use sections already written by other people. In the creation of a folder
documents may have to be collected from different places. In both cases it is
necessary to assemble the final composition from the different available parts.
The final composition has to be of a specific kind (in the first example the
composition must be a document, in the second a folder) and thus belong to
a specific composite concept. During the assembly we have to make sure that
all parts satisfy the requirements which are dictated by the definition of this
composite concept, including the constraints between the parts which must
be fulfilled before assembly is allowed.

The composes function as defined in chapter 6 allows us to check whether
a set of individuals can be used as parts and modules for the instantiation
of an individual of a particular concept. The function checks the structural
properties such as the number and domains of the parts and the different
kinds of constraints between the parts. For instance, given the fact that we
want to instantiate a document given some parts (e.g. title and sections), the
composes function checks whether there is exactly one part that will be a
title part and that this part is a string. It also checks whether there are at
least three individuals that will be section parts and that these are sections.
The first section part must also be an introduction. Further, a check is made
that the title part comes before the section parts.

To instantiate a new document individual we can first check the set of
available parts using the composes function and if the structural properties
are satisfied, a new individual can be instantiated using the assembly function.

Another approach may be to use completion and let the system automatically infer (or propose) new composite individuals. This approach is most
useful when the parts that are not yet used can be partitioned into sets that
have the required structural properties and for which the parts are intended
to belong to the same individual.

9.3.3 Inheritance via Part-of

As we have seen before, description logic systems allow for a dynamic update
of the document base. Information about documents or parts of documents
can be retracted, asserted or updated at any time. However, some of the
information regarding parts may be dependent on information about the
composites they belong to and vice versa. For instance, the supervisors for a
folder include the supervisor for a particular document in the folder. In some
cases the propagation of this information via part-of is done automatically. In
this example, for instance, the definition of a folder contains an **aggregate**
construct, thereby assuring that the supervisors for documents in the folder

are also supervisors for the folder. Also the **same-filler** construct allows for inheriting information via part-of.

However, in some cases this propagation of information does not occur automatically. Assume, for instance, that sections and documents have a last-change attribute indicating the date of the last change to the section or document. Obviously, the last change date of the documents must be the same (if the document changed the last time via a section) or later (if the document changed the last time via a part which is not a section, such as the title) than the latest last change date of the sections. A propagation that we would like to have occur is that whenever a section changes, then its last change date changes and also the last change dates for all the documents to which the section belongs (in the case of sharing) are updated to be the last change date of the section. To be able to perform this propagation we need to be able to find all documents that include this particular section, i.e. we need to be able to traverse the part-of[2] hierarchy for individuals.

In chapter 5 we defined user functions (such as *cl-ind-includes* and *cl-ind-directly-included-in*, see also appendix A) that allow us to gather information about the structure of the individuals. Using these user functions we can write procedures that explicitly use the part-of hierarchy of individuals. For our example, the procedure in figure 9.4 can be used to propagate the last change date from sections to the documents that contain the sections. The procedure should be called whenever a section changes.

```
(defun propagate-last-change-date (sec)
    (let ((docs (cl-included-in-and-concept-instance sec document))
          (lc (first (cl-fillers sec last-change))))
        (dolist (d docs)
            (cl-ind-remove-all-fillers d last-change)
            (cl-add-fillers d last-change lc))))
```

Fig. 9.4. Propagating the last change date.

9.3.4 Recognition of Individuals

Recognition of individuals can be used to check constraints that do not occur in the concepts that are defined in the Tbox. In this way we can verify parts of our domain model. In the document knowledge-base this can be used to verify that a document has particular properties. For instance, if we know that a code review document always has to have four sections, then we can check whether a particular code review document belongs to the concept

---

[2] In this example we can traverse the part-of hierarchy. More generally, we may want to traverse the compositional inclusion hierarchy to include the information about modules as well.

(**and** document (**atleastp** 4 section-p)). If this is not the case, then we know that the document does not fulfill all the requirements yet. To make the result of the verification stronger we can perform a closure over the roles and part names whenever a document is supposed to be finished. For instance, if a document has exactly three sections when finished and the section part name is closed, then the recognition mechanism finds that the document belongs to (**and** (**atleast** 3 section-p) (**atmost** 3 section-p)).

Recognition of documents and parts of documents provides information about the properties of these individuals. This information is important in reasoning involving the reason why the document or part was created and involving the intended use of the document or part. For instance, if we know that the fourth section in a code review document always involves the naming problems in the code, then a section involving naming problems in code is likely to be the fourth section of a code review document. This information may be used when using the section in the instantiation of particular documents.

9.3.5 Retrieval

An important task for a description logic system for document management is to allow for retrieval of documents that contain particular information. This kind of query can often be written as a concept definition. For instance, a project manager may want to retrieve the documents from a particular project (e.g. with the name DL-project) for which John was supervisor. This can be done by querying the system with the following concept description: (**and** document (**fills** project-name DL-project) (**fills** supervisor John)).

The system can also be queried using the system's user functions. In chapter 5 we described some of the user functions for the CLASSIC system. For instance, it is possible to retrieve the fillers for a particular role for an individual, as in the case where we want to know who was supervisor for a particular document. This is discussed and exemplified further in chapter 11.

9.4 Summary

In this chapter we investigated the needs of a project document management system. We showed that our description logic for composite objects allows for a natural representation for documents. In particular, the structure is easily represented and reasoned about in our framework. Further, we showed how basic tasks in such a system can be performed using the inferences of a description logic system. In particular, the possibility of traversing a part-of hierarchy for individuals and inferences regarding the building of composite individuals were shown to be particularly useful. In this chapter we only briefly described the task of retrieving documents from a document knowledge-base. However, chapter 11 is completely dedicated to this task.

10. Learning Composite Concepts

10.1 Motivation

Some recent work investigates concept learning in the context of description logics. Given the fact that first-order logic has been restricted in several ways for its use in the field of machine learning, description logics seem to make another good candidate as a learning framework. However, it is only recently that learning algorithms have been developed within this framework [CH94a, CH94b, FP94, KM94] and we are not aware of any learning algorithms (learning in description logics or other kinds of learning) that incorporate special knowledge about the part-of relation. In this chapter we sketch how we can use our description logic for composite objects to include extra information about this important relation into learning. On one hand we have a relatively rich representation language with an infinite space of possible concepts. On the other hand we have special constructs for handling part-of relations that can be used in the learning algorithm to reduce the overall search space. In section 10.2 we describe the framework that we use and we define the learning task in section 10.3. Two useful operations in learning in description logics are to compute a least common subsumer for two concepts and to associate a concept with an individual that captures as much information about that individual as possible. We describe these operations for our framework in section 10.4. The algorithms are described informally in section 10.5.

10.2 Framework

The framework that we use is the framework introduced in chapter 5. Thus we allow in the language the **and**, **all**, **atleast**, **atmost**, **fills**, **allp**, **atleastp**, **atmostp**, **part-fills**, and **pp-constraint** constructs. Further, we need the definitions of direct part and module for concepts as defined in chapter 6.

Throughout this chapter we use a *standard-family* as an example. Figure 10.1 describes the concept of a *standard-family* which is defined as being composed of a part *husband* that belongs to the concept *man*, a part *wife* that belongs to the concept *woman*, and two *offspring* parts that belong to

P. Lambrix: Part-Whole Reasoning, LNAI 1771, pp. 131-141, 2000
© Springer-Verlag Berlin Heidelberg 2000

standard-family $\doteq$
          (**and** (**allp** *husband man*)
                  (**atleastp** *1 husband*)
                  (**atmostp** *1 husband*)
                  (**allp** *wife woman*)
                  (**atleastp** *1 wife*)
                  (**atmostp** *1 wife*)
                  (**allp** *offspring child*)
                  (**atleastp** *2 offspring*)
                  (**atmostp** *2 offspring*)
                  (**pp-constraint** *married husband wife*)
                  (**pp-constraint** *mother wife offspring*)
                  (**pp-constraint** *father husband offspring*))

Fig. 10.1. A standard family.

the concept *child*. We have the constraints that the *husband* is *married* to the *wife*, the *wife* is the *mother* of the *offspring* and the *husband* is the *father* of the *offspring*.

10.3 Learning Task

The learning task is defined as follows:
  Given:
- the *Tbox* language to describe concepts
- background knowledge described in *Tbox* language $\cup$ *Abox* language
- an example set described in *Tbox* language $\cup$ *Abox* language. We allow the user to present several kinds of information to the learning system. Assume that the concept to learn is $C^\star$. Then the system handles the following cases (positive and negative examples):

    membership and non-membership of individuals:
    - $x \in C^\star$, i.e. a particular individual belongs to the concept to
        learn
    - $x \notin C^\star$, i.e. a particular individual does not belong to
        the concept to learn
    and a set of constraints that $C^\star$ should fulfill:
    - $C^\star \Rightarrow C$, i.e. a particular concept subsumes the concept to
        learn
    - $C \Rightarrow C^\star$, i.e. a particular concept is subsumed by the concept
        to learn
    - $C \lhd_n C^\star$, i.e. a particular concept is a *n*-part of the concept
        to learn
    - $C \lhd_{\mathbf{mod}} C^\star$, i.e. a particular concept is a module of the
        concept to learn

Find:
- a concept description for $C^\star$ that satisfies the conditions in the examples.

10.4 Useful Operations

In the learning algorithms we need generalization and specialization operations. Given two concepts C_1 and C_2 we can generalize to obtain the *least common subsumer* of the two concepts. We present the definition and a computation strategy in this section. As the language contains the **and**-construct, finding a more specific concept for the pair C_1 and C_2 can be defined as (**and** C_1 C_2).

Another useful operation is to associate a concept with an individual. This concept should reflect the properties of the individual as closely as possible. We show a possible way of defining this notion.

10.4.1 Least Common Subsumer

The *least common subsumer* (LCS) of a pair of concepts is the most specific description in the infinite space of possible descriptions that subsumes this pair of concepts [CBH92]. As our language includes the **and**-construct, this LCS is unique. We extend the computation of the LCS in [CBH92] to also cope with the constructs related to part-of shown in figure 10.2.

In figure 10.3 we define a *standard-family-with-boys* similarly as a *standard-family* but where the two *offspring* are *boys*. A *family-with-2-girls* is also similar to a *standard-family* but the two *offspring* are *girls* and we do not have the constraint that the *wife* and the *husband* are *married*. The LCS of the two concepts gives us then a family where the *offspring* belong to the concept *child* and we do not have the *married*-constraint. During the computation we assume that LCS(*boy,girl*) = *child*.

LCS((**and** C_{11} .. C_{1k}),(**and** C_{21} .. C_{2l})) :=
    (**and** C_{1121} ... C_{112l} ... C_{1k21} ... C_{1k2l}) with C_{1i2j}=LCS(C_{1i},C_{2j})
LCS((**all** r_1 C_1),(**all** r_2 C_2)) :=
    if r_1=r_2 then (**all** r_1 LCS(C_1,C_2)) else $\top$
LCS((**atmost** m_1 r_1),(**atmost** m_2 r_2)) :=
    if r_1=r_2 then (**atmost** $\max(m_1,m_2)$ r_1) else $\top$
LCS((**atleast** m_1 r_1),(**atleast** m_2 r_2)) :=
    if r_1=r_2 then (**atleast** $\min(m_1,m_2)$ r_1) else $\top$
LCS((**fills** r_1 i_{11} ... i_{1k}),(**fills** r_2 i_{21} ... i_{2l})) :=
    if r_1=r_2 then (**fills** r_1 i_{31} ... i_{3m})
    with $\{i_{31},...,i_{3m}\} = \{i_{11},...,i_{1k}\} \cap \{i_{21},...,i_{2l}\}$ else $\top$
LCS((**allp** n_1 C_1),(**allp** n_2 C_2)) :=
    if n_1=n_2 then (**allp** n_1 LCS(C_1,C_2)) else $\top$
LCS((**atmostp** m_1 n_1),(**atmostp** m_2 n_2)) :=
    if n_1=n_2 then (**atmostp** $\max(m_1,m_2)$ n_1) else $\top$
LCS((**atleastp** m_1 n_1),(**atleastp** m_2 n_2)) :=
    if n_1=n_2 then (**atleastp** $\min(m_1,m_2)$ n_1) else $\top$
LCS((**part-fills** n_1 i_{11} ... i_{1k}),(**part-fills** n_2 i_{21} ... i_{2l})) :=
    if n_1=n_2 then (**part-fills** r_1 i_{31} ... i_{3m})
    with $\{i_{31},...,i_{3m}\} = \{i_{11},...,i_{1k}\} \cap \{i_{21},...,i_{2l}\}$ else $\top$
LCS((**pp-constraint** r_1 n_{11} n_{12}),(**pp-constraint** r_2 n_{21} n_{22})) :=
    if (n_{11}=n_{21} and n_{21}=n_{22} and r_1=r_2) then (**pp-constraint** r_1 n_{11} n_{12}) else $\top$
For primitive concepts C_1 and C_2: LCS(C_1,C_2) := if C_1=C_2 then C_1 else $\top$
other cases (with different constructors): LCS(C_1,C_2) := $\top$

Fig. 10.2. Least common subsumer

$boy \doteq$
>   (**and**   *male*
>   *child*)

$girl \doteq$
>   (**and**   *female*
>   *child*)

$standard\text{-}family\text{-}with\text{-}boys \doteq$
>   (**and**   (**allp** *husband man*)
>   (**atleastp** *1 husband*)
>   (**atmostp** *1 husband*)
>   (**allp** *wife woman*)
>   (**atleastp** *1 wife*)
>   (**atmostp** *1 wife*)
>   (**allp** *offspring boy*)
>   (**atleastp** *2 offspring*)
>   (**atmostp** *2 offspring*)
>   (**pp-constraint** *married husband wife*)
>   (**pp-constraint** *mother wife offspring*)
>   (**pp-constraint** *father husband offspring*))

$family\text{-}with\text{-}2\text{-}girls \doteq$
>   (**and**   (**allp** *husband man*)
>   (**atleastp** *1 husband*)
>   (**atmostp** *1 husband*)
>   (**allp** *wife woman*)
>   (**atleastp** *1 wife*)
>   (**atmostp** *1 wife*)
>   (**allp** *offspring girl*)
>   (**atleastp** *2 offspring*)
>   (**atmostp** *2 offspring*)
>   (**pp-constraint** *mother wife offspring*)
>   (**pp-constraint** *father husband offspring*))

LCS(*standard-family-with-boys,family-with-2-girls*) = (*family-with-2-children* $\doteq$)
>   (**and**   (**allp** *husband man*)
>   (**atleastp** *1 husband*)
>   (**atmostp** *1 husband*)
>   (**allp** *wife woman*)
>   (**atleastp** *1 wife*)
>   (**atmostp** *1 wife*)
>   (**allp** *offspring child*)
>   (**atleastp** *2 offspring*)
>   (**atmostp** *2 offspring*)
>   (**pp-constraint** *mother wife offspring*)
>   (**pp-constraint** *father husband offspring*))

Fig. 10.3. Least common subsumer of two kinds of family concepts.

10.4.2 Specific Concepts

Specific concepts try to capture as much information as possible about an individual in a concept definition. An individual belongs to its specific concepts and for every concept to which the individual belongs this concept subsumes the specific concepts of the individual. We find the following definition in [DE92]:

> A concept C is a *specific concept* for an individual x with respect to a knowledge base $\langle Tbox, Abox \rangle$ iff
> (i) $x \in \varepsilon[C]$ and
> (ii) $\forall D: x \in \varepsilon[D] \rightarrow C \Rightarrow D$ in Tbox

Depending on extra language constraints there are several possibilities for computing specific concepts. In general it is not possible to completely fit all the relevant information about an individual into a single concept in the language [Scha94]. As a solution to this problem [DE92] defines extra constructs which are only to be used internally by the system but not by the user. Here we associate with an individual x a concept $SC(x)$ which can be defined in our language. We note some properties of this concept in figure 10.6. In the example in figures 10.4 and 10.5 we assume that we have complete knowledge of the world and that all roles and part names are closed.

family ::
    (**and**   (**all** *accounts large*)
            (**part-fills** *husband John*)
            (**part-fills** *wife Mary*)
            (**part-fills** *offspring Marc Jane*))
John ::
    (**and**   *man*
            (**fills** *married Mary*)
            (**fills** *father Marc Jane*))
Mary ::
    (**and**   *woman*
            (**fills** *mother Marc Jane*))
Marc ::
        child
Jane ::
        child

Fig. 10.4. A family.

SC(*Marc*) = *child*
SC(*Jane*) = *child*
SC(*Mary*) =
  (**and** *woman*
     (**atleast** *2 mother*)
     (**atmost** *2 mother*)
     (**all** *mother child*)
     (**fills** *mother Marc Jane*))
SC(*John*) =
  (**and** *man*
     (**atleast** *1 married*)
     (**atmost** *1 married*)
     (**all** *married* SC(*Mary*))
     (**fills** *married Mary*)
     (**atleast** *2 father*)
     (**atmost** *2 father*)
     (**all** *father child*)
     (**fills** *father Marc Jane*))
SC(*family*) =
  (**and** (**all** *accounts large*)
     (**atleastp** *1 husband*)
     (**atmostp** *1 husband*)
     (**allp** *husband* SC(*John*))
     (**part-fills** *husband John*)
     (**atleastp** *1 wife*)
     (**atmostp** *1 wife*)
     (**allp** *wife* SC(*Mary*))
     (**part-fills** *wife Mary*)
     (**atleastp** *2 offspring*)
     (**atmostp** *2 offspring*)
     (**allp** *offspring child*)
     (**part-fills** *offspring Marc Jane*)
     (**pp-constraint** *married husband wife*)
     (**pp-constraint** *mother wife offspring*)
     (**pp-constraint** *father husband offspring*))

Fig. 10.5. Specific concepts in a family.

concept-filler

$$\frac{kb \;\vdash\; x \;\to\; C}{SC(x) \;\Rightarrow\; C}$$

role-filler

$$\frac{kb \;\vdash\; <x,y> \;\in\; \varepsilon[r]}{\exists C : (y \;\to\; C \wedge SC(x) \;\Rightarrow\; (\textbf{all } r \; C))}$$

$$\frac{kb \;\vdash\; <x,y> \;\in\; \varepsilon[r]}{SC(x) \;\Rightarrow\; (\textbf{fills } r \; y)}$$

$$\frac{kb \;\vdash\; \sharp\{y \;\mid\; <x,y> \;\in\; \varepsilon[r]\} = m}{SC(x) \;\Rightarrow\; (\textbf{atleast } m \; r)}$$

In the case where the role r is closed we also have:
$$\frac{kb \;\vdash\; \sharp\{y \;\mid\; <x,y> \;\in\; \varepsilon[r]\} = m}{SC(x) \;\Rightarrow\; (\textbf{atmost } m \; r)}$$

part-filler

$$\frac{kb \;\vdash\; y \lhd_n x}{\exists C : (y \;\to\; C \wedge SC(x) \;\Rightarrow\; (\textbf{allp } n \; C))}$$

$$\frac{kb \;\vdash\; y \lhd_n x}{SC(x) \;\Rightarrow\; (\textbf{part} - \textbf{fills } n \; y)}$$

$$\frac{kb \;\vdash\; \sharp\{y \;\mid\; y \lhd_n x\} = m}{SC(x) \;\Rightarrow\; (\textbf{atleastp } m \; n)}$$

In the case where the part name n is closed we also have:
$$\frac{kb \;\vdash\; \sharp\{y \;\mid\; y \lhd_n x\} = m}{SC(x) \;\Rightarrow\; (\textbf{atmostp } m \; n)}$$

role-filler involving the parts

In the case where the part names n_1 and n_2 are closed we also have:
$$\frac{kb \;\vdash\; (\forall y_1, y_2 : y_1 \lhd_{n_1} x \wedge y_2 \lhd_{n_2} x \;\to\; <y_1, y_2> \;\in\; \varepsilon[r])}{SC(x) \;\Rightarrow\; (\textbf{pp} - \textbf{constraint } r \; n_1 \; n_2)}$$

Fig. 10.6. Specific concepts.

10.5 Learning Composite Concepts

The algorithms are targeted at learning descriptions of composite concepts, i.e. concepts involving part-of. We propose to use a version-space-like strategy [Mit82]. We maintain two spaces: one for the is-a relation (or subsumption) and one for the part-of relation (i.e. parts and modules). The first space is represented[1] by a set $\mathcal{G}$ of concepts that are more general than the concept to learn $C^\star$, a set $\mathcal{S}$ of concepts that are more specific than $C^\star$ and a set $\mathcal{N}$ of individuals which do not belong to the extension of $C^\star$. The second space is represented by a set $\mathcal{C}$ of concepts for which $C^\star$ can be used as a building block and a set $\mathcal{B}$ of concepts which $C^\star$ can use as building blocks. Finally, we also keep information about the possibility or necessity of occurrence of part names. $\mathcal{P}^-$ denotes the part names which cannot occur in the definition of $C^\star$. $\mathcal{P}_n$ is a set of tuples $\langle n, min, max, C \rangle$ for the part names which necessarily occur in the definition of $C^\star$ where n is the part name, min and max specify a superset of the interval to which the number of n-parts in $C^\star$ belongs, and C is a generalization of the domain of n for $C^\star$. $\mathcal{P}_p$ is a similar set for part names which possibly occur in $C^\star$. In this case min and max specify a subset of the interval to which the number of n-parts in $C^\star$ belongs, and C is a specialization of the domain of n for $C^\star$. Finally, we also keep information about which constraints between the parts are possible.

We discuss the learning algorithms informally and point out the extra information we obtain by a special handling of part-of. In the examples involving subsumption and individuals we obtain also extra information about part-of. Similarly, the examples involving part-of provide information for the is-a hierarchy. This extra information leads then to an algorithm which for composite concepts should converge faster to a concept definition. Below we assume that the concept to learn $C^\star$ is *standard-family*.

10.5.1 Learning by Using Concepts and Subsumption

In the case where we know that $C^\star \Rightarrow C$ we have immediately a more general concept and the standard updates[2] can be performed. However, we also know the following: (i) the part names which occur in the definition of C also occur in the definition of $C^\star$, (ii) the part names which occur in the definition of C occur in $C^\star$ with a more restricted number restriction, (iii) the domain for the part name in C subsumes the domain for the corresponding part name in $C^\star$, and (iv) the **pp-constraints** occurring in the definition of C also occur in the definition of $C^\star$.

---

[1] As the **and** of two more general concepts is also a more general concept, and the LCS of two more specific concepts is also a more specific concept, $\mathcal{G}$ and $\mathcal{S}$ are actually singletons or the empty set.

[2] By the standard updates we mean the basic updates of the $\mathcal{G}$, $\mathcal{S}$, $\mathcal{C}$ and $\mathcal{B}$ sets. The updates in the data structures originating from the extra information are straightforward and we do not discuss the actual updates.

For instance if we know that *standard-family* ⇒ *family-with-2-children* (figure 10.3), then *husband*, *wife* and *offspring* must occur in the definition of *standard-family* with N(*husband,C**) = [1,1], N(*wife,C**) = [1,1] and N(*offspring,C**) = [2,2]. We also know that the *husband*-part for *standard-family* is a *man*, the *wife*-part for *standard-family* is a *woman*, and each *offspring*-part for *standard-family* is a *child* (or more specific). Further, the *wife* and *offspring* parts are connected through the role *mother* and the *husband* and *offspring* parts are connected through the role *father*.

In the case where $C \Rightarrow C^*$ we have immediately a more specific concept. We use LCS in the updates. We also know that: (i) the part names which occur in the definition of C are the only possible part names for the definition of C^*, (ii) if some part name occurs in both definitions, then the number restriction for C is stronger than the number restriction for C^*, (iii) if some part name occurs in both definitions, then the domain for the part name in C^* subsumes the domain for the corresponding part name in C, and (iv) the **pp-constraint**s in the definition of C are the only possible **pp-constraint**s in the definition of C^*.

Knowing that *standard-family-with-boys* ⇒ *standard-family* would tell us that the only part names occurring in the definition of *standard-family* can be *husband*, *wife* and *offspring*, although not all need to occur. We know also that for the occurring part names the domains are more general than the ones in *standard-family-with-boys*. For instance, an *offspring* in *standard-family* is more general than a *boy*. Further, the only possible **pp-constraint**s for *standard-family* are the **pp-constraint**s occurring in *standard-family-with-boys*.

10.5.2 Learning by Using Individuals

In the case where $x \in C^*$ we assume that a specific concept for individual x is a more specific concept than C^*. Therefore we can use SC(x) as a learning example.

Having *family* as in figure 10.4 as an example for *standard-family* tells us that SC(*family*) ⇒ *standard-family*.

The examples where $x \notin C^*$ are used to find inconsistencies or concepts for which there is no definition in the language.

10.5.3 Learning by Using Concepts and Part-of

In the case where $C \vartriangleleft_n C^*$ we have a building block for C^* and we know that if (**allp** n A) occurs in the definition of C^* then $C \Rightarrow A$.

Knowing that *young-child* is an *offspring*-part of *standard-family*, leads to (**allp** *offspring* A) occurring in the definition of *standard-family* and *young-child* ⇒ A.

In the case where $C \vartriangleleft_{\mathbf{mod}} C^*$ we have a building block for C^* and we know that: (i) if (**allp** n A) occurs in C, then (**allp** n A') occurs in C^* such that $A \Rightarrow A'$, (ii) for the part names occurring both in C and $C^\star$ no other **pp-constraint**-terms can occur in the definition of $C^\star$ than the ones which occur in the definition of C, (iii) for every part name n the upper bound for the number of n-parts is at least as high for $C^\star$ as for C, and (iv) there is a part name that is defined in $C^\star$ but not in C, or there is a part name n for which the upper bound for the number of n-parts is strictly higher for $C^\star$ than for C.

Let the concept *couple* be defined as in figure 10.7. The fact that *couple* $\lhd_{\mathbf{mod}}$ *standard-family* implies that a *standard-family* defines a *husband*-part which is at least as general as a *man* and a *wife*-part which is at least as general as a *woman*. The upper bounds for the number of these parts is greater than one. We also know that the only constraint between *husband* and *wife* can be that they are *married*.

$couple \doteq$

(**and** (**allp** *husband man*)
          (**atleastp** *1 husband*)
          (**atmostp** *1 husband*)
          (**allp** *wife woman*)
          (**atleastp** *1 wife*)
          (**atmostp** *1 wife*)
          (**pp-constraint** *married husband wife*))

Fig. 10.7. A couple.

10.6 Summary

In this chapter we have discussed the fact that in a system where we have information about the is-a relation and about part-of, the interaction between these two relations may provide some extra information that is not available when we consider the relations separately. This fact can be used in learning algorithms within the framework of description logics. We have extended some standard operations for concepts in description logics to deal with part-of and we have shown how they can be used to learn composite concepts. Further work on the approach is needed. Another approach is described in [LL98] where we define a meta-concept language to describe sets of concepts that satisfy a number of observations. The actual concepts are defined in the same language as the one in this chapter.

Part IV

Application

11. Document Search Using Content, Structure and Properties

More and more information is nowadays being stored in electronic form. For users it becomes more and more difficult to find information in current document bases. Essentially, there are two different ways for a user to find information in document bases. The first way is to browse. The user starts with a particular document and follows links from that document to other documents until her information need is satisfied. However, the user may also not find the desired information and give up, or become distracted and follow other paths that are considered interesting. The second way is to query the document bases using a search engine. The most common kind of search engine is based on an index that relates keywords to documents. The index is created based on an analysis of the text in the documents. The search is then essentially a table lookup in the index. An example of such a search engine is AltaVista ([AltaVista]). This kind of engines is widely used nowadays. They are easy to use and fast and often give the user at least an approximate answer to the query. Therefore, these systems perform well when a user only needs a crude answer to a query or when a user only needs a starting point from which to browse or query further.

Searching for information using this kind of search engines has, however, a number of drawbacks. The query language for these search engines is usually quite simple allowing in most cases for search using keywords and boolean operators (**and, or** and **and-not**) only. The more advanced search engines of this type may allow for queries involving keywords in some predefined parts of documents such as titles, but usually the engines do not support the use of more advanced information about the logical structure of the documents. However, this would be needed when a user, for instance, wants to find a document with a figure that contains certain information in the figure heading or in the notes section. Also, the user cannot use information about properties of documents, such as file size or author information. This may be interesting when a user only wants to load documents to her own workspace with size smaller than a certain maximum size. Therefore, the ability to use logical structure and properties in the query language together with information about the contents of a document, would allow a user to more precisely specify her query needs.

P. Lambrix: Part-Whole Reasoning, LNAI 1771, pp. 145-165, 2000
© Springer-Verlag Berlin Heidelberg 2000

Another drawback is the fact that a user needs to know the exact term that she is looking for. The documents that are returned for a query are the documents that contain exactly the query term (except for possible stemming). The search engine does not take any advantage of general domain knowledge or additional knowledge that a user may have about the domain. For instance, as the laboratory for intelligent information systems is a research laboratory of our computer science department, when a user is searching for documents from our computer science department, also the documents from the research laboratory should be retrieved. The general knowledge may be stored in the form of ontologies or be commonly available. A user or organization may also have her own preferences or classifications of query terms. For instance, both our computer science department and system engineering department do research on security. However, they work within different frameworks. Therefore, when they are looking for information related to their work, they have their own intuitions and preferences on what kind of information they want to obtain. Background knowledge may also be used to reduce ambiguity in the query terms. In all these cases the use of additional knowledge results in the retrieval of fewer non-relevant documents with respect to the user's information need and therefore in a better quality of the answer to the query.

In this chapter we define a model and architecture that allows a user to query a collection of document bases using information about content, logical structure and properties of the documents. We also allow for the use of background knowledge and knowledge about the user during the search. Further, the user can browse the available information (documents as well as background knowledge) and use this to interactively modify queries.

To clarify the scope of this chapter we also point out what we do not cover in this work. We concentrate in this chapter on text document bases. Further, we discuss test results of our prototype implementation, but do not compare these results to other systems. The reasons for this are, as [NB97] mentions, in most cases code is not available, performance depends heavily on implementation, different systems have different goals and thus different structures and such a study needs a theoretical framework that does not exist yet. Finally, we have not integrated relevance ranking mechanisms with the mechanisms needed for querying using information about content, logical structure and properties of documents. This will be one of the directions for future work. However, it is possible to extend our query language with relevance information in the sense of [Seb94].

The remainder of the chapter is structured as follows. In section 11.1 we describe our model as well as the interfaces to our model: the interface to the user and the interface to the document collections. In section 11.2 we describe an architecture for a system that supports our model. A prototype implementation based on this architecture as well as test results are described in section 11.3. The chapter concludes with a discussion of related work in section 11.4 and a conclusion in section 11.5.

11.1 Model

In this section we describe a model that deals with the problem stated above (see figure 11.1).[1] We describe the functionality of the system through its interfaces. First, we describe a query language that allows a user to use information about the contents, logical structure and properties of the document. Then, we describe the interface of the system to the actual document bases where the documents that can be searched reside.

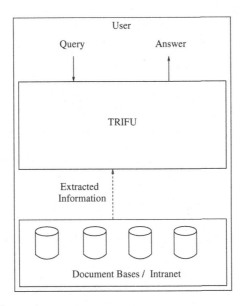

Fig. 11.1. Model overview.

11.1.1 Query Language

As we have seen before, in general, the user lacks the flexibility to state queries involving all the characteristics of a document. This is needed, for instance, in a query to retrieve all documents with a specific word (e.g. "retrieval") in the title or any sub-title of the document, belonging to the documentation of a specific project (e.g. DL-project) and with a specific author (e.g.

---

[1] TRIFU in the figure stands for The Right Information For yoU.

John). This query contains content information (*with a specific word in the title*), information about the logical structure of the document (*in the title* and *belonging to the documentation of a specific project*) as well as other information (*with a specific author*). In figure 11.2 we show an interface where queries using the different kinds of information can be asked. The interface also allows for browsing of the available information using the Lookup field and button.

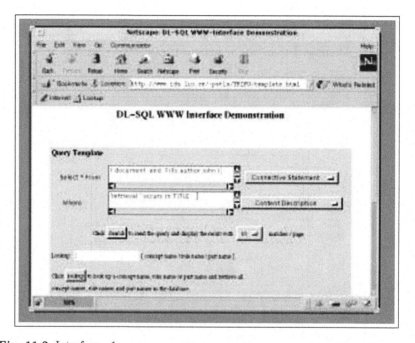

Fig. 11.2. Interface - 1.

A query language supporting all the different kinds of information allows for more precise queries and therefore less documents that are not relevant to a query are retrieved. We define here a base query language that deals with these different kinds of information. Based on a study of current practice and research on structured documents we introduce constructs that should be available in any language that allows for queries using the different kinds of information about documents. The base query language can be extended and for such an extension we refer to section 11.3. We have chosen to use an SQL-like syntax. Below we introduce the syntax and give examples and intuitions. For the semantics of the (extended) language we refer to section 11.3.

Queries about Properties. Queries about properties of documents can be asked using a select-from statement. For instance, to find all documents from a research department we write the following.

> **select** *
> **from** *department-document*

These properties can be combined by boolean operators **and**, **or** and **and-not**. We also introduce a construct **fills** that allows for searching for specific values of a document property. For instance, one could ask for the documents for which John is an author:

> **select** *
> **from** (*document* **and fills** *author John*)

In this query the property of the document is represented by an attribute (author) and we search for a specific value (John).

Content-based Search. The most common way to search for content information is to use keyword search. In our base language we introduce the **occurs** construct to support this kind of search. For instance, to retrieve the documents that contain the word "retrieval", we write the following.

> **select** *
> **from** *document*
> **where** *'retrieval'* **occurs**

We also allow to specify directly in the **occurs** construct which type of parts of documents that we wish to search. For instance, the query

> **select** *
> **from** *document*
> **where** *'retrieval'* **occurs in** *heading*

retrieves all documents that have a heading part (on arbitrary level) containing the word "retrieval".

Boolean queries can be modeled using the **and**, **or** and **and-not** constructs. For instance, to find the documents that contain the words "retrieval" and "logic" we write the following.

> **select** *
> **from** *document*
> **where** (*'retrieval'* **occurs**
>   **and** *'logic'* **occurs**)

Queries about Structure. According to recent research in structured documents (e.g. [SAZ94].) there is a need for querying and retrieval restricted to parts of a document (e.g. by only retrieving titles or specific sections instead of the whole document), for access to documents by their structure (as, for instance, in the query for documents that contain a particular word in a title, or as in the query for the sections that together with a particular title and abstract make up a document) and for querying which combines structural data and non-structural data.

The logical structure of a document can be seen as defining a part-of hierarchy over the document and its parts. For instance, this document contains among others a title, a table of contents and sections while the sections contain sub-sections. We introduce the **includes-some** and **within-some** constructs to allow for traversal of a part-of hierarchy of documents and their parts where the type of the parts is of importance. This allows, for instance, for expressing queries where the scope of the query is not a complete document but only a part of a document. For instance, to find a document where some paragraph contains the word "retrieval" and a figure with "model" in the caption, we perform the following query.

> **select** *
> **from** *document*
> **where includes-some**
> > (**select** *
> > **from** *paragraph*
> > **where** (*'retrieval'* **occurs**
> > > **and includes-some**
> > > > (**select** *
> > > > **from** *figure*
> > > > **where** *'model'* **occurs in** *caption*)))

It is also possible to just retrieve parts of the documents such as in the query to find the sections that are about logic.

> **select** *
> **from** *section*
> **where** (*'logic'* **occurs**
> > **and within-some** *document*)

We can use specific documents in a query as well using variants of the constructs that deal with objects rather than types: **includes-object** and **within-object**. The following query finds all paragraphs of the particular document KR-journal that are about logic.

> **select** *
> **from** *paragraph*
> **where** (*'logic'* **occurs**
> > **and within-object** *KR-journal*)

Further, we allow queries based on the structure of the document that require traversing a part-of hierarchy. For instance, the following complex query finds the sections that together with a particular abstract (paper121-abstract) and title (paper121-title) make up a document.

select *
from *section*
where within-some
        (select *
        from *document*
        where (includes-object *paper121-abstract*
            and includes-object *paper121-title*))

Combining Query Types. The different kinds of queries as described in the previous sections can be combined. As an example we translate the query: find all documents with the word "retrieval" in the title or any sub-title of the document, belonging to the documentation of the DL-project and with John as author. We obtain

select *
from (*document* **and fills** *author John*)
where (*'retrieval'* **occurs in** *title*
        and within-object *DL-project-documentation*)

In summary, the following types of queries are defined by the language:

− queries using information about properties of the documents,
− queries using structural information,
− keyword searches,
− and combinations of the different types of queries above using the connectives **or**, **and**, and **and-not**.

11.1.2 Document Bases

The searchable documents are stored in document bases. The documents may have different formats. The document bases can be heterogeneous. We assume that we can extract the information we need to answer queries as described above, from the documents. There are several techniques to do this including document analysis and text classification. Further, we assume that our system can access the document bases in a uniform way. This could be achieved by defining a uniform way to denote the documents (e.g. a global address) and defining a mapping between the uniform denotation and the local addresses within the document bases.

11.2 Architecture

In this section we describe an architecture that is based on the model discussed in section 11.1. The architecture, shown in figure 11.3, consists of a number of components that interact with each other. We give a high-level overview of the architecture. To obtain an actual system the architecture needs to be instantiated and a number of trade-offs need to be made. In the next section we describe such an implementation.

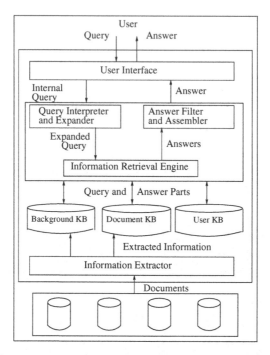

Fig. 11.3. Architecture overview.

11.2.1 Knowledge Bases

An important component in the architecture is the use of knowledge bases. The knowledge bases contain information about the searchable documents, domain knowledge and knowledge about the users. The search for documents is essentially based on querying the different knowledge bases. The information in the knowledge bases is extracted from the searchable documents or imported from already existing ontologies and knowledge bases. We consider three different kinds of knowledge bases.

Document Knowledge Bases. The document knowledge bases contain information about the actual documents. This information includes information about the contents, logical structure and properties of the documents. The content information can include a search index as well as semantic information that is extracted from the documents using document analysis or information extraction techniques. The logical structure of documents is defined by the part-of structure of the different types of documents. Different document types may have different logical structures and documents may belong to different document types. For each document the part-of structures are represented in the document knowledge base. Properties of documents are added manually or extracted automatically from the documents. For instance, we can extract the authors of a document from the document, but annotations from a particular user may have to be added manually.

Background Knowledge Bases. The background knowledge contains information about the domains that can be used in the queries. This includes general ontologies, company-specific ontologies or domain knowledge extracted from the searchable documents. The nature of the information can differ from one part to another. For instance, knowledge bases can contain information about concepts and inheritance, default information, relevance information etc.

User Knowledge Bases. In the user knowledge bases information about the users of the system is stored. This information includes user profiles representing what particular users find interesting as well as preferences of particular users and user-based ontologies. The information can be imported from other information sources, added manually or learned by the system by observing users' behavior or through interaction with the users.

Although the topic of maintenance of the knowledge bases is beyond the scope of this chapter, we are aware of the fact that this is an important aspect when implementing our model in an actual system. There are a number of issues. For instance, we need to decide how and when changes in the documents in the document bases affect the content of the knowledge bases. Another problem that needs to be addressed is how the knowledge bases may change over time. For instance, the user knowledge base may be updated by learning the users' behavior.

11.2.2 Information Extractor

The information extractor extracts different kinds of information from the documents. Information retrieval techniques are used to generate searchable indexes. Document analysis and text classification techniques (e.g. [RJZ89, PJ93, Hoc94, RL94, LC96]) are used to classify the documents with respect to content. When the domain and the kind of queries we want to ask, is known, then also information extraction techniques can be used (e.g. [MUC]). Background information can be extracted using dictionary construction techniques (e.g. [SFAL95]). Information about the logical structure can in a relatively easy way be extracted from structured documents. For instance, the syntax of SGML, HTML and LaTeX define the structure of the documents of these types. For other kinds of documents document structure analysis techniques can be used (e.g. [Hoc94]). These techniques can also be used to extract some information about properties of the documents.

11.2.3 Kernel

The kernel interacts with the user interface and the knowledge bases. The kernel receives a query in the internal language. The query language allows for querying with respect to properties of documents, their logical structure as well as their contents. The answer to the query is computed by interacting with the knowledge bases. The answer is then sent back to the user interface. The kernel consists of three parts: the query interpreter and expander, the information retrieval engine and the answer filter and assembler.

Query Interpreter and Expander. The query interpreter and expander receives the query in the internal query language. The query can be expanded to take background knowledge and user knowledge into account. The background knowledge contains strict information as in ontologies as well as other kinds of information such as, for instance, default information (e.g. [Voo94, LSW98, McG98]). For instance, when we are looking for documents about knowledge representation and the background knowledge contains the fact that description logics is a sub-field of knowledge representation, then the system expands the query to also search for documents about description logics. On the other hand, a user that is new to a particular subject often wants to find typical information about that subject as a starting point. In that case the system can use default information to expand the query. Also, the system can take user-specific information and ontologies into account. The background and user information is obtained from the knowledge bases. The expanded query is sent to the information retrieval engine.

Information Retrieval Engine. The information retrieval engine receives an expanded query from the query interpreter and expander and generates the answer to the query. The information retrieval engine processes the expanded query and decides on which resources need to be used to be able to answer the query. The available resources are knowledge bases containing knowledge about the documents and the user as well as background knowledge. The engine decides on which information should be retrieved from which knowledge bases. The original query is then translated into a number of knowledge base queries. The knowledge base query languages may differ from each other and the internal query language. The results from the queries to the different knowledge bases are combined to provide an answer to the original query. The answer is a list of representations of documents and document parts that satisfy the expanded query.

Answer Filter and Assembler. The answer filter and assembler receives the results of the queries from the information retrieval engine. The answer can be modified using background and user information. For instance, the answer can be modified to take the user's preferences with respect to the presentation of the answer into account.

Using Background Knowledge and User Knowledge. We note that the background knowledge and the user knowledge can be used during different phases. The query interpreter and expander can expand the query and thereby modify the original question. The knowledge may also be used during the actual search by the information retrieval engine. Finally, also the answer filter and assembler may use this knowledge thereby modifying the computed answer. The issue of which phase is best suited to use the information depends on the kind of the information. For instance, the information about how a user would like the answers to be presented, is used most conveniently when the answers to the query have been computed. Other information may be used at different phases. For instance, an ontology may be used to expand a query. This would be necessary if the ontology cannot be used during the computation of the answer. On the other hand, if the information retrieval engine can handle ontological information, it may not be necessary to expand the query. Another example may be the use of security information excluding some users from accessing a number of documents. Depending on the access control mechanism, the access information may be used to expand the query or to modify the answer. Our architecture allows for the use of background and user knowledge in all different stages. For an instantiation of the architecture we have to investigate the different possibilities and trade-offs.

11.2.4 User Interface

The user interface interacts with the user. User queries are stated in an end-user query language which has to allow for queries regarding information about content, logical structure and properties of the documents. These queries are then translated into an internal query language. The internal query language may be different from, but should be at least as expressive as the end-user query language.

The user interface also receives information about the answers to a query and about how these answers should be presented to the user. Based on this information the answers are made available to the user.

11.3 Prototype Implementation and Test Results

In this section we describe our prototype implementation (see figure 11.4) and test results. The prototype implements the architecture in section 11.2.

In our implementation the user can query the system using an SQL-like language. The syntax of the language is described in appendix B. This language is an extension of the language defined in section 11.1.1. With respect to the logical structure of documents it is sometimes useful to be able to state queries involving parts one level down in the part-of hierarchy. Therefore, we have introduced the **directly** qualifier that can qualify the **includes-some**, **within-some**, **includes-object**, and **within-object** constructs. For instance, to find the documents that have the word "retrieval" in their main title, we can use the following query.

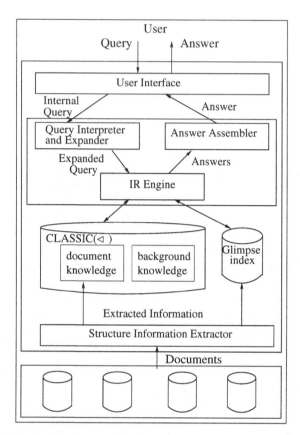

Fig. 11.4. Prototype implementation.

select *
from *document*
where directly includes-some
    (**select** *
    from title
    where *'retrieval'* **occurs**)

The language to query the properties of documents is extended with a number of constructs as well. The **atleast** and **atmost** constructs allow for the representation of number restrictions such as in *a document has* **at least** *1 author*. The **all** construct essentially represents domain restrictions and allows for representation of things such as **all** *authors of a document work at a computer science department*. The **parts-constraint** construct allows for defining constraints between parts as in *the title of a document comes always* *before the sections.* For instance, to find documents with at least two authors and for which all authors work at a computer science department, we can ask the following query.

> **select** *
> **from** (*document* **and atleast** *2 author*
>   **and all** *author computer-science-department-member*)

The internal query language is description logic-based and is shown in figure 11.5, while the semantics is shown in figure 11.6. The choice of a description logic as basis for the internal language is motivated by the following. Description logics can be used to represent both ontological (background knowledge) and object-specific knowledge (information about the documents). The same language can also be used to express queries. It has been shown before [MSST93] that description logics can model the boolean as well as the vector model of information retrieval and thus complex queries can be asked. The use of a description logic for composite objects allows us to query with respect to the structure of a document as well [LP97].

The internal language can be seen as a variant of the end-user language where different constructs are used for ordinary relations (roles) and part-whole relations (part names). The part-whole relations are used to build a part-of hierarchy and define the basis for the support for queries on logical structure of documents. We can map a query in the end-user language in a straightforward way into a query in the internal language. For instance, the query

> **select** *
> **from** (document **and fills** author John)
> **where** ('retrieval' **occurs in** title
>   **and within-object** DL-project-documentation)

is translated to

> (**and** document (**fills** *author John)*
>   (**ir-matches** *"retrieval" title*)
>   (**included-in-individual** *DL-project-documentation*))

The query interpreter and expander receives as input a query formulated in the internal query language. Background knowledge may be taken into account to expand the query. The expanded query is then sent to the information retrieval engine which interacts with the knowledge bases to obtain answers to the queries.

In our prototype the knowledge base component of the system consists of two parts: the description logic system CLASSIC($\lhd$) and the information retrieval system GLIMPSE [WM92, GLIMPSE]. The information about documents resides partly in CLASSIC($\lhd$) and partly in GLIMPSE. The system creates a GLIMPSE index over the collection of searchable documents, thereby allowing for keyword search. The index contains the words in the

<query-description> ::=
    | *<concept-description>*
    | *<structure-description>*
    | *<content-description>*
    | (**and** *<query-description>*⁺)
    | (**or** *<query-description>*⁺)
    | (**and-not** *<query-description>* *<query-description>*)

<structure-description> ::=
    | (**includes** *<query-description>*)
    | (**included-in** *<query-description>*)
    | (**directly-includes** *<query-description>*)
    | (**directly-included-in** *<query-description>*)
    | (**includes-individual** *<individual-name>*)
    | (**included-in-individual** *<individual-name>*)
    | (**directly-includes-individual** *<individual-name>*)
    | (**directly-included-in-individual** *<individual-name>*)

<content-description> ::=
    | (**ir-matches** "*<ir-query>*" [*<concept-description>*])

<concept-description> ::=
    <concept-name>
    | ⊤
    | (**all** *<role-name>* *<concept-description>*)
    | (**atleast** *<positive-integer>* *<role-name>*)
    | (**atmost** *<non-negative-integer>* *<role-name>*)
    | (**fills** *<role-name>* *<individual-name>*⁺)
    | (**allp** *<part-name-name>* *<concept-description>*)
    | (**atleastp** *<positive-integer>* *<part-name-name>*)
    | (**atmostp** *<non-negative-integer>* *<part-name-name>*)
    | (**part-fills** *<part-name-name>* *<individual-name>*⁺)
    | (**pp-constraint** *<role-name>* *<part-name-name>* *<part-name-name>*)

<concept-name> ::=	*<symbol>*
<role-name> ::=	*<symbol>*
<part-name-name> ::=	*<symbol>*
<individual-name> ::=	*<symbol>*

Fig. 11.5. Syntax of the internal query language.

query descriptions:

$\varepsilon[(\textbf{and } A\ B)] = \varepsilon[A] \cap \varepsilon[B]$

$\varepsilon[(\textbf{or } A\ B)] = \varepsilon[A] \cup \varepsilon[B]$

$\varepsilon[(\textbf{and-not } A\ B)] = \varepsilon[A] \setminus \varepsilon[B]$

concept descriptions:

$\varepsilon[\top] = \mathcal{D}$

$\varepsilon[(\textbf{all } r\ A)] = \{x \in \mathcal{D} \mid \forall\, y \in \mathcal{D}: <x,y> \in \varepsilon[r] \rightarrow y \in \varepsilon[A]\}$

$\varepsilon[(\textbf{atleast } m\ r)] = \{x \in \mathcal{D} \mid \sharp\, \{y \in \mathcal{D} \mid <x,y> \in \varepsilon[r]\} \geq m\}$

$\varepsilon[(\textbf{atmost } m\ r)] = \{x \in \mathcal{D} \mid \sharp\, \{y \in \mathcal{D} \mid <x,y> \in \varepsilon[r]\} \leq m\}$

$\varepsilon[(\textbf{fills } r\ i_1\ ...\ i_m)] = \{x \in \mathcal{D} \mid <x,\varepsilon[i_1]> \in \varepsilon[r] \wedge ... \wedge <x,\varepsilon[i_m]> \in \varepsilon[r]\}$

$\varepsilon[(\textbf{allp } n\ A)] = \{x \in \mathcal{D} \mid \forall\, y \in \mathcal{D}: y \lhd_n x \rightarrow y \in \varepsilon[A]\}$

$\varepsilon[(\textbf{atleastp } m\ n)] = \{x \in \mathcal{D} \mid \sharp\, \{y \in \mathcal{D} \mid y \lhd_n x\} \geq m\}$

$\varepsilon[(\textbf{atmostp } m\ n)] = \{x \in \mathcal{D} \mid \sharp\, \{y \in \mathcal{D} \mid y \lhd_n x\} \leq m\}$

$\varepsilon[(\textbf{part-fills } n\ i_1\ ...\ i_m)] = \{x \in \mathcal{D} \mid \varepsilon[i_1] \lhd_n x \wedge ... \wedge \varepsilon[i_m] \lhd_n x\}$

$\varepsilon[(\textbf{pp-constraint } r\ n_1\ n_2)] =$
$$\{x \in \mathcal{D} \mid \forall\, y_1,y_2 \in \mathcal{D}: (y_1 \lhd_{n_1} x \wedge y_2 \lhd_{n_2} x) \rightarrow <y_1,y_2> \in \varepsilon[r]\}$$

structure descriptions:

$\varepsilon[(\textbf{directly-includes } C)] = \{x \in \mathcal{D} \mid \exists\, y \in \mathcal{D}, \exists\, n: y \lhd_n x \wedge y \in \varepsilon[C]\}$

$\varepsilon[(\textbf{includes } C)] = \{x \in \mathcal{D} \mid \exists\, y \in \mathcal{D}: y \lhd^* x \wedge y \in \varepsilon[C]\}$

$\varepsilon[(\textbf{directly-included-in } C)] = \{x \in \mathcal{D} \mid \exists\, y \in \mathcal{D}, \exists\, n: x \lhd_n y \wedge y \in \varepsilon[C]\}$

$\varepsilon[(\textbf{included-in } C)] = \{x \in \mathcal{D} \mid \exists\, y \in \mathcal{D}: x \lhd^* y \wedge y \in \varepsilon[C]\}$

$\varepsilon[(\textbf{directly-includes-individual } i)] = \{x \in \mathcal{D} \mid \exists\, n: \varepsilon[i] \lhd_n x\}$

$\varepsilon[(\textbf{includes-individual } i)] = \{x \in \mathcal{D} \mid \varepsilon[i] \lhd^* x\}$

$\varepsilon[(\textbf{directly-included-in-individual } i)] = \{x \in \mathcal{D} \mid \exists\, n: x \lhd_n \varepsilon[i]\}$

$\varepsilon[(\textbf{included-in-individual } i)] = \{x \in \mathcal{D} \mid x \lhd^* \varepsilon[i]\}$

content descriptions:

$\varepsilon[(\textbf{ir-matches } s)] = \{x \in \mathcal{D} \mid x \text{ contains } s \vee (\exists\, y \in \mathcal{D}: y \lhd^* x \wedge y \text{ contains } s)\}$

$\varepsilon[(\textbf{ir-matches } s\ C)] = \{x \in \mathcal{D} \mid (\exists\, y \in \mathcal{D}: y \lhd^* x \wedge y \in \varepsilon[C] \wedge y \text{ contains } s)\}$

Fig. 11.6. Semantics of the internal query language.

documents together with their place of occurrence and the offsets in the files where they occur. These offsets can then be used to find out in which documents and document parts the words occur. Further, for each document and document part an individual is automatically created in the CLASSIC($\lhd$) system and the part-whole relations between these individuals are instantiated. The addresses of the documents are stored as well. The offsets in the documents representing the beginning of document parts are extracted and assigned to the corresponding individuals. Other information about the documents is currently added by a human user. However, one could imagine that a large part of this information could be extracted from the documents automatically using information extraction or document analysis techniques. Further, we use hash tables that relate CLASSIC($\lhd$) individuals representing documents and document parts to file names and offsets known by GLIMPSE and vice versa.

During the testing of our prototype we have concentrated on HTML documents. The logical structure is extracted automatically from the documents [LSÅ97] and transformed into a <concept-descr> representation as defined in the syntax of the simple language in chapter 5.[2]

The background knowledge is stored in the CLASSIC($\lhd$) system as well. The background knowledge may be general knowledge as well as individual or organizational domain knowledge that may be used to tailor search to the needs and preferences of the individual or organization. It may be new knowledge that is added manually or stored knowledge that can be loaded into the system. This is also true for the information about document types as well as for the properties of actual documents.

The information retrieval engine decides on which parts of the queries are sent to the description logic system and which parts to the information retrieval system. The result of the description logic part is a set of individuals representing documents and document parts. Due to the functionality of the description logic system, relevant background information is taken into account during the search. The result of the information retrieval part is transformed using the word offsets into a list of individuals as well.

The answer assembler combines the results and presents the final result as a list of individuals. The result of the query is presented as a page containing a list of pointers to the documents satisfying the query.

We implemented a number of interfaces to the system. The expert user interfaces require knowledge about the end-user query language. The novice interface presents the user with a template for a query. The user instantiates the template to pose a query. The interface helps the user by showing for each template item the different syntactically correct possibilities. For instance, in the example in figure 11.7 the user has already filled in the **from**-part of the query. For the **where**-part of the query the user can choose via a menu

---

[2] This is also the sub-language of the internal query language represented by <concept-description> together with the **and**-construct.

between *content description*, *structure description* or *connective statement*. In this example the user has chosen *content-description* from the menu. A new template window pops up representing the alternatives for *content-description*. The string that the user wants to search for has to be filled in. The user can choose whether she wants a context as well. A click on a menu displays all the different available contexts. In this example the user has chosen *title*. When this part of the query is constructed as desired, the user clicks on the *ok*-button. Then the new template is removed and the statement is automatically entered in the original template. The result is as shown in figure 11.2.

Fig. 11.7. Interface - 2.

In addition to the fact that the interfaces allow for querying the system using the end-user query language, they allow for retrieval of information about the different types of documents and about the background knowledge. The information that can be retrieved is the definition of document types and concepts in the background knowledge, as well as information about the neighborhood of the types and concepts. In the prototype implementation the neighborhood of a concept consists of the more specific and more general concepts as well as the individuals that belong to the concept. We can browse the information in the knowledge bases by exploring neighborhoods of concepts. This allows for interactive querying where a user can modify a query using the neighborhoods of concepts in a query. For instance, when more answers are desired the query may be made more general, and when less answers are desired the query may be made more specific.

We have tested our prototype system on a collection of 180 HTML documents taken from the web pages of our department. The web pages included information about research and education as well as some other activities at the department. We created a description logic representation of the documents using the method in [LSÅ97]. This program was run under Allegro Common Lisp Version 4.2. We partitioned the document collection into seven parts where part two contained part one, part three contained part two and so on. For each part a GLIMPSE index was created and a description logic knowledge base was instantiated. The background knowledge used in the test contained a description of the structure of the department such as information on the research laboratories and the course leaders.

With respect to the representation of the documents we found that the number of CLASSIC($\lhd$) individuals grows more than linear with respect to the number of documents. (In our experiments we found a ratio between 1.1 and 1.6.) The conversion program as described in [LSÅ97] creates a new individual for every HTML tag found in an HTML document and considers this as a part of the document. A less naive approach would decide on a number of tags that can be considered as parts and only store information about these tags.

In the prototype implementation the loading of the information about the documents in CLASSIC($\lhd$) took about 20 seconds per document for the largest document base. This may be explained by the fact that the system infers possible new information about the documents and classifies each document under the most specific concept to which it belongs. Also, we did not address any optimization issues and used a research prototype implementation of CLASSIC($\lhd$) where efficiency was not a main issue. There is thus room for improvement in the sense of optimizing our prototype as well as in the sense of using faster description logic systems.[3]

We tested the system with a number of different queries involving the different kinds of information. The response time for most queries was at most a few seconds on the collection of 180 documents. As expected, the information that had the most influence on the response time are the queries involving logical structure. These queries require a traversal of a part-of hierarchy of the

---

[3] Recent research in description logics shows that large improvements can be made with respect to efficiency in comparison to the previously available research prototypes. For more information, see the description logic systems comparison section in [FDMNW98].

parts of the documents. However, even for most queries involving information about the structure the response time was a few seconds. We tested a worst case scenario using the query to *find all titles that are included in an HTML document that contains the word "information"*. Most documents in the collection contained the word "information" and all documents were HTML documents. Therefore, the system had to traverse the part-of hierarchy for almost every document to find all titles in the documents. The response time for this query was 3 seconds for the smallest collection (50 documents) and 15 seconds for the largest collection (180 documents).

The expressive power of our query language allows for expressing information about content, logical structure and properties of documents. Therefore, the users could state their queries more precisely than with other search tools that allowed, for example, only for keyword search. The answer sets contained therefore less irrelevant information. Finally, as expected, the use of background knowledge improved the recall of the system.

11.4 Related Work

Although we are not aware of a knowledge-based information retrieval system that allows for querying using information about the content, logical structure and properties of documents, work has been done on the different parts.

In [NB97] a model for representing content information and information about logical structure of documents is proposed. Instead of proposing a particular query language, the authors have chosen to define a number of useful operators. Query languages can then be constructed by choosing a sub-set of the operators. The language proposed in this chapter can be seen as an instantiation of one such language. With respect to architectures of systems following their model, they have experimented with systems where content and structural information is stored in indexes.

Recently, a number of query languages for semistructured data and web query languages have been introduced (e.g. [AQMWW97, FFLS97, MMM97]). One of the main features of these proposals is that the underlying data and their logical structure can be modeled using graphs. To traverse the graphs and thus to query the logical structure of the documents, the query languages support the notion of path expressions. We note that we can model most of the path expressions by combining the **includes** and **allp** constructors of our internal language. We can use the types of the nodes in the paths as well as the labels of the edges. For instance, the types of the nodes are in our case domain restrictions, as in (**includes** *reference*). The labels of the edges are in our case part names, as in (**includes** (**allp** *table-part large-table*)).

Another kind of related work is the work on query languages for structured documents. In [MacL91] a query language is specified for retrieving information from hierarchically structured documents. The language is influenced by

SQL and Nial. Four different categories of search capabilities are considered: simple selection and navigation, simple object selection conditions, contextual conditions and object specification. In [CACS94] the object-oriented database management system O_2 is extended to handle SGML documents. The data model was extended to include ordering information and union of types. The query language O_2SQL is extended with new constructs among which the notion of path variables. In [KM93] SQL is extended to provide access to structured text described by SGML in text-relational database management systems.

Some other recent approaches in information retrieval propose to use a knowledge base to structure and store information. An example of these approaches are the information agents. These systems tackle a slightly different problem, but use similar techniques to provide a uniform query interface to multiple information sources. Examples of such systems are the Information Manifold [LSK95], Infomaster [GGKS95] and SIMS [ACHK93]. The Information Manifold allows a client to superimpose a tailored conceptual organization on an unstructured information space, thereby enriching the usefulness and access to that information. The underlying knowledge base is a description logic system. Infomaster supports a variety of user interfaces to various information sources. Infomaster uses a language that is a combination of KQML, KIF and Ontologies along with the languages native to the information sources, such as SQL and HTML. SIMS uses a description logic system as well and has been tested in a transportation planning domain using Oracle databases.

11.5 Conclusion

In this chapter we have presented a model for querying document bases. With respect to expressivity we have argued that support should be given to allow for queries involving different kinds of information about the searchable documents as well as background information. We have presented an architecture where the main components are a kernel that deals with the search, knowledge bases that contain information about the documents, background knowledge and knowledge about the users, and an information extractor that extracts relevant information from the documents and stores this information in the knowledge bases.

The knowledge in the knowledge bases can be browsed and used to narrow or widen the answer set of documents. One possibility is for the user to interactively query the system. In this case the user evaluates the answer set and uses the information in the knowledge bases to generalize or specialize the query.

The background knowledge and knowledge about documents can be specified for individual users or organizations. In this case the document knowledge base is used to find and retrieve documents that are tailored to the needs of the individual or organization.

An important direction for further work is the extraction of information from documents. Our current implementation deals mainly with the extraction of the logical structure and keywords from documents. One possible direction is to use semantic tags in documents. Then, we could use similar techniques for the extraction of semantic information as for the extraction of the logical structure. Other approaches need to be investigated as well.

Another direction for further work is the automatic creation of domain knowledge for particular users. To this aim we are currently investigating machine learning techniques that, given a number of HTML documents, build user profiles.

Part V

Conclusion

12. Conclusion

12.1 Contributions

In this work we have introduced a framework to introduce representation and reasoning about part-of in description logics. We summarize the contributions.

- We have introduced a model for part-of based on direct part-whole relations (chapter 3). The use of part-whole relations is similar to the approach in [SP94a], but different from most other approaches.
- We have introduced a simple description logic for composite objects (chapter 5). We have shown how part-of can be given first-class status by introducing new constructs in the language. These constructs can be used to define composite concepts and individuals. Further, a part-of hierarchy for individuals was introduced that can be used to answer containment questions. For this description logic an implementation based on CLASSIC exists. Specialized user functions are introduced involving information about part-of.
- An extended language is introduced to provide greater expressiveness (chapter 6). The notion of module was introduced to capture another relation with part-of intuition that was not included in the part-whole relations.
- Specialized inferences involving part-of were introduced (chapter 6). These inferences provide support for the creation of composite individuals given the existence of individuals that can be used as parts and modules.
- The usefulness of the approach was shown in a number of applications. In the agent application (chapter 8) we re-modeled an existing system. The database of the existing system contained much implicit information about part-of, but did not use this information in a specialized way. We showed that using a description logic for composite objects the domain modeling could be done in a much more natural way.
  In the document management application (chapter 9) we analyzed the requirements for this domain. We showed that this domain could be naturally modeled using our approach and we showed that specialized inferences for part-of were useful for the instantiation of documents. The model for documents was carried over to the information retrieval application (chapter

P. Lambrix: Part-Whole Reasoning, LNAI 1771, pp. 169-174, 2000
© Springer-Verlag Berlin Heidelberg 2000

11). We showed that our description logic supports information retrieval of structured documents.

We also showed that a description logic for composite objects may be a useful framework for machine learning (chapter 10). In this case we make use of the interaction of subsumption and the information about part-whole relations to learn composite concepts.

We have already compared our approach with respect to its capability of representation and reasoning about part-of with the other approaches in description logics in chapter 7. We summarize the main points.

The lack of a formal basis for part-of is recognized in the overview article [AFGP96] for most other approaches. We have introduced a formal basis for part-of in our approach that has as its main characteristic that it is based on the notion of named direct parts. The model is very flexible as it allows us to define different kinds of part-whole relations as well as it allows us to combine them in a more general transitive part-of relation. A disadvantage of the model could be that it is very general. Therefore, in general, we cannot make use of specific properties of particular part-whole relations in our framework. This would require an extension to the framework.

We have given part-of first-class status in our description logic for composite objects in two ways. First, we have introduced constructs targeted at part-of. For instance, we have introduced similar constructs for part-of as for ordinary relations. We also introduced constructs that are specific for part-of. This approach provides us with an extended capability with respect to modeling applications and querying the resulting knowledge bases. Our approach is in contrast to the approaches where part-of is represented by predefined roles and where the same constructs are used with respect to part-of and ordinary roles.

Secondly, we have introduced specialized reasoning tasks. This has not been done in other approaches. However, it seems natural that a description logic for composite objects needs to provide services concerning part-of. A natural class of services concerning part-of provides support for the creation or building of composites.

We introduced a part-of hierarchy for individuals that can be used to structure the objects into composite objects. The hierarchy can then be used to query and manipulate a knowledge base containing composite objects. In our applications this hierarchy proved to be of paramount importance. However, the only other approach that introduces a part-of hierarchy for individuals is [SP94a].

By integrating part-of in description logics we were able to study the interaction between part-of and is-a. The interaction can be seen in the different algorithms in the description logic system. For instance, the structural subsumption rules for the subsumption algorithm contain parts related to is-a as well as parts related to part-of. Several of the user functions of our implementation are based on the is-a hierarchy for concepts as well as on the part-of hierarchy for individuals. One interaction that we do not support is the part-sensitive subsumption of [JP89, Ber94]. However, this interaction does not occur in general for every kind of part-whole relation.

We have explored the use of our description logic for composite objects in a number of application areas. Although we do not have fully implemented systems for every application, we have shown the usefulness of our approach. In each of the areas we found that the use of our description logic for composite objects gave a number of advantages such as natural models of the domains, extended representational capabilities, extended query capabilities and specialized services.

12.2 Future Work

In this section we propose some possible extensions to our framework. This list is not exhaustive and further work is needed to reveal other needs. Extensions should be considered with respect to user needs and they depend on the user's application. We introduce each of the extensions on its own and discuss some of the implications. If several extensions were needed for some application, the interaction should also be studied.

Part Name Hierarchy

An extension that may be useful in some applications is to have a part name hierarchy. Then it is possible to specialize the part names. In a soccer team all members could be soccer players. However the member part name in the team could be specialized to distinguish between the goalkeeper, the defense players, the midfield players and the forwards. This could be written as follows.

$keeper \overset{.}{\leq} member$
$defense \overset{.}{\leq} member$
$midfield \overset{.}{\leq} member$
$forward \overset{.}{\leq} member$
$team \overset{.}{\leq}$ (**and** (**atleastp** *11 member*) (**atmostp** *11 member*) (**allp** *member soccer-player*) (**atleastp** *1 keeper*)
(**atmostp** *1 keeper*) (**allp** *keeper goalkeeper*)
(**allp** *defense field-player*) (**allp** *midfield field-player*)
(**allp** *forward field-player*))

An extension in this sense to CLASSIC was proposed in [SP94a].

Inverses of Part Names

Another useful extension would be to allow for inverses of part names. In contrast to roles where the inverse is again a role, the inverse of a part name is not a part name. Thus we may have to introduce another domain of *containment names* to represent the inverses of part names. Hence for a part name n the inverse c is a containment name. The subsumption algorithm and the recognition algorithm have to be modified in a similar way to the algorithms in languages supporting inverse roles.

We may want to allow the same expressivity for containment names as for part names and thus introduce new constructs such as **allc**, **atleastc** and **atmostc**. This would allow us to define items such as (**atmostc** 1 c) stating that for an individual belonging to this concept there is at most one composition via the c containment name. Actually this example expresses that an individual belonging to this concept cannot be shared as a part via the inverse of c.

Parts without Names

In some cases it may seem to be useful to be able to allow a user to state that an individual or concept has an upper or lower bound on the number of direct parts, without requiring that the part names are given. In the case where we have a part name hierarchy we may introduce a part name $\top_P$ which subsumes every part name. Then we can use this part name to express, for example, (**atmostp** $5 \top_P$) indicating that there are at most five direct parts. This would also allow for closing of this part name so that for an individual it is possible to know the exact number of parts.

In the case where we do not have a part name hierarchy, we would need to introduce new constructs. For instance, we may allow (**atleastp** m), (**atmostp** m) and (**allp** C) in the language, indicating that there are at least m direct parts, there are at most m direct parts and that all direct parts belong to the concept C respectively. We would need to update subsumption and normalization rules. Examples include:

$\vdash$ (**atleastp** m n) $\Rightarrow$ (**atleastp** m)
$\vdash$ (**allp** C) $\Rightarrow$ (**allp** n C)
$$\frac{m_1 \; < \; m_2}{\vdash \; (\textbf{atleastp} \; m_2) \; \Rightarrow \; (\textbf{atleastp} \; m_1)}$$

A consequence of allowing parts without part names is that we do not have complete information with respect to the names for the parts of a concept. In the case where incomplete information may present a problem, we still may want to have parts without part names in the query language in a similar way as in chapter 11.

Inheritance via Part-of through Context

In the language defined in chapter 6 we can express inheritance information via part-whole through the **same-filler** and **aggregate** constructs. For instance, in the definition of a folder (**same-filler** *project-name document-p.project-name*) may occur. Thus the inheritance information is placed on the concept level. Values are propagated in the case where we know that the whole belongs to the concept with the inheritance information. For instance, if a whole belongs to a folder, then the inheritance works between the folder and its document parts.

Another approach is to allow inheritance information to be propagated dependent on the context. In this case, too, we define the inheritance information on the concept level and the actual propagation appears on the individual level. However, the propagation is guided by part-of relationships between the individuals. To be able to handle this we may do the following.

We introduce the constructs **included-in** and **includes** as defined in chapter 11. Thus (**included-in** *document*) and (**includes** *document*) represent all individuals that are included in and include a document, respectively. For these constructs we allow the Tbox to contain statements as (**included-in** C_1) $\Rightarrow_T C_2$ and (**includes** C_3) $\Rightarrow_T C_4$. The natural meaning of these statements is then that every individual included in a C_1 is also a C_2 and every individual that includes a C_3 is also a C_4. We say that information is propagated in the context of C_1 propagating C_2, and C_3 propagating C_4 respectively. In the first case we have a propagation mechanism from wholes to parts, while in the second case the information goes from parts to wholes.

For instance, if a cube is defined as a composition of a number of faces, then for a red cube we may want to propagate the color to its parts as well. We could then write (**included-in** *red-cube*) $\Rightarrow_T$ (**fills** *color red*). The fact that a broken part in a device, for instance, causes all the pieces that contain the broken part to be broken can be represented by (**includes** (**fills** *status broken*)) $\Rightarrow_T$ (**fills** *status broken*).

The recognition and propagation algorithms have to be modified to cope with this information. For instance, when handling individual i, we have to move up in the compositional inclusion hierarchy for individuals to find the individuals i' for which $i' \,\widehat{\rhd}^*\, i$. Then we need to check whether i' belongs to a concept that can propagate inheritance information downwards. If this is the case, then this information has to be added to individual i. Similarly, we have to check for individuals i'' for which $i \,\widehat{\rhd}^*\, i''$. Then we need to check whether i'' belongs to a concept that can propagate inheritance information upwards. If this is the case, then this information has to be added to individual i.

Transitivity

In our language we can define part-whole relations for which no particular properties can be given. We also have the part-of relation and compositional inclusion which are derived from the basic direct parts. Part-of and compositional inclusion are transitive. It may, however, be useful to be able to distinguish different kinds of part-whole relations that are transitive. We might introduce a **transitive** construct as in [JP89] for part names. This would provide us with a middle ground between the transitivity of part-of and the non-transitivity of direct parts. However, the transitivity of part-whole relations may affect subsumption in general and thus the algorithms have to be modified to take this new interaction into account. For example, in a language that contains an **existsp** construct as in (**existsp** n C)[1] we have the subsumption relation: (**existsp** n (**existsp** n C)) $\Rightarrow$ (**existsp** n C) when the part name n is defined to be transitive.

Further, the recognition and propagation algorithms have to be modified. For instance, if we know that n is transitive, $i_1 \lhd_n i_2$, $i_2 \lhd_n i_3$, and i_3 belongs to (**allp** n C), then we should not only make sure that i_2 belongs to C, but also i_1 should belong to C. Further, the recognition algorithm should not only check the direct parts, but should also consider the other parts through transitive part-whole relations.

Terminological Cycles

Terminological cycles via part-of in the Tbox may be useful. This would allow us, for instance, to define a document as having sections and a section as having a title, paragraphs and (sub-)sections. In this case we can define documents with an arbitrary level of sub-sections. A careful analysis of the consequences has to be performed.

Cycles via part-of in the Abox are not permitted. They would contradict the mereological assumptions for our part-of relation.

Extending the Specialized Inferences

In chapter 6 we introduced some specialized inferences with respect to part-of. It would be interesting to investigate other specialized inferences inspired by new applications or extensions to the framework. For instance, for the extension of the framework with parts without names a useful new inference could be, given a part and its domain and a concept definition, to find out to which part names the individual could belong.

---

[1] (**existsp** n C) would mean that there exists an n-part that belongs to C.

So, Dear Reader, You have reached the end of this work. You have covered a lot of ground. You have seen how we can talk about part-of and You have seen that the approach we propose is useful in applications. What better to add then as a conclusion than the following: If You ever have a hard time again trying to explain to a machine things involving part-of, why not try to speak our language?

References

[AQMWW97] Abiteboul, S., Quass, D., McHugh, J., Widom, J., Wiener, J., 'The Lorel Query Language for Semistructured Data', *International Journal on Digital Libraries*, Vol. 1(1), pp. 68-88, 1997.

[AFQ89] André, J., Furuta, R., Quint, V., eds, *Structured Documents*, The Cambridge Series on Electronic Publishing, Cambridge University Press, 1989.

[ABN92] Anwar, T.M., Beck, H.W., Navathe, S.B., 'Knowledge Mining by Imprecise Querying: A Classification-based Approach', *Proceedings of the 8th International Conference on Data Engineering*, pp. 622-630, 1992.

[ACHK93] Arens, Y., Chee, C., Hsu, C.-N., Knoblock, C., 'Retrieving and Integrating Data from Multiple Information Sources', *International Journal of Intelligent and Cooperative Information Systems*, Vol. 2(2), pp. 127-158, 1993.

[AMSS88] Arens, Y., Miller, L., Shapiro, S., Sondheimer, N., 'Automatic Construction of User-Interface Displays', *Proceedings of the 7th National Conference on Artificial Intelligence - AAAI 88*, pp. 808-813, Saint Paul, MI, 1988.

[ACGPS94] Artale, A., Cesarini, F., Grazzini, E., Pippolini, F., Soda, G., 'Modelling Composition in a Terminological Language Environment', *Proceedings of the ECAI Workshop on Parts and Wholes*, pp. 93-101, Amsterdam, August 1994.

[AF94] Artale, A., Franconi, 'A Computational Account for a Description Logic of Time and Action', *Principles of Knowledge Representation and Reasoning: Proceedings of the Fourth International Conference - KR 94*, pp. 3-14, Bonn, Germany, 1994.

[AFGP96] Artale, A., Franconi, E., Guarino, N., Pazzi, L., 'Part-Whole Relations in Object-Centered Systems: An Overview', *Data and Knowledge Engineering*, Vol. 20(3), pp. 347-383, 1996.

[At*89] Atkinson, M., Bancilhon, F., DeWitt, D., Dittrich, K., Maier, D., Zdonik, S., 'The Object-Oriented Database System Manifesto', *Technical Report*, GIP-ALTAIR, No. 30-89, LeChesnay, France, 1989.

[Baa90] Baader, F., 'Terminological Cycles in KL-ONE-based Knowledge Representation Languages', *Proceedings of the National Conference on Artificial Intelligence - AAAI 90*, pp. 621-626, 1990.

[BH91] Baader, F., Hollunder, B., 'KRIS: Knowledge Representation and Inference System', *SIGART Bulletin*, Vol. 2(3), pp. 8-14, 1991.

[BH92] Baader, F., Hollunder, B., 'Embedding Defaults into Terminological Knowledge Representation Formalisms', *Principles of Knowledge Representation and Reasoning: Proceedings of the Third International Conference - KR 92*, pp. 306-317, Cambridge, MA, USA, 1992.

[BH93] Baader, F., Hollunder, B., 'How to Prefer More Specific Defaults in Terminological Default Logic', *Proceedings of the International Joint Conference on Artificial Intelligence - IJCAI 93*, pp. 669-674, 1993.

[BHNPF92] Baader, F., Hollunder, B., Nebel, B., Profitlich, H.-J., Franconi, E., 'An Empirical Analysis of Optimization Techniques for Terminological Representation Systems - or - Making KRIS get a move on', *Principles of Knowledge Representation and Reasoning: Proceedings of the Third International Conference - KR 92*, pp. 270-281, Cambridge, MA, USA, 1992.

[Ba*87] Banerjee, J., Chou, H.-T., Garza, J., Kim, W., Woelk, D., Ballou, N., 'Data Model Issues for Object-Oriented Applications', *ACM Transactions on Office Information Systems*, Vol. 5(1), pp. 3-26, 1987.

[BCN92] Batini, C., Ceri, S., Navathe, S., *Conceptual and Logical Database Design: The Entity-Relationship Approach*, Benjamin/Cummings, Menlo Park, CA, 1992.

[BM88] Beech, D., Mahbod, B., 'Generalized Version Control in an Object-Oriented Database', *Proceedings of the Fourth IEEE Conference on Data Engineering*, pp. 14-22, 1988.

[BS92] Bergamaschi, S., Sartori, C., 'On Taxonomic Reasoning in Conceptual Design', *ACM Transactions on Database Systems*, Vol. 17(3), pp. 385-422, 1992.

[Ber94] Bernauer, J., 'Modelling Formal Subsumption and Part-Whole Relation for Medical Concept Description', *Proceedings of the ECAI Workshop on Parts and Wholes*, pp. 69-79, Amsterdam, August 1994.

[BRG88] Bertino, E., Rabitti, F., Gibbs, S., 'Query Processing in a Multimedia Document System', *ACM Transactions on Office Information Systems*, Vol. 6(1), pp. 1-41, 1988.

[Bet93] Bettini, C., *Temporal Extensions of Terminological Languages*, Ph.D. thesis, Computer Science Department, University of Milan, 1993.

[BP91] Bollinger, T., Pletat, U., 'The LILOG Knowledge Representation System', *SIGART Bulletin*, Vol. 2(3), pp. 22-27, 1991.

[Bor92] Borgida, A., 'From Type Systems to Knowledge Representation: Natural Semantics Specifications for Description Logics', *International Journal of Intelligent and Cooperative Information Systems*, Vol. 1(1), pp. 93-126, 1992.

[Bor94] Borgida, A., 'On the Relationship between Description Logic and Predicate Logic Queries', *Proceedings of the International Conference on Information and Knowledge Management - CIKM 94* pp. 219-225, 1994.

[Bo*89] Borgida, A., Brachman, R., McGuinness, D., Resnick, L., 'CLASSIC: a Structural Data Model for Objects', *Proceedings of the ACM International Conference on Management of Data - SIGMOD 89*, pp. 58-67, 1989.

[BP94] Borgida, A., Patel-Schneider, P., 'A Semantics and Complete Algorithm for Subsumption in the CLASSIC Description Logic', *Journal of Artificial Intelligence Research*, Vol. 1, pp. 277-308, 1994.

[BS85] Brachman, R., Schmolze, J., 'An Overview of the KL-ONE Knowledge Representation System', *Cognitive Science*, Vol. 9(2), pp. 171-216, 1985.

[Br*93] Brachman, R., Selfridge, P., Terveen, L., Altman, B., Borgida, A., Halper, F., Kirk, T., Lazar, A., McGuinness, D., Resnick, L., 'Integrated Support for Data Archeology', *International Journal of Intelligent and Cooperative Information Systems*, Vol. 2(2), pp. 159-185, 1993.

[Bra87] Bratman, M., *Intention, Plans, and Practical Reason*, Harvard University Press, 1987.

[BDS93] Buchheit, M., Donini, F., Schaerf, A., 'Decidable Reasoning in Terminological Knowledge Representation Systems', *Journal of Artificial Intelligence Research*, Vol. 1, pp. 109-138, 1993.

[BJNS94] Buchheit, M., Jeusfeld, M., Nutt, W., Staudt, M., 'Subsumption between Queries to Object-Oriented Databases', *Information Systems*, Vol. 19(1), pp. 33-54, 1994.

[Bus87] Bush, R., *Reaction Control System Training Manual RCS 2102*, Flight Training Branch, Missions Operations Directorate, NASA, Johnson Space Center, Houston, TX, April 1987.

[CDL95] Calvanese, D., De Giacomo, G., Lenzerini, M., 'Structured Objects: Modeling and Reasoning', *Proceedings of the International Conference on Deductive and Object-Oriented Databases*, LNCS 1013, pp. 229-246, 1995.

[CLN94] Calvanese, D., Lenzerini, M., Nardi, D., 'A Unified Framework for Class-Based Representation Formalisms', *Principles of Knowledge Representation and Reasoning: Proceedings of the Fourth International Conference - KR 94*, pp. 109-120, Bonn, Germany, 1994.

[CJW95] Cao, Y., Jung, B., Wachsmuth, I., 'Situated Verbal Interaction in Virtual Design and Assembly', *Video Presentation at the International Joint Conference on Artificial Intelligence - IJCAI 95*, 1995.

[Cat91] Cattell, R., *Object Data Management: Object-Oriented and Extended Relational Database Systems*, Addison-Wesley Publishing Company, 1991.

[CACS94] Christophides, V., Abiteboul, S., Cluet, S., Scholl, M., 'From Structured Documents to Novel Query Facilities', *Proceedings of the ACM International Conference on Management of Data - SIGMOD 94*, pp. 1-22, 1994.

[Cru79] Cruse, D.A., 'On the Transitivity of the Part-Whole Relation', *J. Linguistics*, Vol. 15, pp. 29-38, 1979.

[CY91] Coad, P., Yourdon, E., *Object-Oriented Analysis*, Prentice-Hall International, 1991.

[CBH92] Cohen, W., Borgida, A., Hirsh, H., 'Computing Least Common Subsumers in Description Logics', *Proceedings of the National Conference on Artificial Intelligence - AAAI 92*, pp. 754-760, 1992.

[CH94a] Cohen, W., Hirsh, H., 'Learning the CLASSIC Description Logic: Theoretical and Experimental Results', *Principles of Knowledge Representation and Reasoning: Proceedings of the Fourth International Conference - KR 94*, Bonn, Germany, pp. 121-133, 1994.

[CH94b] Cohen, W., Hirsh, H., 'The Learnability of Description Logics with Equality Constraints', *Machine Learning*, Vol. 17, pp. 169-199, 1994.

[Da*90] Dayal, U., Manola, F., Buchmann, A., Chakravarthy, U., Goldhirsch, D., Heiler, S., Orenstein, J., Rosenthal, A., 'Simplifying Complex Objects: The PROBE Approach to Modelling and Querying Them', eds, Zdonik, Maier, *Readings in Object-Oriented Database Systems*, pp. 390-399, 1990.

[DL95] De Giacomo, G., Lenzerini, M., 'What's in an Aggregate: Foundations for Description Logics with Tuples and Sets', *Proceedings of the International Joint Conference on Artificial Intelligence - IJCAI 95*, pp. 801-807, 1995.

[DBSB91] Devanbu, P., Brachman, R., Selfridge, P., Ballard, B., 'LaSSIE: A Knowledge-Based Software Information System', *Communications of the ACM*, Vol. 34(5), pp. 34-49, 1991.

[DE92] Donini, F., Era, A., 'Most Specific Concepts Technique for Knowledge Bases with Incomplete Information', *Proceedings of the First International Conference on Information and Knowledge Management - CIKM 92*, pp. 545-551, 1992.

[DLNN91a] Donini, F., Lenzerini, M., Nardi, D., Nutt, W., 'Tractable concept languages', *Proceedings of the International Joint Conference on Artificial Intelligence - IJCAI 91*, pp. 458-465, 1991.

[DLNN91b] Donini, F., Lenzerini, M., Nardi, D., Nutt, W., 'The Complexity of Concept Languages', *Principles of Knowledge Representation and Reasoning: Proceedings of the Second International Conference - KR 92*, pp. 151-162, Cambridge, MA, USA, 1991.

[DP91] Doyle, J., Patil, R., 'Two Theses of Knowledge Representation: Language Restrictions, Taxonomic Classification, and the Utility of Representation Services', *Artificial Intelligence*, Vol. 48, pp. 261-297, 1991.

[Fah79] Fahlman, S., *NETL: A System for Representing and Using Real World Knowledge*, The MIT Press, 1979.

[FFLS97] Fernandez, M., Florescu, D., Levy, A., Suciu, D., 'A Query Language for a Web-Site Management System', *SIGMOD Record*, Vol. 26(3), pp. 4-11, 1997.

[Fra93] Franconi, E., 'A Treatment of Plurals and Plural Qualifications based on a Theory of Collections', *Minds and Machines: Special Issue on Knowledge Representation for Natural Language Processing*, Vol. 3(4), pp. 453-474, November 1993.

[FDMNW98] Franconi, E., De Giacomo, G., MacGregor, R., Nutt, W., Welty, C., *Proceedings of the International Workshop on Description Logics*, Trento, Italy, 1998.

[FP94] Frazier, M., Pitt, L., 'CLASSIC Learning', *Proceedings of the Seventh Annual Conference on Computational Learning Theory - COLT 94*, pp. 23-34, 1994.

[GGKS95] Geddis, D., Genesereth, M., Keller, A., Singh, N., 'Infomaster: A Virtual Information System', *Proceedings of the CIKM workshop on Intelligent Information Agents*, 1995.

[GI89] Georgeff, M., Ingrand, F., 'Decision-Making in an Embedded Reasoning System', *Proceedings of the International Joint Conference on Artificial Intelligence - IJCAI 89*, pp. 972-978, 1989.

[GI90] Georgeff, M., Ingrand, F., 'Research on Procedural Reasoning Systems - Final Report - Phase 2', SRI International, 1990.

[GP95] Gerstl, P., Pribbenow, S., 'Midwinters, End Games, and Body Parts: a Classification of Part-Whole Relations', *International Journal of Human-Computer Studies*, Vol. 43, pp. 865-889, 1995.

[Gol90] Goldfarb, C.F., *The SGML Handbook*, Clarendon Press, Oxford, 1990.

[GZC89] Güting, R., Zicari, R., Choy, D., 'An Algebra for Structured Office Documents', *ACM Transactions on Information Systems*, Vol. 7(2), pp. 123-157, 1989.

[HPS88] Haimowitz, I., Patil, R., Szolovits, P., 'Representing Medical Knowledge in a Terminological Language is Difficult', *Proceedings of the 12th Annual Symposium on Computer Applications in Medical Care*, pp. 101-105, Washington, DC, 1988.

[Han92] Hanschke, P., 'Specifying Role Interaction in Concept Languages', *Principles of Knowledge Representation and Reasoning: Proceedings of the Third International Conference - KR 92*, pp. 318-329, Cambridge, MA, USA, 1992.

[Hay77] Hayes, P., 'On Semantic Nets, Frames and Associations', *Proceedings of the International Joint Conference on Artificial Intelligence - IJCAI 77*, pp. 99-107, 1977.

[HKNP92] Heinsohn, J., Kudenko, D., Nebel, B., Profitlich, H.-J., 'An Empirical Analysis of Terminological Representation Systems', *Proceedings of the National Conference on Artificial Intelligence - AAAI 92*, pp. 676-773, 1992.

[Hoc94] Hoch, R., 'Using IR Techniques for Text Classification in Document Analysis', *Proceedings of the 17th ACM International Conference on Research and Development in Information Retrieval - SIGIR 94*, pp. 31-40, Dublin, Ireland, 1994.

[IG89] Ingrand, F., Georgeff, M., 'Monitoring and Control of Spacecraft Systems Using Procedural Reasoning', *Proceedings of the Space Operations Automation and Robotics Workshop*, Houston, Texas, 1989.

[IGR92] Ingrand, F., Georgeff, M., Rao, A., 'An Architecture for Real-Time Reasoning and System Control', *IEEE Expert*, pp. 34-44, December 1992.

[IOS87] International Office for Standardization, *Information Processing - text and office Systems - Office Document Architecture (ODA) and Interchange Format (ODIF)*, ISO 8613, 1987.

[ILE88] Iris, M.A., Litowitz, B.E., Evens, M., 'Problems with the part-whole relation', Evens, ed, *Relational Models of the Lexicon*, pp. 261-288, 1988.

[Jan88] Jang, Y., *KOLA: Knowledge Organization LAnguage*, MIT/LCS/TR-396, 1988.

[JP89] Jang, Y., Patil, R., 'KOLA: A Knowledge Organization Language', *Proceedings of the 13th Symposium on Computer Applications in Medical Care*, pp. 71-75, 1989.

[KC90] Katz, R., Chang, E., 'Managing Change in a Computer-Aided Design Database', eds, Zdonik, Maier, *Readings in Object-Oriented Database Systems*, pp. 400-407, 1990.

[KM94] Kietz, J.-U., Morik, K., 'A Polynomial Approach to the Constructive Induction of Structural Knowledge', *Machine Learning*, Vol. 14, pp. 193-217, 1994.

[KLMN90] Kilpeläinen, P., Lindén, G., Manilla, H., Nikunen, E., 'A Structured Document Database System', *Proceedings of the International Conference on Electronic Publishing, Document Manipulation and Typography - EP 90*, pp. 139-151, Gaithersburg, Maryland, USA, 1990.

[KM93] Kilpeläinen, P., Manilla, H., 'Retrieval from Hierarchical Texts by Partial Patterns', *Proceedings of the 16th ACM International Conference on Research and Development in Information Retrieval - SIGIR 93*, pp. 214-222, Pittsburgh, PA, USA, 1993.

[KBG89] Kim, W., Bertino, E., Garza, J.F., 'Composite Objects Revisited', *Proceedings of the Conference on Management of Data - SIGMOD 89*, SIGMOD Rec., Vol. 18(2), pp. 337-347, 1989.

[Koe94] Koehler, J., 'An Application of Terminological Logics to Case-based Reasoning', *Principles of Knowledge Representation and Reasoning: Proceedings of the Fourth International Conference - KR 94*, pp. 351-362, Bonn, Germany, 1994.

[LCSKR88] Laffey, T., Cox, P., Schmidt, J., Kao, S., Read, J., 'Real-time Knowledge-based Systems', *AI Magazine*, Vol. 9, pp. 27-45, 1988.

[Lam92] Lambrix, P., *Aspects of Version Management of Composite Objects*, Lic. thesis 328, Department of Computer and Information Science, Linköpings universitet, 1992.

[Lam96] Lambrix, P., *Part-Whole Reasoning in Description Logics*, Ph.D. Thesis 448, Department of Computer and Information Science, Linköpings universitet, 1996.

[LL98] Lambrix, P., Larocchia, P., 'Learning Composite Concepts', *Proceedings of the International Workshop on Description Logics*, pp. 147-152, Trento, Italy, 1998.

[LM96] Lambrix, P., Maleki, J., 'Learning Composite Concepts in Description Logics: A First Step', *Proceedings of the 9th International Symposium on Methodologies for Intelligent Systems - ISMIS 96*, LNAI 1079, pp. 68-77, Zakopane, Poland, 1996.

[LP97] Lambrix, P., Padgham, L., 'A Description Logic Model for Querying Knowledge Bases for Structured Documents', *Proceedings of the Tenth International Symposium on Methodologies for Intelligent Systems - ISMIS 97*, LNAI 1325, pp. 72-83, Charlotte, North Carolina, USA.

[LP00] Lambrix, P., Padgham, L., 'Conceptual Modeling in a Document Management Environment using Part-of Reasoning in Description Logics', *Data & Knowledge Engineering*, Vol. 32, pp. 51-86, 2000.

[LR93] Lambrix, P., Rönnquist, R., 'Terminological Logic Involving Time and Evolution: A Preliminary Report', *Proceedings of the Seventh International Symposium on Methodologies for Intelligent Systems - ISMIS 93*, LNAI 689, pp. 162-171, Trondheim, Norway, 1993.

[LSJ99] Lambrix, P., Shahmehri, N., Jacobsen, S., 'Querying Document Bases by Content, Structure and Properties', *Proceedings of the Eleventh International Symposium on Methodologies for Intelligent Systems - ISMIS 99*, LNAI 1609, pp. 123-132, Warsaw, Poland, 1999.

[LSW98] Lambrix, P., Shahmehri, N., Wahllöf, N., 'A Default Extension to Description Logics for Use in an Intelligent Search Engine', *Proceedings of the 31st Hawaii International Conference on System Sciences, Volume V - Modeling Technologies and Intelligent Systems Track*, pp 28-35, 1998.

[LSÅ97] Lambrix, P., Shahmehri, N., Åberg, J., 'Towards Creating a Knowledge Base for World-Wide Web Documents', *Proceedings of the IASTED International Conference on Intelligent Information Systems*, pp. 507-511, 1997.

[LC96] Larkey, L., Croft, B., 'Combining Classifiers in Text Categorization', *Proceedings of the ACM International Conference on Research and Development in Information Retrieval - SIGIR 96*, pp. 289-297, Zurich, Switzerland, 1996.

[LSK95] Levy, A., Srivastava, D., Kirk, T., 'Data Model and Query Evaluation in Global Information Systems', *Journal of Intelligent Information Systems, Special Issue on Networked Information Discovery and Retrieval*, Vol. 5 (2), 1995.

[LZS95] Lowe, B., Zobel, J., Sacks-Davis, R., 'A Formal Model for Databases of Structured Text', *Proceedings of the Fourth International Conference on Database Systems for Advanced Applications*, Singapore, 1995.

[Lyo77] Lyons, J., *Semantics*, Cambridge University Press, 1977.

[MacG91] MacGregor, R., 'Inside the LOOM Description Classifier', *SIGART Bulletin*, Vol. 2(3), pp. 88-92, 1991.

[MacL91] MacLeod, I., 'A Query Language for Retrieving Information from Hierarchic Text Structures', *The Computer Journal*, Vol. 34(3), pp. 254-264, 1991.

[McG98] McGuinness, D., 'Ontological Issues for Knowledge-Enhanced Search', *Proceedings of the Workshop on Formal Ontology in Information Systems*, 1998.

[MRI95] McGuinness, D., Resnick, L., Isbell, C., 'Description Logic in Practice: A CLASSIC Application', *Proceedings of the International Joint Conference on Artificial Intelligence - IJCAI 95*, video presentation, pp. 2045-2046, 1995.

[MRT91] Meghini, C., Rabitti, F., Thanos, C., 'Conceptual Modeling of Multimedia Documents', *IEEE Computer*, pp. 23-30, October 1991.

[MSST93] Meghini, C., Sebastiani, F., Straccia, U., Thanos, C., 'A Model of Information Retrieval based on a Terminological Logic', *Proceedings of the 16th ACM International Conference on Research and Development in Information Retrieval - SIGIR 93*, pp. 298-307, Pittsburgh, PA, USA, 1993.

[MMM97] Mendelzon, A., Mihaila, G., Milo, T., 'Querying the World Wide Web', *International Journal on Digital Libraries*, Vol. 1(1), pp. 54-67, 1997.

[Mit82] Mitchell, T., 'Generalization as Search', *Artificial Intelligence*, Vol. 18(2), pp. 203-226, 1982.

[Nap92] Napoli, A., 'Subsumption and Classification-Based Reasoning in Object-Based Representations', *Proceedings of the 10th European Conference on Artificial Intelligence - ECAI 92*, pp. 425-429, 1992.

[NLD94] Napoli, A., Laurenco, C., Ducournau, R., 'An Object-Based Representation System for Organic Synthesis Planning', *International Journal of Human-Computer Studies*, 1994.

[NB97] Navarro, G., Baeza-Yates, R., 'Proximal Nodes: A Model to Query Document Databases by Content and Structure', *ACM Transactions on Information Systems*, Vol. 15(4), pp. 400-435, 1997.

[Neb90a] Nebel, B., 'Terminological Reasoning is Inherently Intractable', *Artificial Intelligence*, Vol. 43, pp. 235-249, 1990.

[Neb90b] Nebel, B., *Reasoning and Revision in Hybrid Representation Systems*, LNAI 422, Springer-Verlag, Berlin, Heidelberg, New York, 1990.

[Ows88] Owsnicki-Klewe, B., 'Configuration as a Consistency Maintenance Task', *Proceedings of the 12th German Workshop on Artificial Intelligence*, pp. 77-87, 1988.

[PL94] Padgham, L., Lambrix, P., 'A Framework for Part-Of Hierarchies in Terminological Logics', *Principles of Knowledge Representation and Reasoning: Proceedings of the Fourth International Conference - KR 94*, pp. 485-496, Bonn, Germany, 1994.

[PN93] Padgham, L., Nebel, B, 'Combining Classification and Non-Monotonic Inheritance Reasoning: A First Step', *Proceedings of the Seventh International Symposium on Methodologies for Intelligent Systems - ISMIS 93*, LNAI 689, pp. 132-141, 1993.

[PZ93] Padgham, L., Zhang, T., 'A Terminological Logic with Defaults: A Definition and an Application', *Proceedings of the International Joint Conference on Artificial Intelligence - IJCAI 93*, pp. 662-668, 1993.

[PJ93] Paice, C., Jones, P., 'The Identification of Important Concepts in Highly Structured Technical Papers', *Proceedings of the 16th ACM International Conference on Research and Development in Information Retrieval - SIGIR 93*, pp. 69-78, Pittsburgh, PA, USA, 1993.

[PS81] Papalaskaris, M, Schubert, L., 'Parts Inference: Closed and Semi-Closed Partitioning Graphs', *Proceedings of the International Joint Conference on Artificial Intelligence - IJCAI 81*, pp. 304-309, 1981.

[Pel91] Peltason, C., 'The BACK System - An Overview', *SIGART Bulletin*, Vol. 2(3), pp. 114-119, 1991.

[Qua95] Quantz, J., *Preferential Disambiguation in Natural Language Processing*, Ph.D. Thesis, Technische Universität Berlin, 1995.

[QR92] Quantz, J., Royer, V., 'A Preference Semantics for Defaults in Terminological Logics', *Principles of Knowledge Representation and Reasoning: Proceedings of the Third International Conference - KR 92*, pp. 294-305, Cambridge, MA, USA, 1992.

[RBKW91] Rabitti, F., Bertino, E., Kim, W., Woelk, D., 'A Model of Authorization for Next-Generation Database Systems', *ACM Transactions on Database Systems*, Vol. 16(1), pp. 88-131, 1991.

[RJZ89] Rau, L., Jacobs, P., Zernik, U., 'Information Extraction and Text Summarization using Linguistic Knowledge Acquisition', *Information Processing and Management*, Vol. 25(4), pp. 419-428, 1989.

[Res55] Rescher, N., 'Axioms for the Part Relation', *Philosophical Studies*, Vol. 6, pp. 8-11, 1955.

[Re*93] Resnick, L., Borgida, A., Brachman, R., McGuinness, D., Patel-Schneider, P., Zalondek, K., 'CLASSIC Description and Reference Manual for the COMMON LISP Implementation Version 2.2', AT&T Bell Laboratories, Murray Hill, NJ, USA, 1993.

[RL94] Riloff, E., Lehnert, W., 'Information Extraction as a Basis for High-Precision Text Classification', *ACM Transactions on Information Systems*, Vol. 12(3), pp. 296-333, 1994.

[RBPEL91] Rumbaugh, J., Blaha, M., Premerlani, W., Eddy, F., Lorensen, W., *Object-Oriented Modeling and Design*, Prentice Hall, 1991.

[SAZ94] Sacks-Davis, R., Arnold-Moore, T., Zobel, J., 'Database Systems for Structured Documents', *Proceedings of the International Symposium on Advanced Database Technologies and Their Integration*, pp. 272-283, Nara, Japan, 1994.

[Sat95] Sattler, U., 'A Concept Language for an Engineering Application with Part-Whole Relations', *Proceedings of the International Workshop on Description Logics*, pp. 119-123, Roma, Italy, 1995.

[Sat98] Sattler, U., *Terminological knowledge representation systems in a process engineering application*, Ph.D. thesis, RWTH Aachen, 1998.

[Scha94] Schaerf, A., 'Which Semantics for Individuals in the Tbox?', *Proceedings of the International Workshop on Description Logics*, pp. 5-8, Bonn, Germany, 1994.

[Schi94] Schild, K., 'Terminological Cycles and the mu-Calculus', *Principles of Knowledge Representation and Reasoning: Proceedings of the Fourth International Conference - KR 94*, pp. 509-520, Bonn, Germany, 1994.

[Schm89] Schmidt-Schauss, M., 'Subsumption in KL-ONE is Undecidable', *Principles of Knowledge Representation and Reasoning: Proceedings of the First International Conference - KR 89*, pp. 421-431, Toronto, Canada, 1989.

[Schm90] Schmiedel, A., 'A Temporal Terminological Logic', *Proceedings of the National Conference on Artificial Intelligence - AAAI 90*, pp. 640-645, 1990.

[SM91] Schmolze, J., Mark, W., 'The NIKL Experience', *Computational Intelligence*, Vol. 6, pp. 48-69, 1991.

[Schu79] Schubert, L., 'Problems with Parts', *Proceedings of the International Joint Conference on Artificial Intelligence - IJCAI 79*, pp. 778-784, 1979.

[Seb94] Sebastiani, F., 'A Probabilistic Terminological Logic for Modelling Information Retrieval', *Proceedings of the 17th ACM International Conference on Research and Development in Information Retrieval - SIGIR 94*, pp. 122-130, Dublin, Ireland, 1994.

[Shi81] Shipman, D., 'The Functional Data Model and the Data Language DAPLEX', *ACM Transactions on Database Systems*, Vol. 6(1), pp. 140-173, 1981.

[Sim87] Simons, P., *Parts - A Study in Ontology*, Clarendon Press, Oxford, 1987.

[SFAL95] Soderland, S., Fisher, D., Aseltime, J., Lehnert, W., 'CRYSTAL: Inducing a Conceptual Dictionary', *Proceedings of the 14th International Joint Conference on Artificial Intelligence - IJCAI 95*, pp. 1314-1321, 1995.

[SP94a] Speel, P.-H., Patel-Schneider, P.F., 'CLASSIC Extended with Whole-Part Relations', *Proceedings of the International Workshop on Description Logics*, pp. 45-50, Bonn, Germany, 1994.

[SP94b] Speel, P.-H., Patel-Schneider, P.F., 'A Whole-Part Extension for Description Logics', *Proceedings of the ECAI Workshop on Parts and Wholes*, pp. 111-121, Amsterdam, August 1994.

[SVSM93] Speel, P.-H., van der Vet, P., ter Stal, W., Mars, N., 'Formalization of an Ontology of Ceramic Science in CLASSIC', *Proceedings of the Seventh International Symposium on Methodologies for Intelligent Systems, Poster Session*, pp. 110-124, 1993.

[SK91] Stonebraker, M., Kemmitz, G., 'The POSTGRES Next-Generation Database Management System', *Communications of the ACM*, Vol. 34(10), pp. 78-92, 1991.

[St*90] Stonebraker, M., Rowe, L.A., Lindsay, B., Gray, J., Carey, M., Brodie, M., Bernstein, P., Beech, D., 'Third-Generation Database System Manifesto', *SIGMOD RECORD*, Vol. 19(3), pp. 31-43, 1990.

[Str93] Straccia, U., 'Default Inheritance Reasoning in Hybrid KL-ONE-style Logics', *Proceedings of the International Joint Conference on Artificial Intelligence - IJCAI 93*, pp. 676-681, 1993.

[Var96] Varzi, A., 'Parts, Wholes, and Part-Whole Relations: The Prospects of Mereotopology', *Data and Knowledge Engineering*, Vol. 20(3), pp. 259-286, 1996.

[Voo94] Voorhees, E., 'Query Expansion using Lexical-Semantic Relations', *Proceedings of the 17th ACM International Conference on Research and Development in Information Retrieval - SIGIR 94*, pp. 61-69, Dublin, Ireland, 1994.

[WJ96] Wachsmuth, I., Jung, B., 'Dynamic Conceptualization in a Mechanical-Object Assembly Environment', *Artificial Intelligence Review*, Vol. 10(3-4), pp. 345-368, 1996.

[WL92] Weida, T., Litman, D., 'Terminological Reasoning with Constraint Networks and an Application to Plan Recognition', *Principles of Knowledge Representation and Reasoning: Proceedings of the Third International Conference - KR 92*, pp. 282-293, Cambridge, MA, USA, 1992.

[WCH87] Winston, M.E., Chaffin, R., Herrmann, D., 'A Taxonomy of Part-Whole Relations', *Cognitive Science*, Vol. 11, pp. 417-444, 1987.

[Wr*93] Wright, J., Weixelbaum, E., Vesonder, G., Brown, K., Palmer, S., Berman, J., Moore, H., 'A Knowledge-based Configurator that Supports Sales, Engineering, and Manufacturing at AT&T Network Systems', *AI Magazine*, pp. 69-80, 1993.

[WM92] Wu, S., Manber, U., 'Fast Text Searching Allowing Errors', *Communications of the ACM*, Vol. 35(10), pp. 93-91, 1992.

[Zdo86] Zdonik, S., 'Version Management in an Object-Oriented Database', *Proceedings of the International Workshop on Advanced Programming Environments*, pp. 405-422, Trondheim, Norway, 1986.

[Åke94] Åkerman, B., *PQM-Instruktioner*, Telia Research AB, 1994.

URLs

[AltaVista] http://www.altavista.digital.com/

[GLIMPSE] http://glimpse.cs.arizona.edu/

[MUC] http://www.muc.saic.com/ (Message Understanding Conferences)

Part VI

Appendices

A. New User Functions

The CLASSIC user functions are described in [Re*93]. In this appendix we show the functionality that we have added to CLASSIC.

Retrieval functions for derived objects

cl-part-name-restrs (derived-object)
  returns a list of part names which are restricted in the derived object.
cl-at-leastp (derived-object part-name)
  returns the minimum possible number of parts for a part name in the derived object.
cl-at-mostp (derived-object part-name)
  returns the maximum possible number of parts for a part name in the derived object.
cl-allp (derived-object part-name)
  returns the domain of parts for a part name in the derived object.
cl-part-fillers (derived-object part-name)
  returns the known part fillers for a part name in the derived object.
cl-pp-constraints (derived-object)
  returns the list of pp-constraints in the derived object.

Retrieval functions for told objects

cl-told-part-name-restrs (told-object)
  returns a list of part names which are restricted in the told object.
cl-told-at-leastps (told-object part-name)
  returns the minimum possible number of parts for a part name in the told object.
cl-told-at-mostps (told-object part-name)
  returns the maximum possible number of parts for a part name in the told object.
cl-told-allp (told-object part-name)
  returns the domain of parts for a part name in the told object.
cl-told-part-fillers (told-object part-name)
  returns the known part fillers for a part name in the told object.
cl-told-pp-constraints (told-object)
  returns the list of pp-constraints in the told object.

P. Lambrix: Part-Whole Reasoning, LNAI 1771, pp. 189-195, 2000
© Springer-Verlag Berlin Heidelberg 2000

Functions for individuals

cl-ind-closed-part-name? (ind part-name)
returns T if the part name is implicitly closed on the individual;
otherwise NIL.
cl-told-ind-closed-part-name? (told-ind part-name)
returns T if the part name is implicitly closed on the individual;
otherwise NIL.
cl-ind-part-name-value? (ind part-name value)
returns T if the part name has the specified value for the individual.
cl-ind-add-part-fillers (di part-name told-part-fillers)
adds a list of part fillers to a part name on an individual.
cl-ind-close-part-name (di part-name)
closes the part name in the individual so that it cannot contain
any more values.
cl-ind-remove-part-fillers (di part-name told-part-fillers)
removes a list of part fillers for a part name on an individual.
cl-ind-remove-all-part-fillers (di part-name)
removes all part fillers for a part name on an individual.
cl-ind-unclose-part-name (di part-name)
removes the told fact that a part name is closed.

Functions for part names

cl-part-name? (object)
returns T if the object is a part name; otherwise NIL.
cl-attribute-pn? (part-name)
returns T if the part name is an attribute; otherwise NIL.
cl-part-names ()
returns a list of all the part names in the knowledge base.
cl-named-part-name (part-name-name)
returns the part name with the given name, or NIL.
cl-define-primitive-part-name (part-name-name &key (attribute NIL))
creates a new part name.
cl-print-part-name (part-name)
prints a part name.

Functions involving the part-of hierarchy for individuals

cl-ind-includes? (ind1 ind2)
returns T if ind2 is part of ind1.
cl-ind-directly-includes? (ind1 ind2)
returns T if ind is a direct part of ind1.
cl-ind-included-in? (ind1 ind2)
returns T if ind1 is part of ind2.
cl-ind-directly-included-in? (ind1 ind2)
returns T if ind1 is a direct part of ind2.
cl-ind-includes-concept? (ind concept)
returns T if there is an individual belonging to concept that is part of ind.
cl-ind-directly-includes-concept? (ind concept)
returns T if there is an individual belonging to concept that is a direct part
of ind.

cl-ind-included-in-concept? (ind concept)
  returns T if ind is part of an individual belonging to concept.
cl-ind-directly-included-in-concept? (ind concept)
  returns T if ind is a direct part of an individual belonging to concept.
cl-ind-directly-included-in-with-part-name (ind)
  returns the individuals of which ind is a direct part with part names.
cl-ind-directly-included-in (ind)
  returns the individuals of which ind is a direct part.
cl-ind-included-in (ind)
  returns the individuals of which ind is a part.
cl-ind-directly-includes-with-part-name (ind)
  returns the individuals that are direct parts of ind with part names.
cl-ind-directly-includes (ind)
  returns the individuals that are direct parts of ind.
cl-ind-includes (ind)
  returns the individuals that are parts of ind.
cl-ind-includes-and-concept-instance (ind concept)
  returns the individuals that are parts of ind and that belong to concept.
cl-ind-directly-includes-and-concept-instance (ind concept)
  returns the individuals that are direct parts of ind and that belong to concept.
cl-ind-included-in-and-concept-instance (ind concept)
  returns the individuals of which ind is a part and that belong to concept.
cl-ind-directly-included-in-and-concept-instance (ind concept)
  returns the individuals of which ind is a direct part and that belong to concept.

B. Query Language

In this appendix we define the end-user query language of the system presented in chapter 11.

<query> ::
    select <selection-list>
    [**from** <from-list>]
    [**where** <where-list>]

<selection-list> ::
    *

<from-list> ::
    <concept-name>
    | <concept-description>
    | (<from-list> **and** <from-list> {**and** <from-list>})
    | (<from-list> **or** <from-list> {**or** <from-list>})
    | (<from-list> **and-not** <from-list>)

<where-list> ::
    <structure-description>
    | <content-description>
    | (<where-list> **and** <where-list> {**and** <where-list>})
    | (<where-list> **or** <where-list> {**or** <where-list>})
    | (<where-list> **and-not** <where-list>)

<structure-description> ::
    [**directly**] **includes-some** <sub-query>
    | [**directly**] **within-some** <sub-query>
    | [**directly**] **includes-object** <individual-name>
    | [**directly**] **within-object** <individual-name>

<content-description> ::
    '<string>' **occurs** [**in** <concept-name>]

\<concept-description\> ::

    top

    | **all** \<role-name\> \<concept-name\>

    | **all** \<role-name\> (\<concept-description\>)

    | **all** \<part-name-name\> \<concept-name\>

    | **all** \<part-name-name\> (\<concept-description\>)

    | **atleast** \<non-negative integer\> \<role-name\>

    | **atleast** \<non-negative integer\> \<part-name-name\>

    | **atmost** \<non-negative integer\> \<role-name\>

    | **atmost** \<non-negative integer\> \<part-name-name\>

    | **fills** \<role-name\> \<individual-name\> {\<individual-name\>}

    | **fills** \<part-name-name\> \<individual-name\> {\<individual-name\>}

    | **parts-constraint** \<role-name\>

         \<part-name-name\> \<part-name-name\>

\<sub-query\> ::

    (\<query\>)

    | (\<sub-query\> **and** \<sub-query\> {**and** \<sub-query\>})

    | (\<sub-query\> **or** \<sub-query\> {**or** \<sub-query\>})

    | (\<sub-query\> **and-not** \<sub-query\>)

\<concept-name\> ::

    \<string\>

\<individual-name\> ::

    \<string\>

\<role-name\> ::

    \<string\>

\<part-name-name\> ::

    \<string\>

\<string\> ::

    \<symbol\>[\<string\>]

\<symbol\> ::

    A | B | .. | Z | a | b | .. | z

C. Symbols

$\Rightarrow$	subsumption
$\lhd_n$	direct part with part name n (n-part)
$\lhd_n^d$	defined direct part with part name n (defined n-part)
$\lhd^*$	part-of
$\lhd_{\mathbf{mod}}$	module
$\widehat{\lhd}$	builds
$\widehat{\rhd}^*$	compositional inclusion
$N(n,C)$	arity of part name n for concept C
$C_{p_1 r p_2}$	**pp-constraint** in the definition of C
$C_{p_1 \ll p_2}$	**order-constraint** in the definition of C
$C_{ap_1 = ap_2}$	**same-filler** in the definition of C
$C_{agg(p.a)=r}$	**aggregate** in the definition of C
$\mathbf{s_T}$	more specific with respect to parts
$\mathbf{g_T}$	more general without specific parts
$gen_{\mathbf{T}}$	more general
$\propto_{1\mathbf{T}}$	preference relation for compositional extensions
$\propto_{2\mathbf{T}}$	preference relation for completions

Lecture Notes in Artificial Intelligence (LNAI)

Lecture Notes in Computer Science